Tai Chi, B

The G

Internal Martial Arts
Before the Boxer Uprising

Also by Scott Park Phillips:

Possible Origins
A Cultural History of Chinese Martial Arts,
Theater, and Religion

Tai Chi, Baguazhang and The Golden Elixir

Internal Martial Arts
Before the Boxer Uprising

Scott Park Phillips

Angry Baby Books
400 W South Boulder Rd. Lot 63
Louisville, CO 80027, USA

NorthStarMartialArts.com
Youtube Channel: Youtube.com/c/NorthStarMartialArtsUSA

First Print Addition May 2019
Also available as an ebook

Library of Congress Control Number: 2019904365
ISBN-13: 978-0-578-49562-0
ISBN-10: 0-578-49562-7

Cover: Haining shadow puppet; Nezha riding wind-fire wheels, Wiki CC 4.0

Publisher's Cataloging-in-Publication Data

Names: Phillips, Scott Park, author.
Title: Tai Chi , Baguazhang and the Golden Elixir : internal martial arts before the Boxer Uprising / Scott Park Phillips.
Description: Includes bibliographical references and index. | Louisville, CO: Angry Baby Books, 2019.
Identifiers: LCCN 2019904365 | ISBN 978-0-578-49562-0
Subjects: LCSH Martial arts—China—History. | Tai chi—China—History. | Martial arts—Religious aspects. | Theater—China—History. | Operas, Chinese. | Hand-to-hand fighting, Oriental—History. | China—Social life and customs. | Taoism—China—History. | BISAC SPORTS & RECREATION / Martial Arts & Self-Defense | HISTORY / Asia / China
Classification: LCC GV1100.7.A2 P45 2019 | DDC 796.80951—dc23

Dedication

For my wife, whose love is my inspiration.

Contents

Chinese Martial Arts: an Introduction 2

What is Tai Chi?   2

We Begin in Darkness   4

What Is Chinese Religion?   9

Theater as a Source   13

The YMCA Conquers China   32

Tai Chi **40**

Fighting without Fighting: How to Beat Up Twenty-Four
    Guards in Thirty-Two Moves   42

Admirals, Pirates, Sages, Generals and Immortals   49

Zhang Sanfeng is an Immortal,
    But what is an Immortal?   64

The Story of Zhang Sanfeng   76

The Golden Elixir in Theater, Tai Chi Texts,
    and Beyond   90

Resisting Disenchantment in the Twentieth Century   100

Making Tai Chi Weird Again   112

Appendix: *San Bao Taijian Xia Xiyangji*   117

Baguazhang..**122**

The Dance of an Angry Baby God   122

Who Was the Best Fighter in China?   132

Mud-Walking Wind-Fire Wheels   136

Indian Origins   138

Weird Weapons   146

Alternative Theories   159

The Ritual Origins of Baguazhang   166

The Nezha Rebellion   182

Creating a New Mythology   188

Baguazhang After the Boxers   198

The Golden Elixir **212**

Acknowledgements   244

Bibliography   248

Notes on Transliteration

I use Tai Chi instead of the more cumbersome and less familiar T'ai Chi Ch'uan or *taijiquan*. I use Baguazhang rather than Pa Kua Chang or the italicized lowercase *baguazhang*. I use Daoism rather than Taoism. I have tried to avoid using Chinese terms in the main text whenever possible to make the book accessible to a broader audience. Otherwise, when I use Chinese terms they are transliterated using pinyin in italics, for example *qi* instead of chi. Chinese characters are sometimes included for easy reference.

Chinese Martial Arts: an Introduction

What is Tai Chi?

On the face of it, Tai Chi is a slow-motion movement art, a dance. A sequence of postures strung together by flowing, silk-like movement. It comes from China and is associated with Chinese identity. Practiced by millions of people around the world, it is an expression of what is sometimes called soft-power, a source of Chinese cultural pride and influence.

Most people will agree it is a martial art. Some Tai Chi schools practice combat testing, competitive bouts, and techniques for dispatching a threat, including weapons training.

The expression meditation-in-motion was coined to describe the positive effects Tai Chi has on the mind. Phrases like "inner-stillness" and "mind-body-integration" are commonly used to describe Tai Chi. Under the guise of stress-reduction, Tai Chi has a cure-all reputation for the hazards of modern life.

Its association with health and healing does not stop there. Tai Chi is widely reported to be good for improving circulation and balance. Anecdotally, it can cure disease, extend one's lifespan, and make us limber in old age.

Although it is controversial, Tai Chi is said to be powered by *qi*, a term mysterious enough to have been translated as *an invisible force which is the source of all life in the universe.*

Anyone picking up this book has probably already heard all this.

As someone who has practiced Tai Chi every day for thirty years, I find the simplicity of this surface gloss a bit embarrassing. My enthusiasm for Tai Chi is huge, and there are millions of us out there. So what is Tai Chi really?

Tai Chi comes from a tradition of theatrical-religious martial skills that use the imagination to create a more animated self, capable of fighting, and of fighting without fighting. It is a ritual. It is a form of body-awareness-renewal that nourishes our interactions with other people and the world. It is a form of whole body storytelling, that comes with its own story. It is a pre-modern form of exercise. Its origins are deep, accessible, and worth investigating.

Baguazhang, Tai Chi's lesser known cousin, comes from a similar theatrical-religious tradition, but its story is different. Baguazhang is a ritual of the spirit of rebellion. It embodies the contradiction of self-sacrifice and invulnerability. It is the embodiment of the greatest fighter, alternating between playful and sadistic, a whirlwind of conflicting emotions, and a dark path to enlightenment.

This book is an investigation of the mythology embedded in the martial arts. We are mythological creatures, or rather creatures who create mythology wherever we go and whatever we do. Re-connecting the martial arts to their mythology is life-affirming. Have you wondered why martial arts are done the way they are done, taught the way they are taught? Not only will this book satisfy your curiosity, whole new worlds open up when we re-vivify Baguazhang and Tai Chi with their original mythologies.

Knowing history unlocks the true content of the art and gives us access to new types of fruition. You may want information that will improve your skills. This book is rooted in the idea that grasping the context these arts were created in is equivalent to having a master key that unlocks Tai Chi and Baguazhang secrets. But I do not believe in spoon feeding. This book is for people willing to do the work.

We Begin in Darkness

I want to write a happy joyful book about Tai Chi and Baguazhang, because that's how I feel about the martial arts I have practiced for thirty years. These arts were created out of joy, not out of darkness and death. Yes, they come from a time when kidnapping and throat slitting were too common. But they were positive solutions to this everyday violence. These arts unleash a comic and playful vision of enchanted discipline. In today's peaceful world, martial arts are an ever growing delight.

But what hangs over this book, and the reason it needs to be written, is a darkness so bleak it is hard to speak of. There is a reason a non-academic American is authoring this book about the history and origins of Chinese internal martial arts. A dark reason. A hundred-million is the callous number thrown around for Chinese people murdered in the Twentieth Century. Twenty-million dead in World War II, millions of those swept away in flood waters intentionally released in a failed attempt by the Nationalists (KMT) to garner a military advantage over the Japanese. Tens of millions intentionally starved by the Communists during the years of the Great Leap Forward (1958-1962); Purges, public executions, mobs, civil war, prison camps, slave labor, street violence, suicide.

From 1899-1901, the Boxer Uprising saw only 100,000 deaths, but the reaction to it cut at the roots of martial arts. It began a process of destruction which brings us to the situation today, where modern martial artists have no solid understanding of where their arts come from.

Let's fix that.

In 1949, at the end of the Chinese Civil War, as the Communists were taking power, the remnants of the Nationalist forces fled to Taiwan. They escaped both the mass murder of the Great Leap Forward (1958-1962) and the Cultural Revolution (1966-1977). One would be forgiven for thinking that the story of the origins of Tai Chi and Baguazhang would have survived there. But Taiwan was under martial law until 1987. Martial arts were called Guoshu, National Arts, and teachers were registered with the authorities. Promoting a non-conform-ing history of the martial arts would have been met with repression. But, as I will show, the damage to historical memory was accomplished much earlier, between 1902 and 1940.

The Cultural Revolution had a profound psycho-emotional effect on Chinese martial arts. The fact that millions died does not tell the story of the cruelty inflicted on hundreds of millions. While it is growing less taboo, it is still hardly talked about and official figures are false. Much of what I know is anecdotal. Stories like this one a friend in Beijing told me: "At one point I got close to my Baguazhang teacher. We were drinking late into the night. I asked him some questions about the Cultural Revolution. He cried for hours." If we could hear them, the most common stories would be about brutalization, witnessing it and being forced to participate in it. Self-Criticism was a practice during the Cultural Revolution in which each person had to stand up and denounce a comrade in specific detail as a class enemy. That person would then stand up and confess, and then accuse someone else. It would go around the circle like this, each person shouting accusations and confessions. These "struggle sessions" happened every day, for ten years. For established martial artists, actors, and religious people, it was an environment of beatings, torture, suicide, and murder.

The Boxer Uprising

The Chinese felt humiliated in the aftermath of the Boxer Uprising (1899-1901). The Boxers suffered terrible losses due to the mass delusion that they were invulnerable to bullets. These rebels fought battles in which theatrical martial arts and religious culture were mixed together— an expression of cultural norms that had been active for centuries. As time passed, people treated the behavior of martial artists during the Uprising as a tragic anomaly, but in fact their behavior was consistent with martial culture at the time. The Uprising continues to affect the way we see Tai Chi and Baguazhang.

Those martial artists who fled to Taiwan with the Nationalists in 1949 were part of the Guoshu movement, exemplars of the effort to cut martial arts off from its roots in theater and religion. Guoshu grew out of

Jingwu, meaning Pure Martial Arts, which expresses the movement's goal of purification. They viewed the influence of religion and theater as diseases infecting martial arts. What began as humiliation became inwardly focused disgust at elements of Chinese culture itself. The Nationalists sought to overcome the stigmatizing slogan, "The Sick Man of Asia." The nationalist leader Chiang Kai-shek wrote, "Avenge Humiliation" on the top of every page of his diary for twenty years.[1] Those days are long gone, but the sense of disgust and indignation from that era still affects how people understand the arts and clouds their ability to see the origins of martial arts. The emotional ghosts of these lingering conflicts inhabits the thinking of both scholars and practitioners in the West.

We can fix this.

Seeing into Chinese culture is not as simple as living in China or being able to speak Chinese. It is Chinese custom to smile at personal tragedy. It is a way of saying, "You are not close enough to me to share that pain." If the authenticity of the smile is challenged, one is likely to get shut out. Or yelled at. A cool defensiveness is common too, "Oh, it wasn't so bad." Or "Oh, that was a long time ago." Or even, "It *was* bad for others, but it was not so bad for me." Add to that, it is considered rude to ask a direct question of a Chinese teacher because it is seen as an attack on their status. Westerners trying to get information about history might happen upon a generous and open-minded teacher—there are many—but the likelihood that this teacher's teacher was also open-minded is slim. This has resulted in a loss of continuity that did not just affect the martial arts. For the last few generations, Chinese Religion has teetered on the brink of extinction. It happened in traditional theater too, where asking a question was answered with a beating.

In Taiwan and Hong Kong people have become more open about discussing these things, but the continuity of enchanted mythology is still blocked by the filters of Twentieth Century trauma and conceit. Mo Yan, who won the Nobel Prize for literature, poetically embodies this frozen ethos— his pen name means, "Don't Speak."

---

[1] Platt 2017.

The story of the Twentieth Century is not all bleak. While the origin mythologies were lost, the arts themselves survived because people protected and preserved them. That is amazing, and the mythology is recoverable because Chinese culture is resilient. The basis for trust has been lost, but the real stories pop up all the time. Reliable sources float around disconnected from other reliable sources, waiting to be assembled and made coherent. This book will provide you with the basis for identifying reliable sources.

While the stated goal of the Communists was to eliminate human nature, they were piggy-backing on the modernist-Nationalist project to break from the past and create a superficial world where only those elements of Chinese culture which were rationally suited to progress could survive. Each of us has something in our pasts which we wish to disassociate ourselves from. We all have moments when we wish we were not so prone to human nature. But in China this desire to disassociate with the past grew into a succession of mass movements, which manifested in hysteria, fear, shame, and disgust. For Tai Chi and Baguazhang to survive, their origins had to be hidden. Like a child not allowed to scream in the dark for fear of discovery by soldiers.

While you read through this book, keep in mind that the beautiful arts we have today have passed through a filter of unimaginable horror. Also keep in mind that secrets were our friends. Keeping secrets and hiding treasures was the smart move. As it turned out, some body-knowledge integrated with enchanted mythology survived in odd pockets of rural China, and we can expect to find more in the future.

This book came about because I followed the advice from my first book, *Possible Origins*. I looked for the sources of Tai Chi and Baguazhang in theater and religion. Theater and religion were inseparable from martial arts in historic China. Finding the answers turned out to be easy. Yes, I have forty years of martial arts practice. Thirty years of world dance-theater training. Twenty years of Daoist studies. A grandfather who was an anthropologist that visited every country on earth and lived naked on an island off the coast of Singapore, sure. But the sources I used to write this book were neither hidden nor hard to find. I simply asked a few questions that no one else had thought to ask.

This book has four voices

One is enthusiastically in love with movement, meditation, martial arts, games, kung-fu movies, magic tricks, vibrant vigorous flying fabulous action-packed fighting displays. The doer. The improviser. The dancer. The voice that squeezes every drop of the nectar of life out of every martial arts movement.

Another voice is concerned with asking the right questions; with the accuracy of historical statements, and getting the right language to articulate precise understandings.

A third voice is concerned with the real consequences of violence and the moral value of self-defense.

And still another voice is that of a student of Daoism, who tries to live by the *Daodejing*, Daoism's most sacred text. In 1995 I began a nine-year intensive study with a Daoist teacher in Santa Cruz California named Liu Ming. This entailed a great deal of reading and practice, which I have written about elsewhere.[2] I practice four Daoist lineage teachings daily. The first two are forms of meditation called Sitting-and-Forgetting *(Zuowang)* and the Golden Elixir *(Jindan);* the third is a form of movement with visualization called Refining-and-Hollowing-Out *(Daoyin)*, the fourth is a dream practice called *Day-and-Night-the-Same*. It is my intention that these Daoist commitments infuse everything I write, teach, and perform.

[2] Phillips 2008, 161-176.

What Is Chinese Religion?

When large numbers of Christian missionaries started arriving in China in the 1800s they thought, "The Chinese are extremely superstitious, but they have no religion." The Chinese Religion, of which martial arts was an important part, was structured on a completely different set of assumptions from Christianity. From the point of view of Chinese Religion, Christianity was not a religion either.

To a Christian, religion is a matter of conscience and a set of beliefs. In contrast, there are four main components of Chinese Religion: the state, theatrical-rituals, text, and the body. I will go through them one by one and show how they each incorporate martial arts. My point is not to show how one type of religion is superior to another, but simply to help readers see the filters and biases both types of religion take for granted.

The State

A major function of ritual is to establish order. Before law was invented, everyone used rituals to create order.

China was a multilingual society and the majority of people were illiterate. Yet a small percentage of scholars were highly literate, and a basic level of literacy was widespread enough to support a dynamic publishing industry and a system of written law. Because of this mix of literacy and illiteracy, successive Chinese dynasties governed using a combination of written laws and official rituals. Both big and small rituals were understood to be part of a giant ritual network that created order and connected everyone together.

The concept of governance in China was called "the mandate of heaven." It was a collective maintained by the ritual rectification of differences. Enormous religious diversity was possible because people participated in rituals which integrated their local traditions into a large flexible cosmology. Whether you were practicing ritual at a home altar with your family, or out in the woods with a bandit army, you understood your ritual actions to be a part of this vast ritual network. This ritual network was a pantheon of deities. Deities were installed locally and managed by independent ritual groups. Yet they were part of one big imagined network. The Chinese thought of this network as an invisible parallel realm occupied by gods, ghosts, ancestors, demons, buddhas, and immortals. The two realms, the seen and the unseen, overlapped spatially. The world we live in—the visible world of forces, influences, and icons—occupied the same space as the invisible world of gods and ghosts. The idea of a separation of Church and State was entirely foreign because religious ritual was a function of the state even at the most intimate levels.

Daoist, Buddhist and Confucian ritual experts all saw their rituals as part of the same imagined network of family, local, regional, and national rituals. Personal prayers, talismans, meditation, oaths, healing, death, and martial arts practices were understood to be forms of ritual conduct that connected one's actions to the functioning of the whole nation. Chaos in heaven and chaos on earth were brought together in harmonious order by these same rituals.

This is not just a theory. The first large group of Chinese to adopt Christianity set off straight away to create a new state. They called their Christian-inspired rebellion Tai Ping (Great Peace) and set up a "New Kingdom of Heaven on Earth." The idea that a religion could be separate from the process of governance did not occur to them. (The Tai Ping civil war lasted from 1863-1878 and claimed twenty-million lives.)

Ritual-Theater

The second component of Chinese Religion was ritual-theater. People understood the ritual elements of performance as effective tools for managing order and chaos. Theater was physical. The basic training was martial arts. Most staged plays had extended fight scenes which were imagined to be taking place within this cosmic network of invisible forces. This imagined realm overlapped spatially with the visible world. A stage was like a window into the unseen world of ghosts and gods. Even the most hilarious comedies were a kind of exorcism in which the audience's uncontrollable laughter was thought to have the power to swallow demons.[3] Chinese Religion birthed as many types of ritual-performance as there are stars in the sky. While Christians thought of religion primarily as a matter of conscience and belief, Chinese saw religion as a ritual performance.

Text

The third component of Chinese Religion is text. Christians have one sacred text, the Bible. China had more than ten thousand. In Chinese Religion, text is capable of invoking the gods. The gods also write new texts through spirit-mediums. The texts of major plays were sacred because they were invocations of the gods. Before a sacred text could be opened and read, one had to perform a ritual. The bare minimum ritual was burning incense while imagining one's intentions being carried on the smoke. Even the texts of Confucian scholars, which sometimes appear secular to modern readers, dealt directly with the practical mechanisms of governance; and the most important mechanism of governance was ritual conduct, a religious act.

The first large group of Chinese Christians, the Tai Ping rebels, contacted the authors of the Bible directly through spirit-mediums. They enacted performances in which characters from the Bible would possess spirit-mediums, bringing the voices of the Bible to life. When the newly established Kingdom issued edicts, they were announced as texts produced from direct consultations with the family of Jesus, Moses, Mary, Noah, and others from the Bible. Hong Xiuquan, the leader of the Tai Ping rebels, learned in one of these spirit-consultations that he was in fact the younger brother of Jesus Christ.[4]

This basic orientation towards Chinese religion is important because physical and aesthetic elements of Baguazhang and Tai Chi come from theatrical-rituals and their sacred texts. These martial arts were part of Chinese religion.

---

[3] Plowright 2002, 47-59.

[4] Spence 1996.

The Body

The fourth component of Chinese Religion is the body. Christians (and Westerners in general) view individual conscience as the battle-ground of righteous action. We contrast this with the body, which we see as impure.[5] In Chinese Religion the body is a site of ritual action. The-ater, martial arts, meditation, spells, and talismans are all ritual actions that transform the body. These actions connect the adept to the vast net-work of everyone else practicing rituals. The physical body is in a dy-namic and reciprocal relationship with the imagined, unseen world.

Roughly speaking, Chinese Religion thought of our body as having two overlapping aspects, a physical body and a ritual body. A ritual body was a collective body. It was shared with the other people we did ritual with. Rituals harmonized, ordered, and aligned groups of people who saw themselves as sharing collective bodies. Practicing martial arts was a way of sharing a ritual body with all those who practiced the same art. The basic unit of a ritual body was a temple.

The average person thought that the actions of a god (or ghost) could affect our physical bodies through a ritual body we shared with them; and vise versa, our physical actions could affect the gods through the same shared ritual body. This reciprocal relationship to the unseen world —through the body—is one of the foundations of martial arts culture. It is also apparent in the family rituals everyone did for their ancestors, which we will discuss shortly.

Having established the four main components of Chinese Religion, the state, theatrical-rituals, text, and the body; it is easy to see how each incorporates martial arts. Now we can build on this basic understanding of Chinese Religion to reveal the context of martial arts in practice.

---

[5] There is an ever widening array of Christian views about the body, such that almost any generalization can be contested. During the period of missionary adventure in China (1870-1940), maintaining a healthy body became ever more important in the definition of Christianity. Still, the dominant Christian view is that the body is the place where un-holy desires stir, and thus, needs salvation in order for transcendence to take place.

Theater as a Source

Historically, in China, theater was everywhere. There were hundreds of different types of theater that people interacted with every day. Like computers or televisions today, theater manifested in innumerable contexts with a wide variety of purposes. China was a large country, with multiple languages, ethnicities, customs, climates, diets, gods, and heroes —and theater was everywhere.

In Shanxi, for example, a typical peasant could watch theater performed by a fifty-person professional troupe thirty times a year.[6] Professionals were hired to perform for every special occasion and for religious festivals throughout the year. A professional actor was trained from a young age in virtuoso kung fu with splits and flips like modern circus acrobats. Either by birth or adoption, actors were in a permanent under-caste, called *mean people*. They could not marry-out, nor were they allowed to do any other work, and they were not legally allowed to live within city walls.[7] They were considered below prostitutes and thieves. Professional actors could be bought, owned, leased, or hired by those who could afford it.[8] And it was a powerful symbol of status to own a whole troupe, or even an individual actor, for home entertainment and to impress guests. The child of a wealthy theater patron might even be given an acting troupe as a plaything. Actors were hired as instructors for martial arts and music.[9]

---

[6] Johnson 2009.

[7] Enforcement of this law varied, but it remained the law of the land until after the Boxer Uprising (1902). See Ye 2003, for a history of the laws, also Johnson 2009, 230.

[8] Food scarcity made long-term or indefinite leases and even bonded servitude viable arrangements. There were also territorial agreements for troupes to serve a region—suggesting that the origins of the mean people *jianmin* caste may have been punishment for serving a previous dynasty. Johnson 2009, 219-234 ; Hansson, 1996; Riley, 1997; Scott 1982; Mackerras 1997.

[9] Volpp 2011; Lei 2006. They were also generally understood to be available for sex. Sommer 2002.

Some theater groups were the residents of a pleasure quarters just outside a big city, called "scholar towns," others travelled the dangerous rivers and roads going from village to village. Villages had their own amateur troupes too, sometimes hundreds of them.[10] Standalone stages were everywhere, and most temples had a stage. The courtyards of temples were designated performing spaces for theater. Traveling troupes could set up massive elaborate theaters made from bamboo and rope in a couple of days, smaller stages went up in hours. Street theater was everywhere too. Participation in theater was the most common thing people did in their free time.

Professional theater was considered an essential part of most local religious events, but communities who could not afford actors could hire puppet troupes instead.[11] Villages also used puppets in religious festivals because they were the most powerful exorcists.[12] The widespread use of puppets had an important effect on the development of the aesthetics used in martial arts. Someone who could move like a puppet, with a mask-like face, was revered as having extraordinary skills.[13] There are elements of puppet theater in all Chinese martial arts. The extreme popularity of onstage fights owes something to the Punch-n-Judy-like antics of puppeteers.

Theatrical processions were a major part of Chinese culture. For example, some processions were led by local toughs with martial skills who would dress up as demon generals, wearing costumes and makeup and carrying theatrical torture implements. Theatrical festivals throughout China were called *"putting on a show for the gods"* because they would take the statues of the gods out of the temples and parade them around the village before taking the statues to the theater and placing them in the

[10] Johnson 2009, 145-149.

[11] *On ritual importance of opera see* Lagerway 2010; *on puppets as substitutes see* Chen 2007.

[12] Schipper 1994.

[13] Plowright 2002, chapters 2, 3, and especially 5, explain the specific connections between Tai Chi and puppets.
Suggested video: Jiaqi Huang. "Nezha Conquers the Dragon King" (a shadow-puppet-inspired animation): https://vimeo.com/101789329

Figure 1. Procession. The Illustrated Australian News, May 26, 1886, cover.

audience. One of these processions could take several days, with dance groups of 8-10 demon generals stopping to perform exorcisms in homes and businesses along the way. Bigger processions would travel from village to village. If they met another group of demon generals carrying a different god, they would have to fight them. There were countless local martial-dance-theater traditions like this, and each village had its own unique traditions. They used masks, makeup, and costumes to invoke the gods and demons, expressing their religious investments with the full

Figure 2. Chinese Theater 1908. (German Federal Archive: Bild 137-004763.)

range of commitment from silent, slow-moving, narrated tableaux on the one hand, to ecstatic, barefoot dances with self-mortification, bloodletting, fire, and explosions on the other.[14] Villagers infused the religious calendar with theatrical events that wove people's lives together. Professional theater performed by a degraded caste was everywhere, but locally diverse lineages and amateur experts were everywhere too. Tai Chi and Baguazhang were part of the theatrical culture of martial prowess that circled around temples and festivals. As I will show, both professional and amateur theater are sources for the physicality and aesthetics of Tai Chi and Baguazhang.

Ubiquitous Violence

Sometimes I hear it argued that theater and martial skills developed out of separate considerations, and are therefore different. In theory perhaps, but in practice they developed in the same bodies because violence, like theater, was everywhere.

War, rebellions, famines, and floods were always happening somewhere in China. Tit-for-tat village wars were so common they rarely made it into the history books. China was a relatively wealthy country for most of its history, and robbery and kidnapping were part of everyday

---

[14] Boretz 2011, 472-484; Boretz 2010; Sutton 2003. Suggested video search: "Bajiajiang."

life.[15] In every era before the Twentieth Century there were bandit armies prowling around, contesting territory, and recruiting loose men. There was a whole legal category of men called "bare-sticks," meaning unmarried, on the loose, and dangerous. By some estimates "bare-sticks" made up 25% of the male population.[16] When bandit armies joined revolutionaries or became religious fanatics, potential for violence increased.

Because violence was everywhere, people had to have ways of defending their bodies, their families, and their property. Everyone was organized into patronage networks of one sort or another. These were large lineage clans or alliances between families, led by a headman or a village council. A patronage network protected the people in it, giving them status within a hierarchy along with duties and obligations. Money collected for seasonal theater performances was also used by patronage networks to repair bridges and fix roads; it was like a local tax. Patronage networks ensured the food supply, kept track of favors, and managed the distribution of labor. If one needed to build a home, their patronage network helped with that. When men-at-arms were needed, the patronage network organized a militia. Martial arts were an integral part of patronage networks. In China, theater, martial skills, and religion were woven together and functioned as a platform for organizing, training, and commanding men-at-arms. Regular experiences with horrific violence spontaneously integrated martial and theatrical skills in the bodies that practiced them. These theatrical-ritual militias have been called "red spears" by scholars, but in practice they had unique local names based in the specific theater-mythology they used during ritual combat.[17] These groups were a relentless source of rural combat resistance throughout the first half of the Twentieth Century until the Communists finally rooted them out by executing their gentry leadership.

---

[15] Robinson 2001; Eshrick 1988.

[16] Ownby 2002, 226-251.

[17] Perry 1980, 269-273.

Fighting as Spirit Possession

A spirit-medium is a person who is possessed by a god, a demon, a ghost, an animal spirit, a legendary hero, a Buddha, or an Immortal. This concept is important for us to understand because it was a key part of the Boxer Uprising (1898-1901) which led to profound changes in the way martial arts were understood and practiced. One characteristic of Chinese spirit-mediums is that they do not remember the experience of being possessed. So, in theory, no one who participated in the Boxer Uprising would remember it. In China there were amateur spirit-mediums, who were possessed only once, and professionals, who were possessed regularly. Literary elite types of spirit-medium would pick up brush and paper and write down the words of a god who possessed the writing brush, not the person. Alternately, a possessed child would write the god's words in sand while a scholar stood by to interpret and write them down. Lowly mediums channelled the recently dead for distraught relatives, allowing the dead to speak through their mouths. Spirit-mediums healed with magic, talismans, or herbs. Others gave entertaining lectures or performed dance. Some chastised and cajoled witnesses to discard their sinful ways and live honest upright lives. Enlightenment practices, sex education, fighting skills, poems, songs, secret histories, games, jokes, and prophecies were all subjects taught by spirit-mediums.[18]

At festivals it was common to play spirit medium games. Here is a description of one from the early Twentieth Century:

> The "Descent of the Eight Immortals" is an invitation of one of the Eight Immortals to descend and to take possession of a man. The man must wash himself and lie on the ground under the moon. Fragrant water is sprinkled around him on the ground; an incense burner with incense, tea, wine and fruits are put beside his head as offerings to the immortal, and a bowl of cold water is placed at his feet. Another recites the "Incantation to the Immortal to Descend" walks around him and burns some paper money on each round. When he has repeated the sentences about three hundred times, the man lying on the ground falls asleep. Then he asks the man: "Master, are you a literary

---

[18] Chan, Margaret 2014, 25-46; Amos 1999; Clart 2003, 1-38; Paper 1995; Seaman 1988, *introduction.*

or a military immortal?" The man in sleep answers. If he is a literary immortal, pen, brush, ink, paper, a plate with sand and a chi-pen must be prepared. Then the man stands up and writes with the brush on paper or with the chi-pen in a plate full of sand. If he is a military immortal, then sword, spear, steel fork and some other weapons are prepared, and he is carried in a chair to a large open space. He chooses a weapon and brandishes it in the air. When he becomes tired, others may ask him whether he will have a pupil or not. If he gives a positive answer, a boy of twelve or thirteen years becomes his pupil. He then continues to brandish the weapon. Finally he is awakened by sprinkling water on his face. It is said that after his awakening he cannot remember anything of what he has done. This game as described above is played in Dongguan.[19]

Actors called the entrance to a stage the "ghost gate" because characters on the stage were dead.[20] The act of putting long dead heroes on the stage brought them back to life. Chinese culture conceptualizes most gods and demons as real people who, long ago, were transformed into deities by extreme actions or circumstances.[21] They are also ghosts. This is obvious in Chinese language where the term *gui* means ghost, the term *shen* means god—and the characters who perform on the stage are called *guishen.*

From a religious point of view, fighting itself was a form of spirit possession. To understand why, it will help to understand what a home altar is. Every Chinese home had two tables in the dining room (and most still do). One table was large enough for the family to eat together. The other table was a small altar positioned against a wall with the names of ancestors written on wooden slats. They used this altar to feed their ancestors. Every day, small food offerings were left on the ancestor-table, along with candles, flowers and incense. This was a symbolic reciprocal relationship with the ancestors. The altar was a way to thank the ancestors, and to remember and receive the fruits of their hard work and upright conduct.

---

[19] Wei-pang, Chao. "Games at the Mid-autumn festival in Kuangtung." *Folklore Studies* (1944): 1-16.

[20] "Ghost portal" *guimen* 鬼門

[21] Kleeman 1994; and Shahar, 1996.

It was a symbolic stage viewed by an imagined audience. The ancestors were observing their own legacy through the conduct of their descendants, as if looking through a window. Ancestors who died with a list of unfulfilled desires could find peace "watching" their descendants achieve their dreams. Ancestors, who suffered and sacrificed so that their descendants would have a better life, could find pride and joy "seeing" the family table full of happy people eating. At the same time, Chinese families expected their ancestors to continue doing the hard work of providing good fortune, from behind the "window" in the invisible world.

However, a person who died on a battlefield, or from suicide, could not be placed on the family altar. They were thought to be so consumed by conflicting emotions like anger and regret that they could cause harm to the family. This sad fate meant that they would not be fed, and they were in danger of becoming homeless, hungry, wandering ghosts. Homeless ghosts would linger in grasses and possess snakes and other things that were close to the ground. From there they could jump to humans and cause them to act violently. In the popular imagination, homeless ghosts were the major cause of violence.[22] This is why Chinese Religion considered fighting a type of spirit-possession. Many Chinese rituals, including Kung Fu, have origins in practices to clear away, or protect against, the influence of homeless ghosts.[23]

To mitigate the violence caused by homeless ghosts, people built shrines to feed them collectively. Seasonal rituals were performed by both Buddhists and Daoists for the same purpose. Both were experts on the processes of death and dying and performed these rituals on behalf of local communities and the state. The purpose of these rituals was to mitigate the potential negative influences of the dead. Over the last thousand years, the integration of such rituals into government protocols and local temple customs created countless Buddhist-Daoist hybrids.

I am doing my best to make this introduction to the religious and theatrical origins of Chinese martial arts accessible to readers who are hear-

----

[22] Meulenbeld 2015.

[23] Phillips 2016.

ing about Chinese religious culture for the first time. It is complex. It took me years to get just this basic understanding. So please bear with me as I make another leap.

In Chinese culture shrines are sites of spiritual power *(ling)*. Shrines for feeding homeless ghosts are just one type among many. For example, there are shrines for famous leaders and for local animal spirits. Over time, some shrines gain reputations for being efficacious in granting people's wishes and other types of empowerment. The occupant or occupants of a shrine are all made of the same stuff. Perhaps we could call it the consolidated essence of human memory and dreams. This is a kind of translation, not the thing itself. But in a sense, all shrines are places for feeding these memories. It is through feeding-rituals, over generations, that the occupants of these shrines become deified.

These feeding rituals are performances. But I must stop myself here and explain, "feeding" is not the right word, only lesser gods receive food offerings. Offerings and symbolic sacrifices are what the gods "eat." Professional opera was used as an offering to thank or appease the gods.[24] Opera storylines were picked based on what people assumed a particular god would like to see. Opera was just one of many types of offerings that were made. The choice and type of ritual offerings in general was important because deities were categorized by the types of offerings they received. For example, demons receive blood offerings, most gods receive incense and flowers, whereas immortals do not require offerings at all but may respond to sincere practice or heartfelt commitments.[25] Both Buddhists and Daoists, in their roles as certified ritual experts, limited and regulated the types of offerings that could be made. Daoist ritual experts, called Daoshi, sometimes called "priests" in English, did not make or participate directly in blood sacrifice, but in other ways they were close to the local ritual traditions of exorcism, healing, and spirit-mediums because they had the power to issue certificates of ritual orthodoxy. A cer-

------

[24] Lagerway, 2010.

[25] The more lively and gritty gods received hard liquor and (probably) pornography.

tificate meant that the cult in question was deemed harmless to the established order.[26]

By precept, Daoist priests did not become possessed. Instead, they used emptiness and quietude to contact and control spirits, ghosts, and gods. That is why meditation was so important, it established emptiness in the ritual expert which gave him or her the power to affect entities in the spirit world. Puppets, which are naturally empty, were used by Daoist exorcists for the same reason. A puppet, especially a marionette, could perform an exorcism while maintaining its emptiness and thereby avoid being possessed. It is because of this capacity that puppet-like movement was treasured by martial artists. The puppet aesthetic is associated with being able to avoid spirit-possession, to, in a sense, fight without fighting. Emptiness was considered the most powerful protector against possession by evil forces.[27] That is a profound difference between Chinese and Western religious traditions.

Given this context it is hard to miss that Tai Chi movement is puppet-like. Because martial performances implicitly threaten to spill blood, and demons are attracted to blood, martial performances functioned within exorcisms as a kind of bait for attracting demons and ghosts so that they could be captured and either killed, imprisoned, or enlisted in service of the good. Being empty like a puppet was both protective and a position of potency for commanding, controlling, subduing, or calming tortured and lost entities in the invisible world. Both Tai Chi and Baguazhang were part of theatrical rituals in this imagined world of chaotic forces—where offerings and deity invocations were integrated into daily life. Actor martial-artists were a type of ritual expert who cultivated the ability to maintain emptiness in motion. The integration of emptiness-in-motion is called the Golden Elixir *(jindan)*. Combined with martial skills, it is what defines the internal martial arts. This idea and the Golden Elixir

---

[26] Schipper 2012, *x*.

[27] Schipper, 1993. It should be noted that the image of a puppet coming to life is a horror story in many different cultures, including China. The possessed puppet and the puppet which cannot become possessed are paired opposites in the unconscious mind. Also see Chan, Margaret 2012.

itself are the subject of the final section of this book. This is not just a general theory of internal martial arts; the specific detailed origins of Tai Chi and Baguazhang fit this cosmology.

Demonic Warfare

Imagine what it was like to lose a small war and have a shrine where your people, who died fighting, were ritually fed. In peacetime, the hope was that these rituals would calm the spirits of the dead so that they would not cause future violence. When another war came along, the meaning of these rituals would shift. They were used to rile up memories of the dead, to motivate people for battle and vengeance, in effect, to enlist the spirits of the dead for warfare.

Because warfare was a regular feature of Chinese life, over the centuries this mechanism became systematized. When homeless ghosts were enlisted for battle, they were called ghost-soldiers. In pre-battle rituals, ghost-soldiers were commanded by demon generals who were themselves ritually conscripted to serve righteousness. These demons were called thunder gods and could be invoked and commanded by Daoist priests and other ritual experts.[28] Over centuries, these rituals became complex seasonal theatrical events where a demonic character went through a series of transformations over several days, passing from demonic to heroic. In Catholicism, the term for transforming a pagan god into a Christian saint is called canonization.[29] Chinese culture was doing something similar in this type of theater, so scholars call it a canonization ritual.[30] This is important because both Tai Chi and Baguazhang are closely connected to the texts of canonization rituals.

Canonization and thunder rituals are important because they explain a number of things which might not be obvious. They explain why

---

[28] Some early versions of this ritual used explosives to reify the awesome power of these gods. If we ever get a cultural history of firecrackers, I suspect we will see a connection to thunder gods.

[29] Canonization by the Catholic Church is a recognition of sainthood; however, the Catholic State, with military power, converted pagan gods into saints via canonization.

[30] Meulenbeld, 2015. The Chinese word for canonization is *feng* 封.

Figure 3. Thunder Gods. Cleveland Museum of Art. (Album of Daoist and Buddhist Themes: Procession of Daoist Deities: Leaf 19) 1200s. Creative Commons 1.0

Figure 4. Garuda, on the entrance to the Porcelain Tower in Nanjing, marking it as a shrine to the battlefield dead. (Excavated). 1500s. Photo: Prof. Gary Lee Todd, Nanjing Museum. Creative Commons 4.0.

Figure 5. Porcelain Tower in Nanjing, "Temple of Repaid Gratitude," constructed during the early-1500s as a war memorial. Destroyed during the Taiping Rebellion. This was a shrine to the battlefield dead. Johan Nieuhof, Het Gezandtschap der Neêrlandtsche Oost-Indische Compagnie, 1665. Maastricht University Library.

theater was taken seriously as a source of martial prowess. They also give us background to understand Daoist rituals that invoked ghost-soldiers as a source of unseen power, as well as rituals for pacifying homeless ghosts as sources of disease and violence. Daoists used emptiness to command ghost-soldiers to serve the community in acts of merit, as did other ritual traditions. The extent to which Daoist ritual was incorporated into warfare is controversial because the lines between what is and is not Daoist are contested. But as we shall see, these rituals connect with the earliest form of Tai Chi.

The major Chinese epics were constructed from canonization rituals. For example, the epic *Journey to the West*— the story of the monkey Sun Wukong traveling to India with his demon buddy Pigsy and the Buddhist monk Xuanzang in search of Buddhist Scriptures to bring back to China— is built around canonization rituals. They fight in nearly every

Figure 6. Zhenwu, Black Flag, painting, source unknown.

episode, and gradually accumulate merit.[31] Indeed, when people went into battle they might do a ritual to become possessed by one of these reformed demons like Sun Wukong or Pigsy, in order to make themselves better fighters. Numerous remote northern villages were using these methods right up to the Communist takeover in 1949.[32] Bottom rung Hong Kong gangsters were still using a small-scale version of deity-possessed fight rituals to develop martial skills in the 1970s.[33] Canonization

---

[31] The meaning of Kung Fu or *gongfu* is somewhat contested outside of Daoist circles. Inside of Daoism, especially in Fujian, it means "accumulated merit," the basic training for becoming a Daoshi (priest). See Schipper 2000.

[32] Perry 1980, 224-237.

[33] Amos 1983, dissertation.

rituals were sources of martial prowess for both combat troops and individuals.

Most of the major Chinese epics developed over several hundred years using improvisation and were codified, compiled, and published in their present forms during a short period called the Wanli era (1573-1620).[34]

Canonization of the Gods (Feng-shenyanyi) is a collection of canonization rituals assembled in a storyline about the transition between the ancient Shang Dynasty and the Zhou Dynasty. It contains the origin story of the god Nezha, China's greatest human fighter. Later in the book I show how Nezha is the aesthetic basis for Baguazhang. This collection of rituals was used to organize militias and played a major role in the Boxer Uprising.

Figure 7. Stealing the Black Flag. From *Xiyangji*, 1597. (Staatsbibliothek, Berlin).

Journey to the North is a collection of canonization rituals for numerous demons and thunder gods subsumed inside the bigger story of the god Xuanwu's (the Mysterious Warrior) thirty-six rebirths before being canonized as the god Zhenwu (the Perfected Warrior).[35] As I will show, the

---

[34] Carlitz 2005, 267-303.

[35] See "Illustrating Grootaers, or, the Principle Gods of Rural Xuan-Da and their Iconographies" http://twosmall.ipower.com/blog/?p=3876 A Guardhouse Temple to the Perfected Warrior was often constructed on the North Wall of Chinese Villages across northern China.
Chao 2011, is a thorough exploration of Xuanwu. Seaman 1980, is a translation of *Journey to the North*.

Figure 8. Black Flags, Contemporary Taiwan.

beginning of the Tai Chi form tells the story of Zhang Sanfeng learning Tai Chi from Xuanwu in a dream. However, that story is not in the standard edition of *Journey to the North*.

There is, however, an epic play called *Journey to the West in a Boat* in which Zhang Sanfeng demonstrates his exceptional fighting skills. In the play, the Emperor of China is an incarnation of Xuanwu but does not know it. Zhang Sanfeng helps to recover Xuanwu's stolen seven-star black flag, which is a symbol of the god's true-form *(zhenxing)* and of his power to unleash thunder and lighting.[36] The seven-star black flag was, and still is, a magical weapon used in Chinese religious communities. It has the power to hold possessing deities down on earth during spirit-

[36] On contemporary uses of the Black Flag see, Chan, Margaret 2016. On true-form, *zhenxing, see,* Verellen 1970, 174.

medium rituals like the ones described earlier. The flag is also used to invoke thunder gods. These plays and the Black Flag are important pieces of the Tai Chi puzzle we will return to shortly.

Keep in mind that these plays or "canonization rituals" were as common as the story of Cinderella is in the West. More than just fairytales, they were the myths and cosmology that local institutions were built on. As we shall see, Tai Chi and Baguazhang come from these myths.

Now that you have this basic background in the religious-theatrical culture of China I can begin to paint for you a detailed picture of the origins of Tai Chi and Baguazhang. But before I do that, it will help to understand the massive changes that Chinese culture went through after the Boxer Uprising. Nearly everyone, including scholars, and educated people raised in China, sees the origins of martial arts through a biased filter. I call this filter the YMCA Consensus.

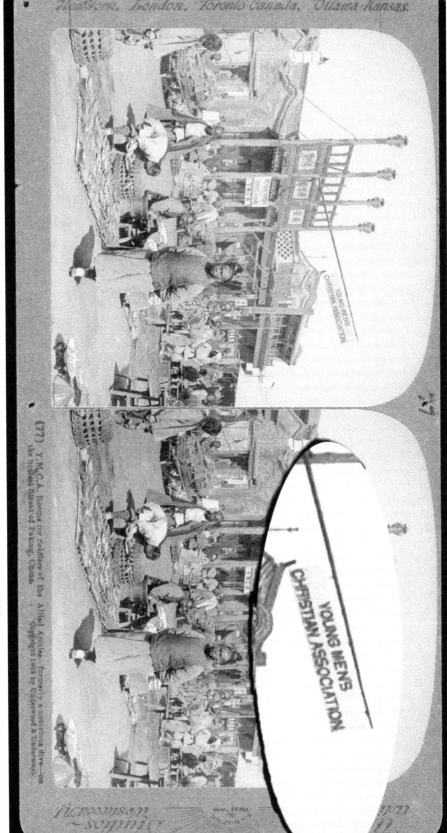

Figure 9. YMCA in China, 1900. Underwood & Underwood 1902.

The YMCA Conquers China

Christian missionaries vastly increased their influence and numbers in China in the second half of the 1800s. These missionaries had expertise in medicine and education. The Young Mens Christian Association (YMCA) was just one of many successful missionary groups; it is a good example because it is well known in the United States for its secular openness and its athletic programs. The YMCA went to China to convert people to Christianity. Their main strategies were to build hospitals and schools, to liberate women, advance ethnic equality, and promote prosperity. About half the missionaries were female and often unmarried.

The Western idea that moral fortitude was akin to clean living with regular exercise got its start in the second half of the 1800s and gained momentum throughout the early Twentieth Century. Scholars call this "Muscular Christianity."[37] By the 1920s it was so successful that the promotion of exercise and displays of robust health became a hallmark of nationalist movements worldwide. As we shall see, in China it took on some unique characteristics.

Originally the YMCA was an urban version of a secret society or gentlemen's club like the Freemasons or the Knights of Columbus. These institutions helped fuel manifest destiny in the American west because a man could come into town, join the Freemasons and instantly have a network of support for finding work and making a life. The YMCA's urban mission was to create network-hubs for class integration where recent arrivals could connect socially with middle class professionals and the creators of industry.[38] The YMCA's success in this project spurred them to integrate this powerful vision into their missionary work in China.

Groups such as the YMCA saw themselves as having a universal vision of redemption without dogma. Like most Protestant sects, they were reflexively antagonistic to rituals which they saw as repetitive, dogmatic,

---

[37] Miracle 2016, 17-43.

[38] Miracle 2016, 17-43.

and superstitious. Since nearly everything in Chinese culture was built around rituals of social organization, groups like the YMCA organized and converted people by offering alternative ways to raise money, organize mutual-aid, and resolve conflicts. Drawing on international connections, they were a counterforce to local patronage networks. They opposed Chinese opera because it put gods on the stage, and they worked to disrupt opera's connection to festival-temple-militia-organizing. They sought to undermine Buddhist and Daoist sources of expertise in healing, funerals, and communal harmony.[39]

Recall that Chinese theater is a ritual tradition in which gods and ghosts perform on the stage using explosive martial prowess. Chinese theater was a major source of conflict with missionaries. Missionary groups forbade Chinese Christian converts from attending theater.[40]

Drought Dragons

The Boxer Uprising (1898-1901) was complex. There are excellent books on the subject already and I do not intend to duplicate them. I have two reasons for discussing it. The first is to explain the role martial arts played in the Uprising. The second is to explain the powerful role the Uprising had in creating Chinese people's modern view of martial arts.

One of the causes of the Boxer Uprising was the conflict between the institution of Chinese theater and groups like the YMCA. In 1898, after widespread crop failures, which were blamed on missionaries whom Chinese labelled "drought-dragons," peasants began training martial arts in groups that swelled into the hundreds.[41] They performed theatrical rituals in which they became possessed by various gods of the theater. The purpose of these rituals was to make them great fighters with magical

---

[39] This issue is complex and is a hot topic of scholarly investigation at the time of this writing. New, indigenously inspired, "Redemptive Societies" modeled on the YMCA found ingenious ways to integrate diverse religious appetites. They created new ways to be Daoist and Buddhist as the old ways were dying. See the three collections of essays edited by David Palmer 2011, 2011, 2012.

[40] In retaliation, village communities banned Christians from attending the theater too.

[41] Clark 2017, 47.

powers, including invulnerability to Western bullets and cannons. They believed their gods were already fighting foreign gods up in the skies and in foreign lands. They set about killing Chinese Christians and foreigners, while destroying infrastructure, especially trains, telegraph lines, churches, hospitals, and schools. Destruction was often indiscriminate because they used fire as a weapon.

The Boxer Rebels were not a cultural anomaly. What they practiced was right in line with a form of martial-religious-theater familiar to all in northern China. However, the particular triggers for the Uprising were unique to the moment, and the government was poorly prepared and split on how to respond.

Initially, Chinese government intentions swung back and forth, alternately opposing and then supporting the Boxers. Large numbers of Chinese Christians flooded into Beijing for protection in the foreign embassies. Thousands were housed next door to the British embassy in the Prince Su Palace after the prince, who opposed the Boxers, agreed to vacate it. Because the Palace was fortified, it soon became a major line of defense. Under the sway of princes who supported the Boxers, the Chinese government made the decision to attack the foreign embassies.[42] That decision triggered an invasion by eight foreign countries, all of which were Christian-identified except Japan. The Eight Nation Alliance wreaked havoc on the port city of Tianjin and looted the Imperial Palace in occupied Beijing. About 100,000 Chinese perished.

The eventual result was the collapse of the last Chinese dynasty ten years later. The Chinese leaders who emerged to replace it had come up through organizations like the YMCA. The founder of the first Chinese Republic, Sun Yat-sen, was a Western-trained doctor who graduated from a Christian missionary hospital school in Hong Kong. Both Sun and Chiang Kai-shek, his eventual successor, were married to the Methodist, Wesleyan University-trained Soong Sisters. They were daughters of Vanderbilt University-trained Methodist missionary turned successful

---

[42] Prince Duan was identified by the foreign armies as the leader of the pro-Boxer princes. Prince Zhuang's Palace was the headquarters of Boxers in Beijing, an altar was set up there as the first place Boxers were to report when they arrive in the city.

business man, Charlie Soong, who was a close friend and advisor to Sun Yat-sen. Another daughter of Charlie Soong married H.H. Kung, who was born to a prominent Shanxi banking family and attended missionary schools. H.H. Kung designed the economic policies of the Nationalist government. Kung and Sun had met in the late 1800s in church and soon realized they both belonged to secret societies which sought the overthrow of the Qing Dynasty.

The influence of Western culture was profound and disruptive but it would be a mistake to think that these changes were simply imposed on China from the outside. During the second half of the 1800s, China was awash with religious strife, secret societies, rebellion, and civil war; China was motivated by lively intellectual debates and experiments to improve society. It was common for Chinese elites to express the view that traditional society was crippling innovations in technology, commerce, the emancipation of women, education, science, and medicine. The Chinese people were looking for change.

In 1898 the Emperor issued an edict declaring that all temples be turned into schools. The idea came from a prominent scholar named Kang Youwei, who hoped to transform China into a single state religion modeled on Christianity in which everyone attended a weekly mass based on the Five Confucian Classics. While enforcement of the edict was initially limited, it was adopted by successive governments as the "Destroy temples to build schools" movement. Half a million temples were confiscated or destroyed by government, local power brokers, and mobs over the next four decades.[43]

In the aftermath of the Boxer Rebellion, the traditional combination of theater, religion, and martial arts were widely and directly blamed for the humiliations China suffered. Suppression campaigns followed. Religious culture that did not conform to Protestant standards was labelled superstition. Religious institutions were pressured to codify doctrine and reform their organizational frameworks to align with Protestant sensibilities. As temples were forcibly confiscated or destroyed, Daoists and Buddhists began devising new individualistic forms of practice and participa-

---

[43]Nedostup 2009; Goossaert 2006, 307-35.

tion. The YMCA and the Red Cross became models for Chinese Religion to re-make itself. Religious organizations had to have outreach, charity, a membership, a regular constituency, a popular moral code for upright living, and other elements of evangelical Protestantism. That which was not "organized" was labeled superstition *(mixin* 迷信*)*. I call this the YMCA Consensus.

From the beginning of the Republic (1912), the YMCA Consensus was the official policy of all political factions. The YMCA Consensus was shared by government supporters and detractors amongst the intelligentsia. In other words, the diverse debates about how to modernize China took place within the YMCA Consensus.

Many forms of local theater went extinct during this period. The survival of local theater was increasingly dependent on severing its connection to the divine—and to the spontaneous—which had long been taken as proof that the gods were present. The YMCA Consensus blamed the culture of traditional theater for bringing catastrophe down on China and holding back progress. The Consensus saw theater as the heart of Chinese resistance to "the good news" modern Western institutions were bringing. Chinese theater put unruly gods and demons on the stage as sources of history, social organization, moral order, and inspiration. The YMCA Consensus saw traditional theater as the enemy. The new government saw festivals which sponsored local ritual-theater as backwards and superstitious, or worse, as an entrenched form of resistance to national unity that had to be crushed. Incidentally, in 1904, the first person to call for the drastic separation of theater from its roots in martial prowess and religious purpose was Chen Duxiu, the eventual founder of the Chinese Communist Party.[44]

The invulnerability practices of the martial arts were an integral part of temple, street, and village theater, and took the brunt of anti-superstition ire. The targeting of theatrical culture began as ridicule and progressed to the fierce anti-superstition campaigns the Nationalists carried

[44] Li 1996, dissertation 60-77.

out from 1926 to 1937 with the goal of eradicating temple and festival centered theater.

On the upside, the changes in theater led to women becoming performers in numbers not seen since the end of the Ming Dynasty (1644). Actors were now free to escape their degraded status as it was no longer imposed by the government or society at large. "Talking theater" was imported and promoted by students returning from Japan.[45]

In the 1920s and 30s new types of theater and new plays were used in "model village" projects. These projects were YMCA funded and they attempted to use the Chinese love of theater as a vehicle for promoting literacy and agricultural reform. These plays also promoted a vision of self-governance and national unity (which in hindsight was rather conflicted).[46] This strategy of using theater was then adopted by the Communists to mobilize against class enemies. [47]

Because the Boxer Uprising was seen as a profound failure of traditional martial prowess, martial arts initially took the brunt of criticism aimed at religion in general. The YMCA Consensus offered a path of survival for martial arts. The Nationalists, who wanted desperately to negate the label "the sick man of Asia," saw exercise and sports as a way to achieve a healthy nation. They thought martial arts might also be leveraged as a source of national pride. Nationalist movements around the world valorized folk dance as a tool for infusing their populations with patriotism. Could martial arts fulfill that role for China? For that to happen, martial arts had to be purified of superstitious and backwards elements. At first this movement was called *jingwu*, pure martial arts, and *tiyu*, physical culture.[48] In 1928 it became known as Guoshu (National

---

[45] Counterintuitively, Beijing Opera rose in popularity during this period because, 1) It was able to weed its repertoire of offending content, 2) The patronage and temple based sources of funding were cut off causing actors to flee to urban areas of the South where they were able to re-establish themselves in a more secular mode. But overall, and over time, the trend was downward.

[46] Merkel-Hess 2016, 89-101; Gamble 1954, 329-407.

[47] Li 1996, 329-377.

[48] Morris 2004, 185-289.

Arts) and was promoted to establish nationalist body discipline. After the Communist revolution in 1949 it was called Wushu.

In a sense, the creation of pure martial arts is inseparable from the tempest of mass killings that ripped through China during the first eighty years of the Twentieth Century. From its inception it was an act of survival partially motivated by hysteria, humiliation, and self-contempt. On the other hand it came out of a desire to preserve some essential part of a great treasure, to create a vision of martial arts within modernity. On one side of this tragedy we have insanity and evil, on the other, strategic attempts to protect beauty. The more complete the picture you and I have of the martial arts before the Boxer Uprising, and the events that changed martial arts throughout the Twentieth Century, the more equipped we will be to distinguish between these two trends.

As I have learned about the mythological content of the martial arts I practice, it has become a map to discovering hidden treasures in every part of my being. Whatever small merit there was in abandoning this content after the Boxer Uprising, it is thoroughly worth re-claiming now.

Humor was, up until the 1930s and even into the 1940s, a central and glorious part of Chinese culture.[49] Humor was also an important part of Chinese martial arts. But Chinese traditions of humor were tortured and crushed in mainland China, beginning in the 1930s before the Communists took power, and after 1949 China became a humorless desert. Of course, humor is part of human nature, and it keeps popping up no matter how many times it gets pounded down. But the story is a bleak one. One reason to know the mythic and cosmological origins of Tai Chi and Baguazhang is so that we can recover the glorious and powerful jester-like energy that they intrinsically embody.

We will return to the Boxer Uprising and look more closely at a few strong and creative voices within the YMCA Consensus when we explore the specifics of Baguazhang's transformation from a theatrical-ritual into a pure martial art. But now we are ready to dive into the history of Tai Chi.

---

[49] Rea 2015.

Tai Chi

The first half of the Twentieth Century saw a fight over the origins of Tai Chi. Initially, everyone said that it came from the Immortal Zhang Sanfeng. The dispute over Tai Chi's origins was not rational. It was an attempt to disenchant Tai Chi from its origins. Readers may or may not be familiar with all the debates, but for now, I will stick with the facts, and later we will return to politics.

My own experience with Tai Chi told me that it must have some roots in the theater. I intuited this because Chen style Tai Chi felt like a performing art. My years of studying Indian dance, mime, theater, and other forms of dance made the theatrical elements of Tai Chi obvious to me, especially the mimed gestures in the Tai Chi form, but to convince anyone else, I would need some evidence. What kind of evidence would be good enough? How about a four-hundred year old play that has Zhang Sanfeng fighting with the named movements from the Tai Chi form?

It was not hard to find this play. It is not an obscure play. There are almost certainly others. I am simply the first person to ask, what are the theatrical origins of Tai Chi?

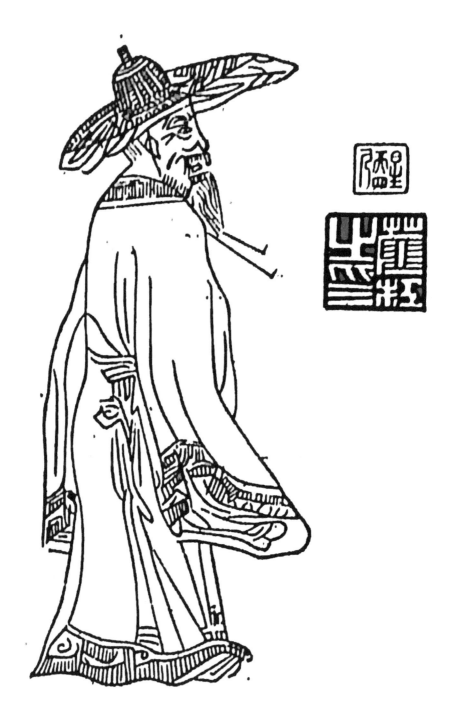

Figure 10. Zhang Sanfeng.

Fighting without Fighting:

How to Beat Up Twenty-Four Guards in Thirty-Two Moves

Our story begins with a short skit about a magical immortal named Zhang Sanfeng, who has hygiene problems. In the skit our immortal effortlessly defends himself against thirty-two attacks unleashed by twenty-four palace guards. Each of the attacks has a name, for example, "face full of flowers technique." Some are the same as the names in the modern Tai Chi form. Nineteen of them match the names used in a famous poem written by General Qi Jiguang in 1563.

This skit is contained inside of a larger play, which is an assemblage of history, stories, poems, and plays with a through-line about the Admiral Zheng He and his journey to faraway lands. The full play has 100 chapters and is called *Sanbao Taijian Xia Xiyang Ji*, which is shortened to *Xiyangji*, and means, *Three Treasure's Journey to the West in a Boat*.[50] The skit about Zhang Sanfeng is mostly in chapter 57, but I have included details from chapters 56 and 58. The preface to the play is dated 1597 but parts of it are decades older.[51]

---

[50] Three Treasures is an honorary name for Zheng He.

[51] The date of the book's preface is 1597, but large sections of the *Xiyangji* are older—see Goode 1976, *dissertation*. The 1590s saw an explosion of publishing that followed improvements in technology and increased wealth. Many of the standard versions of theatrical literature were composed during this decade, all of which were based on earlier versions of these plays, in some cases dating back several hundred years. These would include *Journey to the West*, *Outlaws of the Marsh*, *Three Kingdoms*, and *Canonization of the Gods* —see Carlitz 2005, 267-303.

Zhang Sanfeng Meets the Buddha and Gets in a Drunken Brawl

In the play, the Buddha comes to Zhang Sanfeng to ask for his help in retrieving the Emperor's seven-star black flag. This is the Yongle emperor of the Ming Dynasty who, in the play, is an incarnation of the Mysterious Warrior god Xuanwu, but he does not know it. The flag was stolen by Golden Hair Dao Elder and taken to the island of Java, where it is used as a weapon against the Chinese fleets fighting there. This flag can cause the entire cosmos to be transformed into brown water if it is waved overhead in a circle three times. Thus, the Buddha is in a bit of a bind. Presumably he has the power to take back the magic flag but it would entail violating his vows of non-violence, and no one else has been strong enough to beat Golden Hair Dao Elder, who is more than thirty feet tall, has round eyes, purple whiskers, and wears a white robe with a jade belt and a gold crown.

When Buddha finds Zhang Sanfeng he asks, "Why are you so dirty?" Zhang answers, "The stinking skin bag cannot be escaped."

Buddha asks, "If you cannot escape it, how can you get fruition?"

Zhang then gives the Buddha a comic lecture about the nature of enlightenment. The answers he gives in the text were lifted from one given by the leader of the Eight Immortals, Lu Dongbin, in the earlier published epic *Journey to the East*. I believe this part of the play is meant to be improvised. A debate between Zhang Sanfeng and the Buddha about the importance of having a body is a great set-up for laughs! Actors in this era were expected to improvise much of the dialog.[52]

Zhang Sanfeng agrees to help and goes directly to the capital where his friend Hu is the Secretary of Rites and has access to the Emperor. However, he arrives at night and his friend is not around, so he falls asleep inside the Imperial City in front of the secretary's office.

His snoring is so vigorous that the palace guards at first think it is an earthquake and twenty-four of them rush to investigate. As they approach Zhang Sanfeng, they are overwhelmed by the smell of booze and

---

[52] Carlitz 2005, 267-303.

vomit. They see a filthy man, covered in scabs, sleeping in his raincoat with a large hat and a halberd shaped beard. While his snores continue to vibrate the entire neighborhood, the guards argue about what he is doing there, who he is, and what they should do with him. They speculate wildly. Again, this dialog reads like a placeholder for an extended improvisation. One guard wonders if he is there on official business. Another says he appears to have the attributes of a Daoist official who sleeps like a bow, stands like a pine, walks like the wind, and sounds like a bell. Another says that if they leave him where he is he might get in big trouble. For his own good, they decide to take him outside the city gates to sleep off his intoxication. First one guard tries to lift him but cannot. Then two try, then three, then six, then nine, then twelve, then all twenty-four try to lift him but cannot. They start to get angry and accuse him of faking sleep. One guard lifts the heavy wooden crossbar from the door and smacks Zhang Sanfeng in the head thinking that will wake him. Zhang Sanfeng then says to himself, "Has someone just hit me? I feel strange. I better act before I lose my rotting flesh bag," and he woke up just enough to flick the crossbar with his finger sending it flying through the air for twenty-five li (which is more than ten miles).

A guard then attacks Zhang Sanfeng with **Grand Mountain Crushing Peak** technique but he misses and strikes another guard who responds with **Immortal Dodges Shadow** technique. Another guard attacks Zhang using **Magpie Fights for Nest** technique but he misses, too, and hits another guard who responds with **Crows Feeding** technique. Then another guard offers **Face Full of Flowers**, which is countered by **Pull the Ground Brocade**, then comes **Golden Cock Stands on One Leg** followed by a **Capture Tiger Body Slam**. A **High Four Directions** punch is countered by a **Middle Four Direc-**

tions jab.[53] Then a **Well Railing Four Directions** sweep is met by a **Pound The Mortar Fist**. Then **Tiger Grabs the Head** elicits **Dragon Bares its Claws** and **Standard Phoenix Elbow** brings out a **Reverse Phoenix Elbow**. A **Cannon Fist to the Head** gets back a flying **Diagonal Body Slam**. Now an **Evade with Weakness to Generate Strength** punch is met by a **Cut the Long, Reinforce the Short** smack. A **Single-Tail Whip** meets a **Seven-Star Sword** poke, causing a **Demon Stamping Leg** to bring out a **Continuously Shooting Cannon**. **Down Thrust Up** fist meets **Up Surprises Down** fist. A **Fake Pat on a Leg** triggers a **Fast Pat on a Horse**. A **Sky Full of Stars** slap is met with a **Tiger Grasping the Ground** and finally a **Fire Scorches the Heart** palm is countered by a **Scattering of Flowers Over the Head** punch. While none of these attacks manage to land on Zhang Sanfeng, all the guards lay beaten and bruised.

In the morning, Zhang Sanfeng's friend gets him an audience with the emperor, whose name is Perpetual Happiness (Yongle). During an extended interview, Zhang preaches the Daoist virtue of "knowing sufficiency."[54] This makes the Perpetual Happiness Emperor furious. His anger allows Zhang Sanfeng to capture the Emperor's true-nature *(zhenxing)* in a gourd which he then gives to the Buddha.

The Buddha then uses the Emperor's true-nature to recover the seven-star black flag and defeat Gold Hair Dao Elder in Java. Then the em-

---

[53] The term translated here as "four directions" or "flat" is *siping*. It can mean four directions, level, or flatten. Douglas Wile offers that it may be related to a push-hands control strategy 1996, 42. Marnix Wells (personal communication) offers that it means to "shutdown" one's options, like the Tai Chi move Six Closing Four Sealing—a movement which Louis Swaim suggests refers to marking a crime scene or sealing a demon into a pickle jar. Pickle jars used for this purpose are actually called wells *(jing)*. Wells are symbolically represented by a square surrounded by a circle, like a Chinese coin. On the other hand, *siping* is an opera mode, for instance it is used in the well known opera *Drunken Concubine*. So perhaps this should be translated something like, "tango his face," or "make him sing the Blues." Siping could also be a reference to the "armies of the four directions" cult which is the spatial foundation for every Chinese town. It could also be a reference to a type of counterbalancing technique—Swaim 1999, 188-189; Shahar 2008, 226n.
Given that it is poetic, multiple meanings are intended.

[54] *Zhizu* 知足, from *Daodejing*, Chapter 46.

peror's true-nature is returned to Zhang who is faced with arrest and imprisonment by the emperor's Brocade Guard. However, the emperor is sick and Zhang claims to be able to cure him if given a chance. He is then pardoned after healing the emperor by restoring his true-nature.[55]

What Does It Mean?

These thirty-two fighting techniques are in pairs: "this *quan*" followed by "that *quan*," or this move versus that move. The term *quan*, denoting each technique, is the same word used in Taijiquan or T'ai Chi Ch'uan depending on your transliteration system. It means fist, or punch, or the art of boxing, but here it is used to denote a theatrical movement or action. I took the liberty of using action words like slap, slam, and smack in this translation.[56]

It is likely that many of these named action-moves appear in other plays. For example, *Scattering Flowers over the Head* is a move from the Monkey King epic *Xiyouji*.[57]

I found nineteen of the thirty-two moves in the fight scene above in the thirty-two verses of General Qi Jiguang's famous poem from 1563. The poem is in a book he wrote about his success fighting pirates. I will introduce Qi Jiguang and his poem in greater depth later on, but for the moment, readers who are not familiar with it should know that it is widely cited as the oldest text featuring the movements named in the Tai Chi form.[58] Martial arts historian Tang Hao (1887-1959) found twenty-five of Chen Style Tai Chi's movements in Qi Jiquang's poem, and Gu Liux-

---

[55] I offer my thanks to Marnix Wells for his generous summary of the text. I found some supplementary material in Walter Goode's *dissertation*, 1976.

[56] Many of these techniques are likely plays on language. The named techniques are in bold font for comparisons. Also see Appendix page 117.

[57] Shahar 2008, 132.

[58] Gyves 1993; Wile 1999, 18-35, have both translated Qi Jiguang into English, several versions of the Chinese text are readily available online.
Tai Chi is not the only martial art that has origins in this poem—see Wells 2005, 23.

in (1908-1991) noticed four more, making the total twenty-nine.[59] It should be noted that Qi Jiguang's poem and Zhang Sanfeng's fight scene above both use the number thirty-two, but in the poem it refers to the number of verses, not techniques. There are often two or three techniques blended together in each of Qi Jiguang's verses, whereas in the fight scene there are thirty-two distinct techniques. Tang Hao and Gu Liuxin were able to pick out individual movements in Qi Jiquang's poem by back-checking them against a list of known Tai Chi movement names, but in the poem they all flow together. This makes Zhang Sanfeng's fight scene in *Xiyangji* the oldest explicit use of these Tai Chi martial arts technique *names* to delineate distinct movements.

It is also important to note that the named movements appear to belong to the Brocade Guards he is fighting, with Zhang Sanfeng's movements filling the empty spaces between them.

If we understand Tai Chi in a limited sense, as a unique set of techniques or movements strung together, then both General Qi Jiguang's poem and Zhang Sanfeng's fight scene are incomplete versions of it. The story of Zhang Sanfeng as a great fighter matters because it gave some anonymous actor a reason to devise or assemble a set of body techniques and then attribute them to Zhang Sanfeng on the stage. That could explain why the Tai Chi *form* was created. The Qi Jiguang poem matters because famous generals intrinsically embody martial prowess, and as we shall see, General Qi Jiguang was taught by a direct student of the Immortal Zhang Sanfeng.

In staging this fight scene we could have Zhang Sanfeng dodge each punch at just the right angle so that it hit another guard. Or like a symphony conductor he could delicately guide the guards into each other while dancing around in slow motion. In another version he could take the blows to no effect while laughing, or in the after-hours version he could be vomiting and stumbling about. The text is ambiguous about the staging.

To understand how a poem and a fight scene became the solo ritual of martial prowess we now call Tai Chi, we need to further explore the

[59] Wile, 1999, 11.

history of the period in which these two works were created. To do that we need to know what the play *Xiyangji* is about and why General Qi wrote his poem. The play is a fictional account of a famous explorer named Admiral Zheng He, whose story you will enjoy. General Qi Jiguang is famous for his success fighting pirates. While fighting pirates, General Qi became the student of a sage named Lin Zhao'en, who then connected him with the Immortal Zhang Sanfeng. All of that will be covered in the next section.

Figure 11. Qi Jiguang (1528-1588).

Figure 12. Lin Zhao'en (1517 - 1598) 林兆恩 (Early Qing Dynasty Portrait).

Admirals, Pirates, Sages, Generals and Immortals

The play's name, *Sanbao Taijian Xia Xiyang Ji*, means *Admiral Zheng He's Journey to the West in a Boat*. It is often referred to by the shortened name *Xiyang Ji*. *Sanbao* literally means *Three Treasures*, which was an honorific given to Zheng He signifying his canonization as a god of the theater and his canonization by the state. Three Treasures implies the attainment of three types of wisdom, Buddhist, Daoist and Confucian.[60] Admiral Zheng He was a real person, but the play fictionalizes him. Literary historian Lu Xun thought that the play was allegory and political commentary about General Qi Jiguang, who was still alive when the play was being composed. In other words, Zheng He may be a stand-in for General Qi Jiguang in the play. To understand why this substitution might work theatrically, we need a little more background on Admiral Zheng He.

His father, a rebel Muslim, died fighting in Yunnan, when Zheng He was just ten years old. Zheng He was castrated and made a servant of Prince of Yan, who would eventually become the Perpetual Happiness Emperor, Yongle. Zheng He was loyal, became a military leader, and was then put in charge of one of history's most famous and amazing journeys of exploration. The Yongle Emperor commissioned an armada of three hundred ships, including sixty-two giant treasure ships. He sent Admiral Zheng He in command of seven journeys to explore lands as far away as East Africa, Mecca, India, and all the countries of Southeast Asia.

The seven voyages took place between 1405 and 1433. They brought back exotic animals like giraffes, elephants, and ostriches. They also

---

[60] The name San Bao, Three Treasures, has numerous meanings. 1) *jing, qi, shen*, 2) "*Compassion, Conservation, and Not-Imagining-Oneself-to-Be-the-Center-of-the-World*."—from the *Daodejing* chapter 67. 3) Buddha, Dharma, and Sangha. But keeping with our need for humor and irony, 4) all castrated eunuchs like Zheng He kept their three treasures (their genitals) in a box.

brought back enormous amounts of imperial tribute from the many countries they visited, as well as emissaries and their entourages. The voyages followed local trade routes that were already in existence; but word of these giant treasure ships, with their advanced technologies and fantastic trade products, vastly increased the number of ambitious traders making voyages to the South China Sea.[61]

China got increasingly wealthy from trade. But when the Yongle Emperor died, his successor ended the voyages and acted to cut off trade. Not much is known about Admiral Zheng He after the time of his final voyage in 1433.

The Chinese government expected all other countries to subordinate by bringing tributary gifts. On receipt of the tribute, the Emperor would then show his magnanimity by giving gifts in return. Over the centuries a custom developed in which traders and merchants would travel to China accompanying the tributary envoys and spend a few months buying and selling while they were in the country.[62] Envoys also brought performing artists on these voyages for entertainment and as imperial gifts.

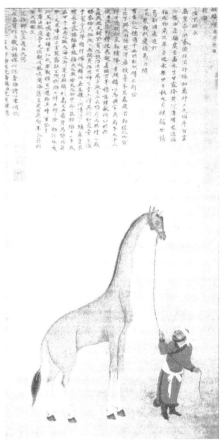

Figure 13. Tribute to the Emperor from Zheng He's voyages. Ch'i-lin (Giraffe), Ming Dynasty. National Palace Museum, Taipei.

Although technically illegal, trade along China's Southern coast increased, along with vast pirate navies which were there to "facilitate" it.

---

[61]Dreyer 2007.

[62]Reid 2010, 16-17.

Independent merchant ships were illegal but were "facilitated" because trade was making people rich. Over time, merchant ships routinely carried letters of envoy from various monarchs claiming they were delivering tribute, when in fact they were just trading with the locals on the South coast of China. The Portuguese arrived to join the game in the early 1500s, and the Dutch and Spanish soon followed. Peoples from all over South East Asia were illegally trading along the coast. At various times between Admiral Zheng He's voyages in the early 1400s and the time the play with Zhang Sanfeng was published, 1597, the government instituted commercial suppression campaigns. Those campaigns blurred the distinction between merchants and smugglers. Merchants increasingly needed weapons and armed networks of ships to ensure safe passage. As pirate navies developed to serve this need, merchants become pirates in the eyes of the state. The value of this trading area became important to countless industries and interests, and soon vast pirate forces began to control the South China Sea.[63]

The Portuguese brought guns which were sold and copied locally. The Japanese had sulfur and the Chinese had saltpeter, which are the two ingredients necessary for making gunpowder. They needed each other's ingredients. This was a perfect storm for increasing the mix of trade and violence. The number of pirates swelled to some 40,000 men and women.[64]

Around 1550, the Chinese emperor instituted a major crackdown on coastal trade. He decided to destroy the pirates and root out their strongholds. The first groups of Chinese soldiers got slaughtered or fled the field. Because many Chinese living on the coast were part of the pirate smuggling operations, soldiers often found themselves cut off from supplies and surrounded by hostiles. And if that were not bad enough, there were these Japanese super-pirates called the *wokou*, meaning dwarf bandits. But they were known in Japan as Water Lords. Just one of these guys with superior steel blades could take out a beachfront of Chinese soldiers.

---

[63] Antony 2012, 481–501; Brook 1999, 202-207 & 229-233.

[64] Antony 2003.

The Chinese could not even get close without getting sliced. Or so the stories tell us.

Next, the government put out a call to martial artists. Fighting monks and local experts from all over the country came to test their skills fighting pirates.[65] Overall, the policy did not work, but the Southern coastal region now had representatives from all the best fighting systems hanging around its teahouses. (Remember this if we ever invent time travel.)

Enter General Qi Jiguang (1528-1588). He had already made a name for himself by coming up with novel ways to fight the Mongol cavalries which had been attacking the capital city, Beijing. Arriving at the coast in 1555, he realized that his armies were inadequate, and promptly set out to rebuild them from scratch.[66] He recruited new soldiers, invented weapons, developed training methods, and implemented new fighting strategies, and formations. One of his ideas was to use five-man teams to fight *wokou;* one member of the five-man team had a long tree branch covered with leaves that he would shake in the face of the *wokou* while the other four would charge in with sturdy shields, spears, and swords. His ideas worked. He cleared the coast of pirates. Then, when he was finished (around 1564), he published a book called *New Treatise on Disciplined Service.* It has eighteen chapters. Chapter fourteen is the poem discussed above, with a short introduction about unarmed martial skills. The title of the poem is *Quanjing Jieyao Pian*, which Douglas Wile has styled *Essentials of the Classic of Pugilism.*[67] In the introduction, General Qi explains that he tried training the troops with several different styles of unarmed combat. All the styles had problems, but by combining the best from each style a person could develop enough skill to have a real advantage. Although unarmed combat skills were not directly useful for battle, General Qi felt the bravery they instilled was good for morale. The thirty-two verses are rhymed like a Broadway musical with narrated stage combat.

---

[65]Gyves 1993.

[66] Huang 1982, 156-188

[67] Gyves 1993; Wile 1999.

As mentioned above, this poem contains twenty-nine of the movement names from Chen Style Tai Chi, but it is more like a song than a poem.

Here is the opening of the poem:

Tie your coat and come outside,

Single Whip with sudden stride,

Without the courage to advance,

Sharp eyes fast hands will have no chance.

Golden Rooster stands on top,

Present your leg then sideways chop,

Rush in low and trip the bull,

They cry to heaven loud and full.

—translation by Chad Eisner[68]

Qi Jiguang's book had a big impact, editions were published in Korea and Japan by the end of the 16th Century. Following his initial success, the court again sent him north to fight the Mongols. While there, he developed a plan to completely restructure the entire Chinese army. Had he been allowed to re-invigorate the military, the Ming Dynasty might not have collapsed two generations later in 1644. Initially he had some powerful supporters, but the political winds shifted and he was accused of sexual improprieties.[69] He retired to his home village and republished his book in 1584. However, for reasons unknown, the new edition did not

---

[68] https://chinesemartialstudies.com/2018/10/01/martial-classics-the-poetry-of-motion-qi-jiguang-in-verse/

[69] Huang 1982, 184-188

Figure 14. *New Treatise on Disciplined Service*, Qi Jiguang, 1564.

include the original poem about unarmed combat.[70] He died alone and penniless in 1588. Without General Qi Jiguang's military reforms, the dynasty fell to Manchu invaders from the North in 1644. The Manchu forced all Chinese men to wear their hair in a queue, which symbolized that they were slaves who could be tied up at night by their hair. It was a tragic and profound end to a way of life. The suffering the Chinese people experienced being conquered by the Manchu inspired the development of increasingly subversive theatrical-religious-martial arts.

That is the standard story. Now for the hidden part.

Three in One: Zhang Sanfeng in Popular Religion

The sage Lin Zhao'en (1517-1598) came from a gentry family of Fujian province, on China's southern coast. Having rejected the official examination system, he set out to teach Confucian studies combined with Daoist Golden Elixir meditation techniques and Chan Buddhist philosophy. This became known as the Three-in-One Religion (Sanyijiao).[71]

Lin's innovations included the idea that people could integrate Golden Elixir practices into their daily lives. This led to numerous publications and community temples for teaching and practicing the Golden Elixir. His Fujian home was a commercial society with growing wealth and an appetite for new freedoms. Lin Zhao'en was a charismatic popu-

[70] Gyves 1993.

[71] Dean 1998; Lui 1976, 149-174.

larizer.[72] His fame and influence grew steadily during his life and continued to grow after his death. He claimed to be a direct student of the Immortal Zhang Sanfeng, the main character of the skit described earlier.

Between 1540 and 1560, he developed a following through teaching, doing exorcisms, healing, offering guidelines for experts in ritual, and sharing a powerful talisman called Correct Qi.[73] His talismans were written on a piece of paper and infused with cosmic efficacy through ritual actions.

Even before General Qi Jiguang arrived in Fujian, the sage Lin Zhao'en was organizing the defense of the coast.[74] He used his Correct Qi talisman against disease, false mediums, and blood-thirsty pirates. He performed rituals to guard against attacks and aid in winning battles. His rituals treated pirates as demonic spirits. Organizing local gentry, he also raised large amounts of money to pay for soldiers and defensive constructions. His Correct Qi talisman was a kind of demonic warfare, or war-magic, a type of performance which is often overlooked as an origin of martial arts.[75]

When pirate attacks led to siege battles, where many people were crowded together behind city walls, plagues broke out and corpses were everywhere. Lin Zhao'en's fame increased as he led essential efforts to collect corpses and sponsored the rituals to enshrine these battlefield dead so they would not become homeless ghosts (a process we explained earlier).[76]

Even pirates came to respect Lin's reputation and would make offerings at his temples. At one point, pirates overran his home region, slaugh-

---

[72] Dean 1998, 20.

[73] Zheng Qi Fu 正氣符, see Dean 1998, 77.

[74] Dean 1998, 53.

[75] Farrer 2016, 1-24.

[76] Dean 1998, 77.

tering nearly everyone, but they left Lin Zhao'en, his family, and his property undamaged.

Around 1560 General Qi Jiguang contracted an incurable disease and was about to die when he received a visit from Lin Zhao'en, who healed him.[77] Lin used two healing methods. First, he did a ritual to resolve grievances brought by the ghosts of those wrongfully killed.[78] Second, he taught Qi Jiguang the first stage of the Golden Elixir meditation. General Qi Jiguang and the sage Lin Zhao'en became good friends, they worked together in mutual admiration and regularly exchanged letters over a twenty-year period. Qi Jiguang was among Lin's most famous disciples. In 1562, a year before General Qi Jiguang published his famous *Military Treatise* (and poem), Lin donated five acres to build a temple for Qi Jiguang, and had a statue of him installed there.[79] Temples of that size had stages because they doubled as theatrical centers. Lin Zhao'en built many temples and shrines in his lifetime.[80] People came from all around to meet the sage as his reputation grew.

Many officials wrote to Lin to ask advice on how to practice the Golden Elixir. In 1561, during Qi Jiguang's successes in Fujian, Lin Zhao'en printed a spirit-channeled collection of Golden Elixir poems attributed to Zhang Sanfeng. Then in 1579, Lin began meeting with Zhang Sanfeng at night in his home to receive instructions and guidance directly from the Immortal.[81]

The sage Lin Zhao'en's life is filled with accounts of the miraculous. For example, in 1578 a light descended on his boat and announced the

---

[77] Dean 1998, 106-107.

[78] This widespread Chinese idea is that there is a court in Hell where the dead can lodge complaints against the living. The ritual likely involves negotiating some sort of restitution.

[79] There is some scholarly speculation that temples for living heroes are attempts to ensure a position in the heavenly hierarchy after death. Building a temple is certainly a dramatic way to show appreciation. But it may have been a place to pray for success in battle, protection from curses, and serenity in peacetime. The temple likely designates Qi Jiguang as a commander of ghost-soldiers (guibing) in the unseen world.

[80] Dean 1998, 88 & 113.

[81] Dean 1998, 82.

re-birth of the Maitreya Buddha. In 1585, Sakamuni Buddha descended from the sky and handed over all of his powers to Lin. Some of Lin's writings are called sutras because his followers consider them the direct words of the Buddha.[82]

In 1591 Lin donated a large amount of money to support official sacrifices to General Qi Jiguang, who died in 1588. The connection between Lin Zhao'en and Qi Jiguang invalidates nearly all Twentieth Century commentators, who claim General Qi Jiguang's martial arts were devoid of theatrical and religious content. Prominent men in General Qi Jiguang's time routinely sponsored theatrical performances, both as entertainment for the troops and to build goodwill with the local populous. There is every reason to believe he did this as well. General Qi participated in ritual exorcisms and practiced a version of the Golden Elixir directly attributed to the Immortal Zhang Sanfeng. General Qi was himself worshiped within the Three-in-One Religion. He was canonized as a type of god who could muster heavenly troops (ghost-soldiers) to achieve victory in battle.

Lin Zhao'en's fame as an exorcist continued to grow alongside his fame as an expert on the Golden Elixir. His published writings multiplied, and his many disciples incorporated his methods of spirit-writing into communal rituals. Lin completed the immortal embryo the year of his death in 1598. This was one year after the publication of the play, *Xi Yangji*, which featured Zhang Sanfeng's extraordinary martial prowess. Lin Zhao'en's merit was so great that it caused the rebirth of forty-eight generations of his family in heaven.[83]

The Three-in-One Religion founded by the sage Lin Zhao'en continued to grow. Three-in-One temples often featured a statue of Zhang Sanfeng on the martial side of the altar and regularly channeled the Immortal's words using spirit-writing methods.[84] At its peak in the 1670s,

---

[82] Dean 1998, 86-93.

[83] Dean 1998.

[84] Altars follow the logic of imperial court, where the martial side was the right side, and the civil or ministerial side was the left. In war time they switched positions because of the convention that the Emperor always differed to the left. (Daodejing chapter 31)

there were Three-in-One temples in Beijing, Shandong, Zhejiang, Jiangsu, Jiangxi and in every prefecture of Lin's home region Fujian.[85]

Beginning in the 1700s, the Three-in-One Religion was banned. They were labeled a White Lotus heterodox cult, triggering crackdowns, arrests, burnings of Lin Zhao'en's writings, and the destruction of temples.[86] The White Lotus label was used widely during that era to justify bans against groups practicing the combination of martial skills and the Golden Elixir.[87] Lin Zhao'en had also announced the re-birth of the Maitreya Buddha, which became a common feature of millennialist rebel groups. These often rebellious and millennialist martial-elixir groups played a role in the origins of Baguazhang as well, as we shall see later in this book.

The Three-in-One Religion was successful in going underground, as many groups were. Three-in-One re-emerged in the first half of Twentieth Century, only to be completely suppressed again in 1949 during the Communist Era. Since the reforms of the 1980s, it has seen a massive recovery, with Three-in-One temples now all over the Fujian region. In Fujian, Zhang Sanfeng is again being channeled by spirit-writing groups.[88]

Going West in a Boat

In Chapter 57 of the play *Xiyangji*, Zhang Sanfeng defends against attacks by twenty-four palace guards using a nascent version of Tai Chi. To understand why, we need to understand what the play *Xiyangji* is about and the cultural context it was written in. We have already covered the main character Admiral Zheng He's journeys in the early 1400s, but the play is also a social commentary on the way the Ming Government was handling commerce, culture, and conflict in the second half of the late 1500s when it was written. There are fight scenes throughout the

---

[85] Dean 1998, 17.

[86] Dean 1998, 17.

[87] Naquin 1985, 255-291.

[88] Dean 1998, 173-177.

Figure 15. Sea battle with guns, *Xiyangji*, 1597. (Staatsbibliothek, Berlin).

play, along with magic, gods, and demons. Admiral Zheng He visits Mecca, Hell, and numerous weird countries; including a land with only women (bummer for a eunuch like Admiral Zheng He). It is well known that Admiral Zheng He was a Muslim in real life, yet in the play he tries to convert the countries he visits to Buddhism.

Xiyangji is an allegorical commentary on the legitimacy of the Ming Dynasty and China's struggles to comprehend and interact with the larger world. It plays on the irony of General Qi Jiguang's success fighting pirates in the mid-1500s. The government's own policies made coastal trade illegal. If the government had allowed legal trade, those smugglers might have become honored contributors to the wealth of the nation, and the number of pirates might never have grown to the size of a navy. By 1567, the rules against trade were mostly lifted anyway, and positive changes began happening.[89] The new and diverse commercial environment began making people rich. The irony is that Qi Jiguang's successes a decade earlier were probably all for not. The trend was toward commercial prosperity and increasingly diverse international markets anyway.

---

[89] Brook 1999, 204.

Xiyangji is a commentary on all of this, including the growing influence of foreigners. The Jesuit Matteo Ricci (1552-1610) landed in Macao in 1582, and began dazzling people with his maps of the world, technology and sciences. At the same time, demand for Chinese trade products exploded; the highly valued silks and ceramics of course, but everything from mass produced nails to talking parrots were being created for export.[90] This exciting trade and cultural exchange had mind expanding effects. Ricci's translation of Confucius, combined with the commercial success of so many Chinese products, nourished and inspired the Enlightenment back in Europe.[91] In China this commercial and cultural expansion fostered the milieu that created Tai Chi.

Xiyangji is a commentary on what was an amazing time to be alive. During the Wanli era (1573-1620) there was an explosion of commercial and private publishing. Countless plays that had been handed around and worked on for generations as manuscripts were published for the first time. Most of China's great epics took on canonical forms in this period.[92] This was a performance-oriented publishing movement. Acting troupes worked intimately with the playwrights to perfect these plays and the art of presenting them.[93]

The literati in China were a group of people who had gone through intensive training in literature and history to become government officials. At that time being a government official had the potential to make one's whole extended family rich and powerful. But, despite the growing wealth and size of the population, the government would not expand the total number of government officials. After passing the government placement exams, qualified people waited with the slim hope that they might get an appointment in their later years. Faced with this uncertain potential, huge numbers of literati simply decided to live for pleasure.

---

[90] Brook 1999, 204-207

[91] Israel 2006, 640-657.

[92] A whole industry sprouted up to create travel guides, and entertainment guides for merchants and literati—see Rubiés & Ollé 2016, 259–309.

[93] Carlitz 2005, 267-303.

Their favorite thing to do was theater. At the same time, there was a growing merchant class, which wanted to raise its social status by contributing to, and participating in, this high literati culture of pleasure.[94] It was a cauldron for creativity. This is the scene that General Qi Jiguang and the sage Lin Zhao'an lived in. Their milieu, the one that created Tai Chi, was a mix of theater, religion and martial skills.

The author of the play *Xiyangji* is unknown. The preface was signed by Luo Maodeng in 1597, but little is known about him. This type of 100-chapter play is a composite, an assemblage.[95] It includes re-writes of numerous other works of theater, and incorporates works of history and poetry as well as fight scenes from other plays.[96] Thousand-page plays like this one were rarely performed in their entirety because it would take weeks. A few chapters at a time were enough to fill an evening of entertainment. After midnight actors would improvise the same plays with sexually explicit material. Parts of *Xiyangji* had been workshopped in front of live audiences and passed around as manuscripts for experimentation and commentary for a generation before being incorporated into the final text. That was normal for the time. Comic martial theater of this sort was developed by actors and writers together using improvisation. Parts of the three Zhang Sanfeng chapters were lifted from earlier plays, histories, and fiction. These sorts of plays within plays functioned as standalone works that could be published or performed independent of the larger work. For all these reasons, it is possible that the Zhang San-

---

[94] Volpp 2011.

[95] This type of play was part of the same trend as the Three-in-One Relgion, namely to combine Daoism and Buddhism in a Confucian frame work as a platform for sectarian proselytizing—see Mair & Seaman 2005, 467.

[96] The play has been used as a source for the claim that some of Zheng He's treasure ships were as long as five-hundred feet! Indeed, the author of *Xiyangji* used many sources. It is not an original work in the modern sense because he lifted many bits from here and there. He took fight scenes and other element from the *Journey to the West*, *Canonization of the Gods*, and *Journey to the East*, which was popular before 1550. He drew directly from actual histories too—see Duyvendak 1953; Gregory 2014, 10-28; Ptak 1985, 117-141. See Walter Goode 1976, 199-228, on the sources of the Zhang Sanfeng chapters, it also contains a summary and bits of translation; unfortunately he skips over the Zhang Sanfeng fight scene. Barbara Witt created an annotated bibliography of *Xiyangji* commentaries covering multiple languages. Witt 2016.

feng chapters are as old as Qi Jiguang's poem from 1563; certainly some of it was. It is a strong possibility that they both drew on a common source, now lost or overlooked, perhaps a live play about the Immortal Zhang Sanfeng. The primary way people learned about Immortals was from watching plays—plays about Zhang Sanfeng must have been common since every scholar who has ever written about Zhang Sanfeng has stated that he was ubiquitous during this period.

The correlations between General Qi Jiguang's poem and the Zhang Sanfeng fight scene in *Xiyangji* suggest several possibilities. The author of the Zhang Sanfeng fight scene may have used Qi Jiguang's poem in order to borrow Qi's reputation for martial prowess. Or he may have intended to mock Qi Jiguang's poor judgment for including unarmed combat in a military treatise. Alternately, Qi Jiguang's poem is a rhyming song that can be read as a joke, one he included in his book as an example of entertaining the troops while building morale. This could explain why he later removed it. Both authors treated open-hand martial skills and theatricality as a unified subject.

Qi Jiguang acknowledges in his introduction that his movements are a composite of several styles, and some of them are theatrically named, like Monkey Fist, and Thousand Stumble Zhang's Stumbling Techniques. [97] Is Thousand Stumbles Zhang another name for the drunken Zhang Sanfeng? None of the named styles are military training. Obviously, both General Qi Jiguang and the author of *Xiyangji* drew on previ-

---

[97] Yang-style Spear also comes from theater as does Eagle Claw Wang (King) which is probably Garuda, Shaolin fighting and drinking monks were the subject of farces, etc... Here is the full Qi Jiguang on styles from Gyves 1993, 35:

"Among the past and present fist specialists, the Song Great Founder [Song Taizu] had the Long Fist system with 32 positions. Moreover there are six pace and fist techniques, the Monkey Fist, and the Feinting Fist. The famous positions each have their own names, but in reality they are quite similar and scarcely differ from one another.

Looking at Master Wen in the present day, we have the 72 moving fist methods, the 36 combining and locking techniques, the 24 counter-spy techniques [qi tan ma], the 8 flash flips, and the 12 short strikes. These are the best of the lot. As for Lu Hong's 8 blows, while they are firm, they do not measure up to Min Zhang's short strike. The leg techniques of Shangdong's Li Bantian, Eagle Claw Wang's grappling methods, Thousand Stumble Zhang's stumbling techniques, Zhang Bojing's strikes, the Shaolin monastery stick fighting art, together with the Green Field cudgel methods, all stand as equals. Mr. Yang's spear arts together with the open hand, fist, and quarterstaff skills, are all famous to the present day."

ous works of theater, or directly from the martial expertise of actors in their milieu. Versions of the epic play *Journey to the East* featuring fighting drunken immortals were already popular by the mid-1500s, so popular that Eight Drunken Immortals Fist is the first empty-hand style *(quan)* ever mentioned at Shaolin Monastery.[98]

General Qi Jiguang and his fellow countrymen witnessed a nascent form of Tai Chi when they watched Zhang Sanfeng fighting on the stage. Tai Chi was a blend of stage combat and anti-pirate morale-building at its beginning, but it was other things too. To help us understand those, the next section explores what Zhang Sanfeng was in people's imagination.

---

[98] Shahar, 2008, 120

Zhang Sanfeng is an Immortal,

But what is an Immortal?

The standard translation for the Chinese word *xian* is "immortal." The character for *xian* is made up of a person and a mountain, a mountain-man if you will. Long ago, the word was used to refer to people with wings who lived on mythical mountains and subsisted on mist and dew. As time passed, the word accumulated new meanings, and it came to refer to a person who had transcended death in some way. This is an open-ended concept which covers the vast territory between an informal metaphor and a pivotal religious doctrine.

Ghosts, Gods, Demons and Immortals

As explained earlier, deceased family members become supportive ancestors when they were placed symbolically on the family altar and ritually fed. But only family members who died natural deaths could be fed on the altar. Those who died in battle or from suicide could not be placed on the family altar and were in danger of becoming homeless ghosts. They were fed in communal shrines. Such a person would be called a ghost or a *gui* in Chinese.[99] A person who died committing an act of heroism, virtue, or self-sacrifice might get his own shrine, and if a community were to make regular offerings or sacrifices to him, the deceased could eventually become a god. This is why the sage Lin Zhao'en created a shrine for General Qi Jiguang. The word for such a person in Chinese is a *shen;* which is imperfectly translated as a deity or a god. When a person dies having spent a lifetime doing horrible things, he might also get a shrine and receive offerings or sacrifices. The idea is that such a person might experience regret while being tortured in hell, which

---

[99] Vincent Goossaert says everyone becomes a *gui* when they die, but for most it is a temporary transitional state (Keynote 2016 International Conference on Daoism, Paris).

Figure 16. Ghosts and Demons. Reed College Hell Scrolls.

would motivate him to use whatever lingering influence he might have to benefit the living. These people are called demons or *mo* in Chinese.[100]

An immortal is similar but different. There are different types of immortals and each person who becomes an immortal has a unique path. Their paths are generally distinct from gods, ghosts, and demons in that they take their body with them at the moment of death or transcendence. The founder of religious Daoism, Zhang Daoling (34-156 CE), rose up in broad daylight with his dogs and chickens. Daoism is not a belief-based religion, everyone is free to take that description literally, or as a metaphor, or both. As a metaphor, for example, at the instant of his death everyone around him, including his dogs and chickens, felt lightness and ease at the perfect completion of a life well lived. Nothing about

---

[100] A general distinction between these types of beings can also be made by considering what kind of offerings or sacrifices are made to them. For instance, demons get blood sacrifices like chickens, dogs and pigs, higher gods get flowers and incense, weaker gods get booze and money, even porn.

his death brought people down. All the feelings he left behind in people's hearts were uplifting and light. That is one meaning of immortal.[101]

Some unknown number of Daoist immortals were so potent during their lives that they were able to achieve the ideal of total anonymity. Others are remembered by hagiographies (religious biographies). An immortal is a person whose life becomes an inspiration in people's collective imagination and on into the realm of storytelling and ritual. In practice, most immortals were teachers who contributed to Daoist methods and understanding. As lore, they become part of the theatrical and religious landscape.

But I risk oversimplifying things. Chinese language commonly uses compound words, so ghost, *gui*, might become ghost-soldier or *guibing*. Both gods and demons are referred to as *guishen* (ghost-gods) or *shenmo* (god-demons), reflecting the idea that a demon can become a god through acts of merit, or the opposite, a god can become a demon through bad behavior. There are many other compound words like *taishen*, great-god, or *xianshen*, immortal-god. Because these are terms used in theater, playwrights freely made up new combinations to suit exciting plots, which then became part of religious practice. The categories of what happened at death were unruly. With the Buddhist notion of re-birth added into the mix, dozens of hybrids were envisioned. What all of these beings had in common is that they could possess the living. They could be channeled as voices, martial arts instructions, healing songs, or spirit-writings, and they could appear in dreams.

But setting that aside, the most common way to become an immortal was the Daoist practice called the Golden Elixir. It is also called making the immortal embryo. It is a meditation technique that uses visualization to transform one's body. In the theater, the Golden Elixir often becomes a magical pill which confers extraordinary fighting ability.

---

[101]For a conservative erudite view of immortals—*see* Campany 2002, 98-102; Raz 2012, 38-90.

Who is Zhang Sanfeng

Whether the Daoist Immortal Zhang Sanfeng was a real person or a composite of different people is a minor academic question. It is significant only for attempting to pin down the early history of how he came to be remembered as an immortal, which is not our concern here. It is widely agreed among scholars that by the late Ming Dynasty Zhang Sanfeng was established as an immortal and was regarded as a fantastic teacher of the Golden Elixir.

Like most people in China today, I first heard about Zhang Sanfeng as the immortal creator of Tai Chi. Too much has been written attempting to debunk Zhang Sanfeng's association with Tai Chi. It is as misguided as trying say Santa Claus has nothing to do with Christmas. It is particularly odd because little else has been written in English about Zhang Sanfeng.[102] Today he is primarily known in the English-speaking world as the creator of Tai Chi. As of this writing there are only two scholarly works about Zhang Sanfeng, a short essay by Anna Seidel (1970) and a re-working of a dissertation by Wong Shiu-Hon (1993). There are also two books which tangentially record Zhang Sanfeng's place in popular culture: a book about sex practices by martial arts historian Douglas Wile (1992), and Kenneth Dean's book about the Three-and-One Religion (1998), which we have already discussed at length. Nearly every mention of the Immortal in English quotes Anna Seidel to the effect that Zhang Sanfeng was ubiquitous in the latter half of the Ming Dynasty, yet no follow-up work has been done. Wong Shiu-Hon surveyed texts from the Daoist canon and historical documents for evidence of a real person named Zhang Sanfeng. In passing he mentions that the play *Xiyangji* has an appearance by Zhang Sanfeng, which is how I discovered the fight

---

[102] The two most well known Chinese scholars of martial arts in the first half of the Twentieth Century, Tang Hao and Xu Zhen, were advocates of the YMCA Consensus. Their "findings" have been repeated uncritically by many scholars, for example, Lorge 2011, 219; Henning, 1994, 1995. The debunking was a two part project. First it was necessary to separate the Golden Elixir from martial arts. Only then could Zhang Sanfeng be separated from Tai Chi. The best scholarly example in English is Stanley Henning, who drew extensively on Tang Hao. But almost every scholar who has mentioned Zhang Sanfeng took a stab at it.

scene.[103] Douglas Wile's book is a translation with commentary on poems about sex and the Golden Elixir attributed to Zhang Sanfeng. Between these four sources there was just enough to piece together a description.

Zhang Sanfeng is a trickster, akin to the American Br'er Rabbit or the West African Anansi the Spider. He is dirty and sloppy in appearance. He has a big round straw hat. He wears a raincoat year-round with a belt. He carries a wand-like ruler. His skin can be filthy and covered in scabs. He has a silvery beard the shape of a halberd blade. He impersonates people, and is otherwise easily mistaken for a bum. He can travel long distances fast, taking giant steps, flying, or traveling by dream. He is known for healing people, sometimes by scraping off bits of his skin to make into medicine pills. He gives mysterious gifts. He can predict the future. He can make plants grow and he gives out magic seeds. He has the ability to smell horrible or pleasant at will. He is also known as Zhang Lata, which means lazy or sloppy. Sanfeng means three peaks, which has many possible meanings depending on the story.[104] For instance, it can mean the integration of Buddhism, Daoism, and Confucianism. But three peaks is also a sexual reference for the tongue, the nipples, and the vagina—walking that taboo line between sex-educator and trickster.[105] Finally, he is known for bestowing the Golden Elixir of immortality in the form of meditation instructions or a magic pill.

This is important because the origins of Tai Chi became unspeakable in China during the Twentieth Century. When the obvious could not be stated because of political repression, Tai Chi's origins slowly became unknown. Zhang Sanfeng's transgressive nature provided a strong reason for denying his connection to Tai Chi. Theatrical immortals have the power to transgress social and political hierarchies. The Golden Elixir was and still is a powerful method for transcendence, which is why I discuss it in depth in the final section of this book.

---

[103]Wong 1993, 29-30.

[104] These are the variant characters for his name: 张三丰, which might imply that he was extremely good-looking and charismatic.

[105] Wile 1992.

In theater and storytelling, the term *xian* (immortal) has even more meanings. The channeled voice of a work of spirit-writing is often called a *xian*, even if it is a god *(shen)* being channeled. In northern China, spirit mediums themselves were called *xian'er*, connoting an intimate, or a lesser immortal. The patron saints of brothels were fox-immortals called *hu-xian*, a term sometimes shortened to *xian*. Brothel channeling games in which sexy tales were transmitted via *xian* were wildly, and secretly, popular among the literati. There are many erotic texts attributed to Zhang Sanfeng, apparently conflating him with fox-spirits as the transgressive force inspiring lusty adventures. Transcendence, martial skills, and risqué humor all came together in popular spirit-writing games, both inside and outside of brothels.[106] This mix of ingredients also created Tai Chi.

In the Twentieth Century General Qi Jiguang became a symbol of rationalistic obedience and military strength for both the Chinese Nationalists and Communists, but only after his temples were destroyed. The truth is that General Qi Jiguang was a devotee of the immortal Zhang Sanfeng, the independent trickster and symbol of spontaneous freedom.

A Rough Description of Three Types of Daoism

Readers may not know that there is a debate among scholars of Daoism about whether or not various forms of popular or peripheral Daoism should be considered Daoism at all. Both sides make valid points. I will wade into this complex debate only to sketch answers to these two questions: How did Zhang Sanfeng fit into Daoist religion? And how did the cult of Zhang Sanfeng function in popular culture?

Ritual

The *Daodejing* (Forth Century B.C.E.) is Daoism's most sacred text, it is attributed to Laozi. Around the year 50 C.E. a man named Zhang Daoling went into retreat in a cave on Crane-Call Mountain and when he came out, he started teaching the *Daodejing* and healing people. Over a

------

[106] Kang 2005, 60.

period of a thousand years, the followers of Zhang Daoling developed an elaborate ritual tradition that embodies the teachings of the *Daodejing*. This tradition is called Orthodox Daoism (Zhengyi Dao) or Celestial Master Daoism (Tianshi Dao). It is a family tradition passed on in lineages of priests called Officials of the Dao or Daoshi. Male and female priests are both called Daoshi and are generally married. Tai Chi does not appear to be linked to Orthodox Daoism.

The *Daodejing* has been an influence on countless Chinese arts, including Tai Chi. In the future it may be possible to construct an argument, that because Daoist ritual and Tai Chi both use Golden Elixir visualizations in motion, Tai Chi evolved from Daoist ritual. As I will show in the next section, mimed elements of Daoist ritual give coherence to the opening movements of Tai Chi; however, how those elements of Daoist ritual got into the Tai Chi form is an unanswered question.

Monasteries

As Buddhism from India and Daoism from China came into contact and conflict with each other, they adopted each other's practices and doctrines and developed new ones. To summarize and simplify a long and complicated history, about a thousand years ago Daoism and Buddhism got together and had two children.

The first child was called Chan, or Zen in Japanese. This is a form of Buddhism built around one of the central practices of Daoism called sitting-and-forgetting or *zuowang* (it has many other names). This practice is non-conceptual. It is simply a posture of stillness. It is the foundation for other forms of Daoist practice.

The second child was called Quanzhen (Complete Perfection). It created Buddhist-like monasteries for celibate monks to practice both sitting-and-forgetting *(zuowang)* and the Golden Elixir of immortality *(jindan)*. Quanzhen's most sacred site is Mount Wudang. Research on martial arts practiced on Mount Wudang before the Twentieth Century is currently uncharted territory and politically fraught. But even conservative scholars believe there was something martial brewing up there. We just do not know what.

Hermits

China has always had hermits. People would go into the mountains and experiment. Hermits have been a great source of creativity and innovation, often interacting with both Buddhism and Daoism. After a time of experimentation in the mountains, hermits would sometimes come back to civilization and heal, teach, or perform magic. People called this, "Coming down from the mountain." During the 1500s, wandering hermits who taught people strange techniques, like how to eat insects and breathe the *qi* of pine trees, were so common that *hermit* became a job description.[107] Hermits are often called "immortals," and Zhang Sanfeng is clearly from this tradition. The Quanzhen monastic traditions claims Zhang Sanfeng as a sort of bad-boy progenitor—but everyone knows, and his name suggests, he was never good at following monastic rules.

Zhang Sanfeng represents an independent streak in Chinese Religion, a wild-man outside of established norms, free, creative, and unpredictable. Zhang Sanfeng is not Daoist by some definitions, but it is safe to say that the followers of the Three-in-One Religion consider him Daoist as do most Chinese people.

Improvisational Theater

Zhang Sanfeng was an immortal and a theatrical character, demonstrating the close relationship between theater and religion. It is a good bet that the comic role Zhang Sanfeng played in *Xiyangji* was improvised by actors and spirit-mediums as a stand-alone character for entertainment or to perform healing rituals. In *Xiyangji*, he does not fight in the conventional sense. He fights without fighting. He has powers.[108] The Buddha recruits Zhang Sanfeng to do a task related to violence, but it does not involve any direct killing. In the story, he is recruited to use his

---

[107] Cass 1999.

[108] In Chinese theater, there is a kind of hierarchy of violence, where the more powerful and enlightened a character is, the less likely they are to use force directly. This theme is explored in several parts of *Xiyangji*, including this one.

unique set of skills to solve a problem. It is similar to the Hollywood convention where a comic superhero is recruited to get a nuclear weapon back from a villain. Zhang Sanfeng is an interesting case because he is associated with comic powers, healing, preaching upright conduct, teaching about the Golden Elixir, and sex work. He has all five of these attributes even before martial art skill is tagged on. Such a wide range of things to be famous for is a big potential outlet for improvisation. It is easy to imagine Zhang Sanfeng employed for improvised comic interludes, working the crowd, teasing and taunting; or wandering through the audience dressed as a smelly bum upsetting tables and stealing people's drinks. Even better, a female Zhang Sanfeng with a beard and a raincoat stumbling all over the audience and making funny sexual puns. Female theater troupes were common during the Ming Dynasty.[109]

In how many different contexts could one expect to encounter a Zhang Sanfeng performance? He was the subject of casual family storytelling. He was a puppet. He was an actor on a stage. His animated antics were enacted live by street performers and storytellers. He was channeled by spirit-mediums for healing, entertainment, and wisdom. He was a disembodied voice channeled through spirit-writing. He was installed on altars as a statue. And he was channeled for certain types of festivals and secret-society games. All of this was happening all over China in fabulously diverse ways.

Zhang Sanfeng was a popular figure, but little research has been done about his role in theater. As yet, other than the book you are reading, there is nothing written in English about Zhang Sanfeng in theater. There were entire troupes of Daoist actors who toured around performing stories of the Eight Immortals. The characters in these plays were known and loved by everyone. These partially improvised plays influenced the creation of martial arts. Remember the first mention of

---

[109] Since female troupes were banned in 1644, after the fall of the Ming Dynasty, Chinese "Opera" became a kind of museum of the Ming Era, using language, clothing and other conventions to maintain nostalgia for freer times. A fist made with the right hand covered by the left symbolized the sun and the moon together, which is the Chinese character for "Ming" Dynasty; it was used as secret sign language to mean, "Bring back the Ming," and it is still used in most Chinese martial arts schools as a greeting—see Lei 2006.

"*quan*"—hand combat— at Shaolin Monastery was Eight Drunken Immortals Style.[110]   In the Yangshen region, Daoist theater troupes performed competitively against Buddhist troupes! They would take turns performing on either side of the river in a cosmic duel of theatrical prowess. As soon as one troupe finished, the whole audience would jump up and run across the bridge to see the other troupe perform. The audience would run back and forth like this all night.[111]

Now that the roots of Tai Chi have been identified in theater and religion, there is no longer a missing link. The field is now open for others to come along and find the rest of the connections. As we leave General Qi Jiguang and the play *Xiyangji* behind, we move on to discover more connections between the early expressions of Zhang Sanfeng's art, and the art of Tai Chi as it is practiced today. Next we examine the Tai Chi form itself for theatrical and religious content.

Figure 17. Zhang Sanfeng.

---

[110] Drunken Eight-Immortals Fist *Zhu Baxian quan*— Shahar 2008, 120.

[111] Mark 1999, 407.

張三丰

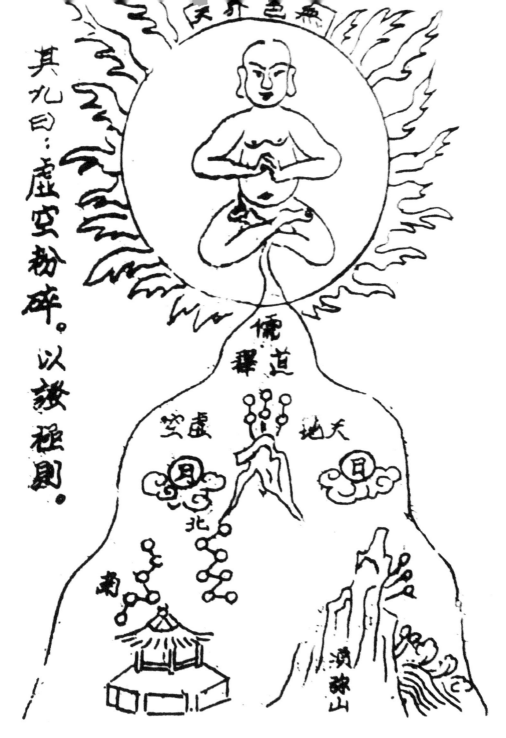

18. "Shattering the void to experience the One," from *Chart of Inner Landscape*, Lin Zhao'en.

The Story of Zhang Sanfeng

The Zhang Sanfeng Tai Chi story begins by noting that he practiced the Golden Elixir living on Mount Wudang. He had a dream in which the god Xuanwu, the Mysterious Warrior, taught him a way to cultivate the Golden Elixir within martial-arts movements. The next morning, while watching a snake and a crane fighting, he remembered his dream. As he watched the animals darting back and forth, in and out of stillness, he saw the same teaching he had received in the dream. He was then able to embody this in practice. Later he was called to the capital. Along the road, he encountered a hundred bandits whom he easily defeated. After that, he passed his knowledge on to a few worthy disciples. As I will show, the Tai Chi form tells this story.

According to Douglas Wile in his Lost Tai Chi Classics (1996), the oldest written version of this story is in the following 1669 *Memorial for Wang Zhengnan*, written by Huang Zongxi:[112]

> The Shaolin Temple is famous for its fighting monks. However, their art stresses only offense, which allows an opponent to take advantage of this for a counter-attack. Then there is the so-called Internal School that uses stillness to control movement and can easily throw an opponent. Therefore we call Shaolin the External School. The Internal School originated with Zhang San-feng of the Sung dynasty. Zhang Sanfeng was a Daoist immortality seeker of the Wudang Mountains. Emperor Huizong summoned him, but the roads were impassable and he could not proceed. That night in a dream he received a martial art from Xuanwu and the next morning he single-handedly killed more than a hundred bandits.[113]

---

[112] Many non-martial accounts of Zhang Sanfeng predate the epitaph; the earliest written account is dated 1431—Wong 1993, 3.

[113] Translated by Douglas Wile 1996, 26.

In the same book, Douglas Wile tells us that in the Wuyang County Gazetteer there was the following entry:

> The "Cave of the Immoral Zhang" at West Pass is traditionally regarded as the site where Zhang Sanfeng realized immortality. The Fugou Gazetteer says that the people of Fugou believed Zhang Sanfeng left his body in the T'ai-chi Temple on the Wudang Mountains. An image of him may still be seen there. He wore a copper cymbal as a straw hat, which he allowed the people of Fugou to strike without becoming angry, for he was very good-natured. The people of Wuyang also believed that Zhang Sanfeng was a native of Wuyang and that they have the exclusive privilege of striking his hat.[114]

This story is humorous and theatrical, perpetually posing the question, "Will he get angry *this* time we hit the cymbal?" It suggests a type of enlightened non-aggressive *(wuwei)* responsiveness, based on the notion that problems and disturbances, like the sounds of cymbals, are self-resolving. That is not to imply getting angry is somehow unenlightened, but rather that naturally appropriate conduct is a measure of the fruition of Daoist cultivation. Being good-natured is a simple way of demonstrating the ease with which ill fate resolves itself when one's conduct is not driven by aggressive passions. The cymbal is also a hallmark of theatrical martial arts; it is the most martial of the instruments. It represents explosive power, the sonic embodiment of chaos used as a counterpart to the drum, the sonic embodiment of order.[115]

---

[114] Wile 1996, 110.

[115] In the opera, percussion gongs are categorized as *wu*, martial, and drums as *wen*, civil.

The Chen Style Tai Chi Form as Dramatic Storytelling

This section has been published elsewhere and is a detailed description of the mime used in Chen style Tai Chi.[116] *I highly recommend watching my video of this. The video may be easier to quickly comprehend than the written version, watch: "The Cultural History of Tai Chi."*[117]

The names of the individual Tai Chi movements are strange and evocative. They suggest an iconography of hidden meaning. But there is a straightforward narrative structure that ties them together. The beginning of the Tai Chi form follows a pattern of ritual invocation that was historically common.

In Chen-style Tai Chi, the beginning movement is raising and lowering the arms. In theatrical contexts, this movement means *start the music*, and is similar to a conductor of Western classical music holding up a baton.[118]

The second movement, called *Play the Pipa*, has several layers of meaning. A *pipa* is a type of lute. This musical beginning parallels the use of music at the beginning of Daoist rituals to invoke the world coming into existence from *hundun* (which means undifferentiated chaos). Land rises out of this oceanic chaos, represented by wave-like movement of the hands. The mythic-historic origins of ritual begin with the invocation of a resident female shaman (廟巫), popularly called a *pipa diviner* (琵琶卜), perhaps because she played the instrument in a trance.[119] The earliest divination in China was done on sheep's scapula bones, also called *pipa* (琵琶骨). Adding an element of dark humor, this *Tai Chi* movement mimes a folk punishment for public fighting, breaking the scapula bones of the belligerents, and *pipa* (枇杷) is also the *sound* of breaking bones.

---

[116] Some of the material in this section is the same or similar to material in both Phillips 2016 & 2019 *Journal of Daoist Studies.*

[117] The Cultural History of Tai Chi — https://youtu.be/CAKBqB5vUeE

[118] Riley, 1997.

[119] Meulenbeld 2007, 49 *dissertation.*

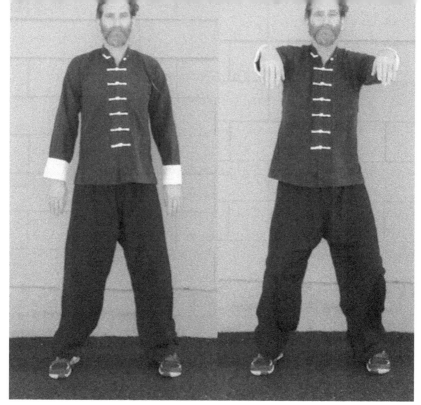

Figure 19. Start the Music.

The next movement involves stepping forward with the left side of the body, while pushing both arms to the right side, dragging of the right leg and then stamping the ground. This represents the male ancestor of all shaman, Da Yu; miming stopping the floods and unifying The Nine Kingdoms; he is half-man, half-bear—that's why he drags his leg. In Daoist ritual he emerges from *hundun* to create the gods.[120]

The third movement is called *Jingang Pounds the Mortar (Jingang daodui* 金剛搗碓*)*. Jingang is the formal name for the Vajra guardians of the Buddha, but in popular culture refers to any martial deity with super-human strength. Stamping the ground while pounding the right fist in

---

[120] Riley 1997, 105-110.
This could alternately be Pangu, who wears a bearskin and emerges in Daoist ritual from *hundun* to create the gods, see Meulenbeld 2015, 200-202.
Stopping the floods was a major theme in China and we will address it again when we discuss Baguazhang. Millions upon millions of people died in Chinese floods. Before (the mythic) Da Yu, virgins were sacrificed to appease the river gods. Da Yu stopping the floods also means an end to blood sacrifice, which was a major goal of early Daoism.

Figure 20. Play the Pipa.

Figure 21 Land rising, Da Yu, Jingang Pounds the Mortar.

Figure 22. Hundun.

the left palm marks a sudden transformation.[121] One then mimes grinding and drinking medicine. This represents Xuanwu (the Mysterious Warrior) ingesting the Golden Elixir.

The next movement, *Lazy About Tying One's Coat,* is immediately proceeded by a crossing of the open palms into the shape of a butterfly.[122] This gesture means *"waking from a dream"* in *Kunqu* style opera, and is otherwise a common convention in Chinese storytelling.[123] The butterfly represents the ancient Daoist Zhuangzi dreaming he is a butterfly, which

[121] The sudden change (*bianhua*) is a common theatrical convention with roots in Tantric Buddhism and Daoist ritual, deities are invoked one after another as intermediaries used to approach *the Dao*—Mair, 2013 18-19; Robinet, 1993, 153.

[122] Another name for Zhang Sanfeng is Zhang Lata (張邋遢) meaning sloppy because he was a *lazy* dresser.

[123] Chen, F. P. L., 2007.
Lecture demonstration about *kunqu* in Peony Pavilion by Sheila Melvin, China: The Power & Glory of the Ming Dynasty, February 10, 2012, Herbst Theatre, San Francisco.

Figure 23. Grinding the Golden Elixir.

is dreaming he is Zhuangzi; when Zhuangzi awakes he can no longer be sure if he is indeed Zhuangzi or whether he is in fact a butterfly.[124]

Next, a martial figure in broad, low, stance draws his fingers down the front of his body and makes a circling motion at the *dantian* (center of the body) while opening the fingers one by one. This circling movement is nearly identical to the mime used in *Kathak*, a dance from North India I studied. In Kathak it is done in front of the chest to mean *opening the heart in all directions like a lotus flower*.[125] As simple mime, this communicates the words: *Sink the qi to the dantian and release its power in all directions*. Again, going with the humorous interpretation, it mimes Zhang Sanfeng waking from a dream of Xuanwu and putting on his pants.

---

[124] I recommend the David Hinton translation of the *Zhuangzi* 1998.

[125] I spent six years studying Kathak with Pandit Chitresh Das.

Figure 24. Drinking the Golden Elixir.

The next movement mimes putting on a big straw hat and then stroking a beard in the shape of a halberd blade. These two characteristics match the earliest descriptions of Zhang Sanfeng.[126] This is followed by tying a belt, and the mime here is quite similar to that used for tying a belt in Kathak, used when showing Lord Krishna putting away his flute. This is Zhang Sanfeng tying his belt and putting away his magic ruler. One of his other names is Zhang Lata, which means *lazy*.

———————————————

[126] Wong 1993, 3.

Figure 25. Butterfly (Waking from a dream)

Figure 26. Lazy About Tying One's Coat.

You are probably thinking, why is mime from Indian dance in the Tai Chi form? This type of mime was spread throughout Asia; I just happen to know the meanings of these movements from my experience with Indian Dance. The specifics of how Indian dance ended up in China plays

Figure 27. Kathak dance: "Opening the heart in all directions like a lotus

Figure 28. Zhang Sanfeng Puts on his Hat and Strokes his Beard.

Figure 29. Zhang Sanfeng Ties his Belt.

Figure 30. Single Whip, a snake, and a crane.

a bigger role in the Baguazhang section of this book. But it is uncontroversial that South Asian entertainers traveled with merchants and envoys on their voyages to China.

Next is *Single-whip (danbian)*, where a single hand strokes a beard while lifting the leg into the air and stepping out into a broad stance. This movement is used for presenting a new character in Beijing Opera. *Single-whip* mimes a pole with a rope tied to one end called a *whipping* in nautical parlance, which is used for loading and unloading baskets from a

Figure 31. Brush-knee (crane and snake chasing each other).

boat. One of the most distinctive martial techniques of Tai Chi is the use of the body as a counterbalance to external forces rather than using force directly against force. *Single-whip* is a symbolic display of the counter balance principle in action.[127]

Yet *Single-whip* also uses extended fingers in the direction of the gaze as a way to mime *looking out into the distance*. And what would Zhang Sanfeng see? A snake fighting a crane!

The next move called *White Crane Spreads its Wings* is preceded by a snake movement, which is followed by *Brush-knee*. The name *Brush-knee* is purely descriptive. Each hand chases the other, alternating and never quite catching up. It mimes a crane and a snake chasing each other.

All variants of the first Chen routine that I know follow this pattern. Some forms repeat the *Jingang Pounds the Mortar*, another *Single-whip* to the other side, and some add an additional movement of a butterfly moving in a complete circle.

Following the storyline, Zhang Sanfeng then sets off on a journey to the capital through the mountains where he encounters and fights one hundred bandits. Since all Tai Chi movements are mimed fighting, the rest of the routine could simply be Zhang Sanfeng fighting bandits. But there are other possibilities.

---

[127] According to Xiang Kairan, in Beijing in 1928 it was called elixir transformation, using words of the same pronunciation (*danbian*) (Brennan 2016).

Further Analysis of the Story

A few Tai Chi form names come from literature.[128] For example, *Needle in the Bottom of the Sea* is a reference to the monkey Sun Wukong taking a pillar from the undersea palace of the Dragon King. The movement mimes Sun Wukong putting the pillar, which becomes his signature magical weapon, behind his ear and then naming it "needle." *Fair-lady Works the Shuttles* mimes, "The Sun and Moon rose and fell like the shuttles of a weaver's loom." It is a visual display of a quote repeated throughout Xuanwu's canonization epic *Journey to the North*, it means *a lot of time passing*.[129] *Seven-star Punch* invokes the seven-star black flag, used by spirit-mediums and in the play *Xiyangji* (see page 28). High Pat on a Horse is a colloquialism for a spy, and the movement mimes looking and listening while hiding behind a horse.

Perhaps the story is a tableau of Zhang traveling amongst the stars meeting various gods and immortals. *Golden-cock Stands on One Leg* refers to the story of the door-gods Yu and Lü, who stood beneath a sacred tree on which sat a golden rooster. Yu and Lü guard the doors of communication between men and gods. The *Golden-cock* movement mimes two mirror-image figures carved out of peach wood (like an exorcist's sword) and carrying reed ropes for capturing ghosts.[130] Is Zhang comically fighting all these gods to attain canonization? Are the one hundred bandits god-demons *(shenmo* 神魔*)* gaining merit through the play of battle? As Zhang journeys through the stages of transformation on his return to *the Dao*, are the bandits he defeats transformed along with him? This would follow the general pattern of theatrical exorcism where both winners and losers eventually achieve redemption.

---

[128] Storytellers in northern China used self-parody to enact violent scenes, often using names to reference fights by characters in other plays. For instance, in a husband and wife scene played by a solo storyteller, the wife might strike her husband with a Monkey-King-Spins-the-Dragon King slap, causing the storyteller to turn suddenly and slap himself. Knowing this about the use of named fight moves in performance opens up more possible interpretations for the Tai Chi form as mimed theater.

[129] Seaman 1987.

[130] Esposito 2004, 361

There are so many different types of ritual-theater that existed during the Qing Dynasty, it is difficult to pin down which type it was. *Jiaoben* or "prompt books," for example, were epics in skeletal form used by story-tellers to recall pivotal verses in stories that can span hundreds of years and take weeks to perform.[131] Tai Chi has the structure of a prompt book for an illiterate storyteller. Imagine a whole-body storyteller who acted out all the characters and the fight scenes himself. Each posture would unfold into a complete narrative, and then transition into the next episode. Literate and illiterate storytellers alike combined large amounts of memorization with improvisation. The individual Tai Chi postures could be these bookends or climax points in a modular epic. It fits. Un-less we find the complete epic in written form it will remain speculative. But I doubt that anyone has even looked.

In my own experiments with public performance, Tai Chi is en-hanced by live narration. For example, at the moment I'm doing *Cloud Hands*, I narrate, "Suddenly the fog rolled in. Unable to see, Zhang San-feng fought on. As the fog cleared bandits lay around him in a heap."

The meaning of the entire Tai Chi form is still elusive. Getting the full picture will require people steeped in Chinese culture who are willing to examine the question. If I could assemble this much of the story work-ing on my own, imagine what a team of experts could do? But the truth is, no one else has looked at this because until now the working assump-tion has been that Tai Chi is a pure martial art completely devoid of the-atrical origins or ritual purposes. The sad truth is that Chinese society went through a traumatic destruction. The origins of martial arts were esoteric before the society went through a process of brutalization, misin-formation, propaganda and mass murder in several traumatic waves over the last hundred and twenty years. The problem is not that the informa-tion is all gone, it is that the criteria for assessing who to trust and how to ask disappeared.

---

[131] Ge 2001, 81-83.

The Golden Elixir in Theater,

Tai Chi Texts, and Beyond

Chinese people have long associated the Golden Elixir with fighting prowess in the theater.[132] Likewise, in popular religious contexts, they associated invulnerability powers with Golden Elixir practices. Martial arts and popular religion scholar Meir Shahar traces invulnerability magic back to India in the Tenth Century.[133] By the Fifteenth Century, every man, woman, and child in China knew that the Golden Elixir could make you a better fighter because it was a common theme in theater. Invulnerability and immortality are obviously closely linked. After all, if I am an immortal and we fight, I have already won. All comic fight scenes incorporate some element of invulnerability.

In Hollywood, when you want to say a lot in a short time, you need a montage. With a montage you can squeeze years of fight training into fifteen seconds. In the Chinese theater they got the same effect by having heroes ingest a pill or drink a potion to instantly attain the Golden Elixir, rather than having to stage years of inner cultivation. While Zhang Sanfeng is known for distributing such pills, he himself spent years in self-cultivation and dream practices.[134] Tai Chi is a form of theater, so at the beginning of the form we mime drinking the Golden Elixir.

---

[132] The terms Golden Elixir *(jindan)* and Inner Elixir *(neidan)* are largely interchangeable.

[133] Shahar 2012, 119-128. While Shahar's examples are compelling, Daoist rituals producing invulnerability to naked blades date back to its inception in the Second Century C.E.—see Kleeman 2016, 297.

[134] The type of invulnerability that Zhang Sanfeng acquired from cultivating the Golden Elixir made him insubstantial—weapons either miss him or appear to pass right through his body as if it was a cloud. I have identified three types of inner elixir that confer invulnerability; *iron (tiedan)*, *gold (jindan)*, and *lotus (luandan)*—*impenetrable, insubstantial,* and *indestructible.*
The pills are an analogy for the teachings themselves, and represent the archaic idea of an actual elixir of magical substances. We will return to this subject in the final section of this book.

In the next section we will look at a series of texts which describe using the Golden Elixir to establish extraordinary martial prowess. Each of them explains the concept of internal martial arts *(neijia)*. These literati authors were immersed in the world of theater in which the Golden Elixir conferred martial arts prowess, and apparently they believed it. When General Qi Jiguang wrote about open hand fighting he doubted its efficacy; yet he became a practitioner of Zhang Sanfeng's Golden Elixir. The following texts assert that martial arts combined with the Golden Elixir produce real unique fighting skills. This is a case of life imitating art.

How to Fight With the Golden Elixir?

Before we look at these pre-modern texts, let us dip into the concept from a modern point of view. There is no place in the cosmos where the laws of physics do not apply. Better fighters make better use of physics. In addition, they use misperception, misdirection, disorientation, illusion, and deception.

The integration of the Golden Elixir into martial skills produces a more accurate perception of reality so that one can better utilize the underlying physics of fighting, while simultaneously tricking the opponent into misreading one's movement. One of several ways it does this is by discarding all the extra effort that goes into maintaining social status—like identity communication, and dominance-submission signaling. This shift removes all force against force contact and replaces it with fighting into emptiness. It would be difficult to attain this type of integration without first developing heavy contact skills because one must learn what *not* to do.

From my own experience playing rough with combat experienced professionals, at a certain threshold of experience some people automatically start to fight into emptiness and discard the baggage of social status and identity. Why? Because we are innate predators. Certain stimuli trigger automatic training and play, which create profound changes in one's movement and perception. With the right positive feedback loops emotional and physical intensity can cause the body to spontaneously teach itself to see and move differently. It is this fundamental aspect of human nature that the Golden Elixir method uses to transcend illusion and experience reality. In the language of the Golden Elixir, the fruition of this practice is an inversion, fake *(xu)* becomes real *(zhen)* and real becomes fake.

The Golden Elixir practice only begins once the practitioner has established the experience of emptiness, clarity, effortlessness, and stillness. It then becomes possible to shift the order of one's perception-action loops such that one becomes more animal-like and more spontaneous. It is a particular way of simultaneously moving and perceiving. For Daoists, this order of perception-action is primeval simplicity, the source of creativity. I will return to this subject in the final section on the Golden Elixir.

The Later Texts on Tai Chi

Writings on internal martial arts before the Twentieth Century either credit Zhang Sanfeng or the Golden Elixir as the source of martial prowess. Here are the details.

Memorial for Wang Zhengnan 1669 & 1676

This text, which we mentioned earlier (see page 76) is a memorial for a martial artist named Wang Zhengnan. The first part was written in 1669 by Huang Zongxi. The second part was written by his son seven years later in 1676. The son, Huang Baijin, was a disciple of Wang Zhengnan and gives a detailed description of the art. The father's memorial describes what a great guy Wang was and how well he fared when he got into fights. The most notable fight was against soldiers carrying swords. He disarmed and defeated each of them by grabbing their swords with his bare hands, at least implying that he had some invulnerability to edged weapons. Both father and son tell us that the art comes from Zhang Sanfeng.[135]

Martial arts historian Douglas Wile did an extensive study of the father's other writings. He concludes that Huang Zongxi was a fundamentalist Confucian who had low regard for Golden Elixir practices. Huang Zongxi even comments on the sage Lin Zhao'en of the Three-in-One religion, accepting his Confucian and Buddhist credentials but calling his Golden Elixir teachings heterodox. At the time he was writing, the Qing Government was about to carry out a campaign of destruction against Three-in-One temples. Without more information I cannot tell whether Huang supported or opposed the crackdown. Huang's main criticism of the Golden Elixir is that there were too many false teachers and he had a friend who had become a devotee of one such teacher and subsequently died of dementia.

Wile rightly notes that, at the time, anyone reading the references (both father and son make) to Zhang Sanfeng would conclude that the Golden Elixir was integrated into the martial art. However, noting Huang Zongxi's anti-Golden-Elixir stance, Wile searches for an alternate explanation. Inner Elixir *(neidan)* is a common alternate name for Golden Elixir *(jindan)*. According to Wile, the text uses the term "inner" in inner lineage *(neijia)* to refer to China, which has just been invaded by the "outer" Manchu. He posits that Zhang Sanfeng is used in the text as a "symbol of Chinese culture and nationalism."[136]

The problem with this theory is that people would still take Huang's words to mean that the martial art integrates the Golden Elixir. Even if readers got his secondary allegory, it does not diminish the more obvious meaning. Furthermore, if Huang Zongxi was a Confucian fundamentalist, to the right of Mencius, would he use sex-pot drunken-wild-man Zhang Sanfeng as a symbol of Chinese cultural pride? Seems like a

---

[135] For a side by side comparisons of Huang Baiji, Chang Naizhou, and modern Tai Chi see, Wells 2005; Wile 1999. The full text with translation is available here, Brennan 2014; https://brennantranslation.wordpress.com/2014/08/29/boxing-methods-of-the-internal-school-nei-jia-quan-fa/

[136] Wile 1999, 42-44.

stretch. Unfortunately, this theory has received traction from other authors.

It is also worth noting that, in naming Zhang Sanfeng, Huang was referencing a theatrical character. The reference could mean that the origins of the martial art's prowess come from the blend of stage combat and the Golden Elixir. It was common for actors to practice the Golden Elixir. Famous actors were courted by Quanzhen Daoists because, as Laozi said, "The Dao is like water, it seeks the lowest of the low." Actors were the lowest social caste. The original gate to the main Quanzhen temple on Mount Wudang was a pass-through stage. People would have to pass under the stage where a live performance was taking place to enter the main courtyard during festivals. To get inside you had to follow the Dao, you had to go lower than the lowest of the low![137]

In Huang Baijin's description of the inner lineage, he explains, "Zhang Sanfeng studied Shaolin and then reversed its principles."[138] I take this statement literally. It rings true to me as a practitioner of both Shaolin and several internal martial arts. The common conception of the Chinese word *nei* to mean *inner*, points to the inner elixir as its source, but the word also means *inward*. Shaolin is reversed by changing all outward force to *inward* force. Instead of a normal "root," we create a reverse root. Instead of outward strength we develop inward strength called *neigong*. *Neigong* is a self-arising realization/actualization about the nature of human movement that comes from the practice of the Golden Elixir combined with martial skills. I will come back to these concepts in the last chapter.

---

[137] Huang Zongxi's reference to Wudang may have been pointing to an inversion of social values that arose in the aftermath of the Manchu conquest.

[138] Shahar 2008,176.

Figure 32. Internal Martial Arts From Chang Naizhou's Writings, 1781.

Ningbo Gazetteer 1735

The Ningbo Gazetteer includes a biography of martial artist Zhang Songxi, who lived in Fujian during the Ming reign period (1522-1566). That is the same place and time that General Qi Jiguang was fighting pirates and the sage Lin Zhao'en was "studying" with the Immortal Zhang Sanfeng (see page 54). This Gazetteer says the art came from Zhang Sanfeng, who learned it in a dream from Xuanwu. Like Huang Zongxi, he also names the art the Inner Lineage *(neijia)*. We now know this legend was well known in the region because it was the subject of theatrical performance.[139]

---

[139] Wile 1999, 68-69.

Chang Naizhou 1781

Marnix Wells and Douglas Wile have both done extensive analysis and translation of the work of Chang Naizhou (1724-1783), a martial artist and literati who left an elaborate description of his art with drawings.[140] His explanations of theory have numerous overlaps with the later *Tai Chi Classics*. Judging by the drawings, his art looks different from Tai Chi, but some of the named movements are the same. It may be that the quality of movement was similar. There is no claim of association in this text with Zhang Sanfeng. However, Chang Naizhou identifies the Golden Elixir as the source of his martial prowess.[141]

1850~ The Tai Chi Classics

These five or so short poems are by far the best-known writings on internal martial arts, with some forty translations in English.[142] I was introduced to them by my teacher George Xu in about 1990 when I was attending his class six days a week and classes were five hours long. At one point we studied the Tai Chi Classics line by line. We took one line

---

[140] Wells 2005, *passim;* Wile 1999, *passim.*

[141] Chang Naizhou includes a section comparing internal martial arts to medical concepts of the body. As Andrew Schonebaum explains in his book *Novel Medicine, Healing, Literature and Popular Knowledge in Early Modern China* (2016), it was common in this period to include medical cures and concepts in published works, including theatrical fiction. To the modern reader it may seem confusing or forced, but it can also be understood as clarifying and drawing distinctions.

[142] The taijiquan classics are: 1) *Taijiquan jing*, attributed to Zhang Sanfeng, 2) *Taijiquan lun*, attributed to Wang Zongyue, 3) *Shisan shi xinggong xin jue*, attributed to Wu Yuxiang, 4) *Shisan shi ge*, 5) *Dashou ge*. For an excellent translation—see Swaim 1999. Probably composed in the mid-Nineteenth Century—see Wile 1996. The five Classics were first published in 1912 by Guan Baiyi—see Davis 2004, 33.
In the last fifteen years four groups of additional texts have appeared which seem designed to either undermine or foster particular lineage claims. This makes their provenance suspicious and their authenticity questionable. One of the texts traces Tai Chi's origins to a temple for Zhang Sanfeng—see Wile, 2017.
The Chen family claims to be the original source of the Tai Chi Classics, but their claim is based on documents which were lost in a fire at the home of Guoshu propagandist Tang Hao.
Brennan (2013) has translated the Wu Family Tai Chi Classics which he dates to 1875, although not published until 1983. Most of the text is dedicated to describing the art in terms similar to the standard five. The last three section are attributed to Zhang Sanfeng and position the art as one which combines martial skills with the Golden Elixir.

of text per week and together we explored it with the goal of full comprehension and embodiment. These poems were either written or compiled by the Wu brothers, the literati students of Yang Luchan (1799-1872). They were first made public in 1912. In addition to the classics there are some recently discovered texts that are similar in content. They are all dated sometime after 1850 and were transmitted through the Yang and Wu family Tai Chi lineages.

The first of "the classics" is attributed to Zhang Sanfeng as the progenitor of the art. There is no way of knowing if these texts were produced through spirit-writing, or group spirit-writing, but that would be the norm for works attributed to Zhang Sanfeng.

The second two classics are attributed to Wang Zongyue. Douglas Wile reviews the many controversies about who Wang might have been. In short, it has become an issue of insurmountable conflict particularly for those who wish to attribute a pure-martial origin to Chen style Tai Chi. Wile points out that Zongyue means *revering* Yue, referring to General Yue Fei (1103-1143).[143] Wells agrees, translating his name as "lineage of Yue," and points out that Fei means "flying."[144]

Yue Fei was a popular martial character on the stage, which is where a Chinese person would have learned about him. He is an incarnation of the Buddhist guardian Garuda. Here is the story: One day the Buddha was giving a teaching and a bat-girl flew by and farted in the Buddha's face. Garuda, who is a giant bird, the archenemy of dragons, and a thunder god, swooped in and killed the bat-girl. Garuda's transgression caused him to go to hell and then be reborn as a human. That is when he became Yue Fei (See Picture).[145]   The Wang in Wang Zongyue means king. Garuda is a king and is depicted wearing a crown. Zongyue refers to the endless cycle of rebirth Garuda and Yue Fei play over and over on

---

[143] Wile 1996, 111.

[144] Wells, 2005, 7-11.

[145] Hsia 2004, 149, 154, 448n.
The Yue Fei story is one of the most common stories told on murals of the hell realms (Reed College: Chinese Hell Scrolls; updated 2019). Hell realm re-enactments were a standard ritual element of the New Year's celebrations in many parts of China.

Figure 33. Yue Fei in Hell. Reed College Hell Scrolls.

the stage. This is of course a spirit-writing name too. Wang Zongyue like Zhang Sanfeng is a name given as the source of spontaneous inspiration for a channelled text.[146] The Yue Fei Garuda story was a universally known "hell story" depicted during New Year's celebration rituals, so every man, woman, and child would have been familiar with this meaning. It is astounding that such widespread knowledge could be obscured in the Twentieth Century to the point that it would go unrecognized. The effects of the mass murders should not be underestimated.

---

[146] Yue Fei is credited as the source for several different martial arts, most notably Xingyi-quan (see page 159).

Resisting Disenchantment in the Twentieth Century

In the last chapter we saw that the earliest writers associate Tai Chi with either the Golden Elixir or Zhang Sanfeng, who was a teacher of the Golden Elixir. This became less and less acceptable over time. In the wake of the humiliation and destruction left by the Boxer Uprising, the Golden Elixir was implicated as a false source of martial prowess and invulnerability to bullets. Since Daoism was strongly associated with the Golden Elixir, it was subject to the same criticisms. In response, Daoists set out to remake the Golden Elixir within the framework of the YMCA Consensus. Recall that the YMCA Consensus is the movement to separate religion, martial arts, and theater, and to annihilate superstition. Daoist modernizers reframed the Golden Elixir as a personal cultivation practice rather than one linked to ritual.[147] They scientized it by describing it in terms of anatomy, physiology, physics and even DNA. They glossed it as a self-improvement practice connected to moral piety, as a path to becoming a better person. Under the YMCA Consensus, the Golden Elixir had to stand alone, without its connection to ritual, martial arts, medicine, art or theater.

By the 1920s the new Chinese state was consolidating power. All Chinese religions struggled against the charge of superstition and accusations of unethical practices which were bad for the nation. Buddhists adopted more effective defensive strategies than Daoists did, even as they both saw massive numbers of temples confiscated. Localized communal-religious practices and festivals were even less effective at defending themselves against the onslaught. For example, Dragon Court temples, which were ubiquitous in northern China, were completely wiped out. This was true for hundreds of other commonplace religious traditions. There were a few loopholes in the Nationalist system. One such loophole allowed some local temples to avoid the charge of

---

[147] Liu Xun 2009.

superstition by claiming they were dedicated to a real person in history, not a god; and therefore not a deceptive, irrational, cult. In these cases, the temples were re-categorized as patriotic memorials.[148] At this time, martial arts were treated like religion, because that is what they were. They defended themselves against the charge of being superstitious primarily by adopting pure-martial arts platitudes, like those of the Jingwu Society (also see page 201)—they also enacted a strategy that paralleled temples claiming to be patriotic memorials. They concocted lineages that could be traced back to a real person, rather than a god, an immortal, or a mystical animal. It was even better if that historic progenitor was a patriotic military figure.

There was another loophole in the anti-superstition laws that affected the new doctrine surrounding Tai Chi. The Nationalists concocted a strategy to preserve the "ancient" Confucian temples by reframing them as pro-government and secular, along with a handful of other quasi-mythic ancients, like the Yellow Emperor. The implicit assumption was that a certain amount of irrationality was tolerable if a religion was ancient, and the model for this was Christianity, whose central figure Jesus Christ was two thousand years old. Thus, one strategy practitioners used was to say that Tai Chi was thousands of years old, based on the principles of the *Yijing (I Ching)*.[149] This explanation found its way into numerous books.

Getting back to Zhang Sanfeng, practitioners re-framed Zhang Sanfeng as a real person and made him the first in a lineage of real people. The explicit connection between the Golden Elixir and Tai Chi was increasingly considered superstitious by those who wrote about Tai Chi (although the idea lingered on). Those promoting the strategy of making Zhang Sanfeng a real person hoped to sever the explicit connection between the Golden Elixir and Tai Chi. They hoped to give legitimacy to Tai Chi as a rational form of Chinese body-science. Here it is helpful to think about Tai Chi as a kind of mobile temple. Temples were being shut

---

[148] Nedostup 2009, 78-91.

[149] It was also a trickster maneuver because the "principles of the Yijing" was a coded way of saying the Golden Elixir.

down unless they could prove they had some value to the state. Tai Chi attempted to be a mobile temple for patriotic notions of internal power and inner strength *(neijin* and *neigong)*. [150] A less superstitious Tai Chi could be a Chinese version of the YMCA Muscular Christianity. In addition to being a path to moral strength, Tai Chi training mimicked the free circulation of commerce and new ideas. After all, Tai Chi is the embodiment of flow. The early boosters of Tai Chi thought that by making Zhang Sanfeng a real person they could distract people from his obvious theatrical origins and diminish the enchanted dimensions of the art.

The Tai Chi Classics, published in 1912, were used to concoct the Tai Chi lineage. One classic was attributed to Zhang Sanfeng and another was attributed to Wang Zongyue. As explained earlier, Wang Zongyue was Yue Fei, the reincarnation of Garuda, but the ambiguity of the name allowed people to pretend it was the name of some unknown person in the lineage. Practitioners then constructed a lineage that passed through Wang Zongyue back to Zhang Sanfeng. When Chen stylists appeared on the scene in the 1930s, they attempted to insert a distant Chen ancestor named Chen Wangting into the lineage. He was a man of some military association who fit well with the deceit of pure-martial origins. [151] But the anti-superstition forces kept growing in strength.

The original religious story that Tai Chi comes from the Immortal Zhang Sanfeng made sense in a culture where knowledge can come from trance, dream, and possession by spirits from the unseen world. But Zhang Sanfeng was a problem for the new state. Not only was he associated with the Golden Elixir, but also with humor, taboo sexual theater, channeling, magic, unruliness, and being a trickster. When you are trying to institute national order, military discipline, and civic unity, you do not want the most popular martial art in the country to be about flipping the

---

[150] Ng 2016, *dissertation*—discusses the origins of the terms *neigong* and *neijin* and how they were used in early Twentieth Century political discourse to posit a uniquely Chinese way of being strong.

[151] Contemporary Chen family sources claim that they maintained secret family documents that show the complete lineage. I have no doubt that a few Chen family members practiced Tai Chi for several centuries, but the modern lineage idea is a political one. Not only can it not be authenticated, it also serves to obscure the origins of the art.

world upside-down. While the newly inked lineages were still drying it became necessary to disassociate Zhang Sanfeng from Tai Chi in order to save it. This great debunking effort was spearheaded by Communist historian Tang Hao. But it was only possible in the aftermath of the silly claim that Zhang Sanfeng was a real person. It worked because practitioners themselves were publicly dismissing the connection between Tai Chi and the Golden Elixir.

Since that time, the strange question, "Do you believe Zhang Sanfeng was a real person," has become a litmus test for those with "correct thoughts." Tang Hao went further, claiming that the source of Tai Chi's pure-martial military prowess came from Qi jiguang and not from Zhang Sanfeng at all. Under the YMCA Consensus, this was an even better lineage origin for Tai Chi because it satisfied the "patriotic-ancestor" standard for secularized religious practice.

It is an open question how Tai Chi spread from the 1870s, when it was just a few guys doing Yang style, to the 1930s, when it became the most widely practiced martial art in China.[152] According to oral histories, sometime around 1870 Yang Luchan began teaching Tai Chi at the palace of Prince Duan. I am inclined to believe it. But I would be remiss if I did not point out that at the time those oral histories were written down, Prince Duan was blamed for the Boxer Uprising and was presumed dead. (He was hiding in Gansu for twenty years but no one knew that at the time.) During the Uprising Prince Duan was the most public supporter of the Boxers, advocating their anti-foreigner mission and believing in their invulnerability to bullets. The Eight Nations Alliance wanted his head. At the moment there is no material evidence of Yang Luchan's connection to Prince Duan, but we know for certain it was an emotionally charged claim.[153]

---

[152] Chen style was not known outside of Chen village until 1928 when Chen Fake began teaching in Beijing, at that time Tai Chi was already popular.

[153] Someone with means and access could settle this question. There were diaries and photographs and other forms of documentation in Beijing in 1870. If there was an amazing martial artist living with the Prince, someone probably noticed it and wrote about it.

Tai Chi spread as a remedy for the ills of foot-binding. Under the influence of groups like the YMCA, the Chinese people ended the practice of foot-binding from 1890 to 1910. Influential speakers and writers, in conjunction with local governments, promoted the idea that arts like Tai Chi were the ideal therapy for training recently unbound feet to walk normally again. The majority of women still had bound feet in 1900, and by 1930 it had become rare. Ironically, reformers began teaching martial arts in missionary schools within a few years of the Boxer Uprising, especially in women's schools. Many of these schools were run by the YMCA, whose anti-foot binding concept was that the body should be naturalized in the image of the Christian God. Educators toured the country making speeches directed at women, using the "hook" that having bound feet inhibits a women's ability to practice martial arts. If you want to be a great female fighter, you cannot have bound feet.[154] Needless to say, a feminist movement was afoot.

The obvious contradictions at play here are one of the reasons this story has not been told. Was the YMCA pro-martial arts or anti-martial arts? The answer is both. Reformers loved the idea of taking Chinese traditional movement training, divorcing it from its origins, and repackaging it as an expression of the new Protestant ideal. They envisioned a naturalized body in God's image—a healthy body—capable of leading in the creation of a new rational, hygienic, and preferably Christian, Chinese State.

Imagine these educational boosters giving speeches about women's empowerment and martial arts. The young women hearing these speeches would see in their mind's eye the familiar image from opera of young female heroes fighting on the stage. But at the time, men, dressed as women, were fighting on the stage with fake-bound-feet. What a strange moment of re-myth-making this must have been; women emulating men, emulating women, emulating men. In that first decade of the Twentieth Century something called soft calisthenics was taught in these women's schools. It evolved into Tai Chi calisthenics, an exercise-art per-

---

[154] Personal communication from Dorothy Ko on the spread of martial arts teaching in girls schools. On using Tai Chi like practices to re-learn walking see Ko 2005, 104.

formed at the 1936 Olympics.[155] From 1925 to 1934 the Nationalists promoted women's martial arts and declared it equal to men's. But then in 1934, the same year that martial arts movies (Wuxia) were banned, women were banned from the Central Guoshu Institute.[156]

The healing reputation of Tai Chi is a mess to sort out. The Golden Elixir has healing powers, that is the reason it was taught to General Qi Jiguang back in the 1500s. Later, the Immortal Zhang Sanfeng as a powerful healer, lent his reputation to Tai Chi to such an extent that early in the Twentieth Century it was simply self-evident that Tai Chi was good for health, especially for the effete and the elderly, and even in YMCA schools. By the 1950s both the art and its reputation were spreading abroad. In the 1980s in the West, assertions about Tai Chi's health benefits began filling a gap left by impersonal and aggressive forms of Western medicine. By the 1990s it was common to hear that Tai Chi could cure anything. That enthusiasm was largely replaced by Qigong towards the end of the 1990s. The enthusiasm has since tapered off, but it has not disappeared because people continue to report that it works.

For hundreds of years the Golden Elixir was at the center of the cult of traditional Chinese medicine. Chinese culture was saturated with knowledge and enthusiasm about healing. The average Chinese grandmother had a substantial body of effective household healing strategies available to her. Literature was intertwined with medicine, especially comic and romantic literature. Books and other sources of information about cooking, bathing, massage, exorcisms, talismans, martial arts and every other aspect of daily life were infused with medical knowledge. Medicine was everywhere but was not an organized medicine with a unifying set of principles. It was an assortment of traditions transmitted through lineages of amateurs and experts. The Golden Elixir was the

---

[155] Morris 2004, 185-229.

[156] The reason given for the exclusion of women was the prevalence of sexual harassment.

best medicine in this menagerie. During the Ming Dynasty the Golden Elixir was the first part of medical curriculums.[157]

All the martial arts that made it through the Twentieth Century, including Tai Chi, were redefined by the Nationalists as purely for fighting, but they were also promoted for their obvious health benefits, creating a lasting paradox. We might even call this the YMCA paradox. Chinese martial arts were slotted into the formula attributed to Western boxing—a healthy body makes a healthy mind, makes a moral person, makes a healthy nation.[158] The old traditional story and the new YMCA story are different but they overlap.

The Nationalists labeled traditional medical knowledge as backwards and superstitious. Experts in herbal medicine, *moxa* and acupuncture resisted this by starting several teaching hospitals in Shanghai in the 1920s. These were modeled on missionary teaching hospitals. This helped define and defend the profession of Chinese medicine during the Nationalist era.

The Communists were even more anti-Chinese medicine than the Nationalists, amplifying the charges that it was backward and superstitious. Most bio-medical doctors, trained in missionary schools, fled in 1949. Those who chose to stay or could not escape were in high demand for their skills, but were also persecuted in several waves of violence over the next twenty years. In the 1950s, the lack of doctors and medical infrastructure was so acute, the Communist Party decided to rehabilitate traditional medical knowledge and knit it together in a synthesis of biomedicine and an assortment of traditional therapies to form the deceptively named Traditional Chinese Medicine (TCM). At the same time, the Communists applied this anti-ritual, anti-religion, anti-theatricality process to martial arts warm-ups, *daoyin*, and all sorts of merit-accumulating movement-meditation practices—to create what became known as

---

[157] Hsu 1999 ,187

[158] See Judkins 2018, "Zhang Zhijiang, Father of the Guoshu Movement," about a Chinese Christian General who had his troops practice "traditional" martial arts. Also see Nedostup 2009, 45-46, where the same general played a role in advocating for religious freedom defined in Christian terms.

qigong. Today, teachers commonly impose this sort of scientization on Tai Chi by overlaying it with TCM concepts and terminology, and by fatuously asserting bio-mechanics as the true source of authenticity.

In the decade after the Cultural Revolution, people were desperate to process the emotional trauma of being survivors. But in the 1980s, the psychological concept of being depressed was still a thought-crime and traditional religious customs for processing emotion had been obliterated. In an ironic twist, the newly invented qigong was the only politically correct outlet for healing grief. It exploded into what people called *qigong*-fever. Every morning masses of people were shaking and screaming and crying and dancing in the parks. They were doing whatever they needed to do to heal, and they called all of it *qigong*. Numerous mass *qigong* cults appeared at this time to help facilitate this release; the best known is Falun Gong. These *qigong* fever cults were then violently suppressed at the end of the 1990s.[159] In response, martial artists reasserted their "pure-martial" origins to distinguish themselves from these groups. These are resilient ghosts.

Morality and Myth

The exploration of moral ambiguity was a traditional element of theatrical martial prowess, because it embodied the movement routines of bandits and demons alongside those of immortals and heroes. The YMCA Consensus replaced that openness with the idea that martial arts should instill clean living and moral rectitude. During World War One, hundreds of thousands of Chinese joined YMCA work camps in Europe, where Western Boxing was the primary leisure activity. After they returned from the War, many became political leaders and social influencers, spreading the YMCA idea of martial arts as moral rectitude. As noted in the introduction, as the YMCA became the model for studying martial arts, it also became an ideal location to take a martial arts class. The Jingwu Society emerged as a Chinese version of the YMCA and spread like wildfire. Under Chiang Kai-shek, these ideals became fully

---

[159] Falungong is the best known qigong fever cult, but there were many, with the total number of participants approaching one hundred million—see Palmer 2007.

Figure 34. Boxing Match. YMCA Camp WWI, France, 1918. Imperial War Museum.

nationalized. The state paid purified martial artists to promote Guoshu (National Arts) as a way to make the nation stronger. Today, the vast majority of Chinese and Westerners continue to view martial arts through that YMCA filter. [160]

The Wushu movement, created after 1949, proceeded to prioritize a virtuosic, non-narrative, non-ritual, athletic performance style. While still consistent with the YMCA Consensus, the Communists incorporated ballet and acrobatics to the exclusion of martial skill. Their stated goal was to eliminate human nature and replace it with a rational mass aesthetic. For Tai Chi, that meant the creation of competition-forms,

[160] The true reach of the Jingwu movement and the Guoshu movement after it, is not known. Film made by Gables show bits of martial arts rituals from the late 1920s https://youtu.be/RFtpjR6uYnI Also see Gables 1954, 329-407. Those rituals were targeted by the Japanese during their invasion and were eventually wiped out in the Mainland by the Communists after 1949. Lion Dancing thrived in Hong Kong and outside Mainland China, as did some lesser known rituals in Thailand, Malaysia, and Indonesia.

Figure 35. Theatrical Procession. YMCA Camp WWI, France, 1918. Imperial War Museum.

short-forms, and elements of standardization that had little to do with the original art. The Communist promotion and control of Wushu inadvertently re-created an underground pure-martial movement, which then re-emerged after the Cultural Revolution.[161]

In the 1990s, Wudang Shan, Zhang Sanfeng's home in some versions of the story, was re-opened. Daoist culture, sparse through the 1950s, was eliminated from the mountain during the Cultural Revolution. At last count, five lineages of Monastic Daoism (Quanzhen) had returned to the mountain. Each lineage teaches martial arts there. The arts they teach have a pure-martial character, but also a unique flowing quality. By most accounts they are martial arts from other parts of China, like Yang Style Tai Chi for example, that are mixed with some local Daoist movement

---

[161] Amos 1983, dissertation.

Figure 36. Northern Shaolin, YMCA Camp WWI, France, 1918. Imperial War Museum.

traditions. The origin claims of these martial arts and invented lineages may only go back as far as the 1930s. The severe breaks in continuity are for the most part acknowledged by Wudang Daoist initiates, who are faithful to precepts of sincerity and integrity. To my knowledge the subject of the history of martial arts on Wudang Mountain is only available as fiction in the movies. I suspect that if we start looking for Daoist theater, we will find the origins of Wudang martial arts and it will be exciting indeed. The original gate of Wudang Shan sponsored by the Yongle Emperor (1360-1424) was a stage for performing theater during festivals.[162]

Foreign martial artists were some of the first and most adventurous tourists to enter China from the end of the Cultural Revolution (1977) to

---

[162] Called "a pass-though gate"—see Hong 2016.

the 1990s when business travel started to eclipse them. Foreigners' visits to Wudang Mountain, asking to meet Daoists and learn martial arts, were a significant factor in the re-establishment of Daoism there. Likewise, the extent to which martial arts in general have been politically rehabilitated is due in part to interest from abroad. Still, with so many Daoists tortured and murdered in the Twentieth Century, the comeback is a miracle in process. It is still on shaky ground. That being said, culture is incredibly resilient and optimism can be found in both preservation and innovation.

Making Tai Chi Weird Again

One of the reasons why mythology is so important is that humans are wired for it. Take it away and we experience a gap in meaning. Gaps in meaning tend to get filled unconsciously. On the one hand we have New Age triviality and on the other hand we have uniform Tai Chi mass performances in the service of Communism. Neither of which would be possible if it were not for the gap in meaning left by the disappearance of Zhang Sanfeng. One of the funnier things trotted out to fill the gap in meaning is the idea that Tai Chi is a pre-industrial "combat-science." People are welcome to put all their eggs in that basket. In practice they are going to lose a lot of eggs to disillusionment.

Tai Chi is a fighting art, but it is so much more. When it comes to meaning, the human mind is a pluralist. We can handle multiple meanings simultaneously. Singular meaning leads to exhaustion and death. Mythology is never singular. It is a collection of meanings that enrich each other. This is an issue which is central to Orthodox Daoism. Ritual, meditation, and *daoyin* all contain the seed idea that we can travel back to the source of meaning and then return refreshed and renewed. In Daoism this is called, "Returning to the source." Daoists happily insert ourselves into mythologies by traveling in dream and ritual back to our cosmological origins. We rediscover the source of mythic inspiration and then return with updated ways of seeing and doing. This is another reason why Daoism is so theatrical. Stage performance and participatory theater are great ways to tap into the collective unconscious and leverage it for communal rejuvenation.

Tai Chi comes from the weirdness of this mythology and ritual-theater. Our participation in slow-motion martial arts is itself a form of resistance to all attempts to normalize it.

Internal martial arts originally meant the Golden Elixir mixed with theatrical-ritual fighting skills. From the beginning, Tai Chi was a combination of fighting skill, religion, and theater. The theatricality of it is key because stories matter, mythology matters, imagery matters, improvisation matters, metaphors matter and the ability to transcend or master identity is a life-changing experience in all realms of being. The fighting style of Tai Chi is unique. As an aesthetic, there is no consensus on why it is performed slowly, yet it continues to attract dedicated seekers of beauty and weirdness. Zhang Sanfeng's inspiration is to fight like an immortal, without fighting, invulnerable, a comic trickster, open minded, capable of healing in multiple dimensions, responsible, weird and free. That is worth fighting for.

One More Time From the Top

Tai Chi has its origins in the blend of Chinese theater, religion and martial skills. Both theater and violence were everywhere, and everywhere they were integrated into the religious life of the Chinese people.

Spirit-mediumship played a role in China's unruly theatrical-religious traditions. These practices have been a constant source of theatrical and martial inspiration and consternation for China's organized religious landscape. Moving in the opposite direction, the inner elixir travelled from Daoism into heretical cults with millennialist visions and morphed into new religious movements throughout the last five hundred years. People incorporated martial skills into village militias, bandit culture, and secret rebellions. Tai Chi fell somewhere in that mix. That is the ocean Tai Chi was floating on.

In Chinese culture, possession cults were widespread and even fighting could be understood as a form of possession. The practice of enshrining and symbolically feeding those who died violent deaths led to elaborate thunder rituals and other forms of demonic warfare.

Those practices became integrated with the theater, enmeshed in literature, and refined in Daoist ritual. Sworn-brothers (see my book *Possible Origins*, 2016) used possession to train martial skills. The seven-star black flag was widely used to hold the possessing deities down, and to command them. It is also a representation of the god Xuanwu's true-form. Widespread use of the seven-star flag denotes Xuanwu's awesome power as a sort of puppeteer of the gods, invoked as a commander of thunder gods during war rituals.

The late Sixteenth Century play *Xiyangji's* middle chapters showcase Zhang Sanfeng who is tasked with extracting Xuanwu's true-form and giving it to the Buddha, who uses it to steal back the seven-star black flag, which is capable of turning the entire cosmos to brown water. Zhang Sanfeng's awesome drunken fight scene with twenty-four brocade guards is the oldest use of the named Tai Chi moves as distinct movements. It has a close relationship to General Qi Jiguang's thirty-two verse poem on open-hand combat, which suggests they draw from a common source. That Zhang Sanfeng fight scene has a few of the pieces of Tai Chi, but it is incomplete.

Xiyangji, which contains the fight scene, is a play about Admiral Zheng He's journeys of conquest. The play's subtext is the Ming Dynasty's struggles with pirates and its difficulties grappling with massive social and cultural changes brought about by the growth of commerce. Qi Jiguang's book on reforming the military is often portrayed as a paragon of rationality. But the reality is that General Qi was enmeshed in the religious culture of his time and wrote a rhymed song about how fun martial arts are, which, seen in context, was a performance for boosting troop morale.

Qi Jiguang maintained a twenty-year relationship with Fujian's most famous sage-healer, Lin Zhao'en. Lin healed him using a ritual for the unresolved dead which was a form of demonic warfare. Lin also taught Qi Jiguang a version of the Golden Elixir which he claimed to have learned from the immortal Zhang Sanfeng. Lin Zhao'en's Three-in-One Religion was highly theatrical. Even today, its lay practitioners learn the Golden Elixir and practice spirit-writing and other forms of ritual performance.

Xuanwu taught Zhang Sanfeng in a dream, as recorded in the Memorial for Wang Zhengnan (see page 97). This is the same story I found in the mime of the Chen style Tai Chi form.[163] Zhang Sanfeng was a popular immortal throughout China. The beginning of the form parallels Daoist ritual. It also contains a plethora of movement names

---

[163] It can be identified abstractly in other styles of Tai Chi too.

that come from theater, a type of theater that was built around canonization rituals.

That was Tai Chi at its beginnings; complex and multi-layered. Yet it is still difficult to say what Tai Chi is today. It is a framework for a larger story. A ritual that confers the protective powers of unseen gods and immortals. It has all the elements of an exorcism. Emptiness in motion is the traditional source of potency for battles with the invisible world. It is a public dedication of merit for a whole community. The sheer volume of detailed mime is proof of its connection to community theater. But it also has elements of a private ritual like those done by Daoist priests in Taiwan where exorcistic puppet shows happen behind closed doors and are done exclusively to an audience of the gods.

If Tai Chi is Daoist it comes from the weird open-ended Daoism of hermits and actors, not from the orthodox rituals of Zhengyi or the monastic traditions of Quanzhen. Tai Chi fits seamlessly with dream practice, where it becomes the gateway to controlling one's bodily motion as an infinite actualization in night-time stillness. The movements and visualizations of Tai Chi are driven by the practice of the Golden Elixir (*jindan*), to which we have dedicated the final chapter of this book. Tai Chi contains layers of myth and meaning which give it ritual potency.

Tai Chi has its origins in a type of theater that made people better fighters. A theater that animated people with the physical morality to avoid fights by being lively, spontaneous, and responsive. Tai Chi is a fighting art that makes inner stillness its highest priority. Tai Chi was not created by people who experienced life as short and cheap, but rather it was made by people who cherished every breath as a glorious treasure, people who were committed to kinesthetic beauty.

How did Tai Chi end up being spread by hippies? And how did hippies get the idea of *fighting without fighting* from a play published in 1597 that almost no one has heard of? How did that idea seep through despite attempts to suppress it?

I think the answer is simple but not obvious. Historically in China, theater was the most common way for the average person to learn history. Understood as ritual, theater was a way of instilling in people a sense of history. History in books is linear and explicit. Ritual approaches to instilling history are holistic and embodied. Daoist rituals, for instance, are embodiments of history through dance, music and storytelling. Tai Chi is ritual-dance-theater. It tells the story of its own creation in a dream of Zhang Sanfeng. Like Daoist ritual, the opening movements tell the story of the world coming into being, and the role of shaman rulers and trance-mediums in defining our present reality (even if that story was unknown). The movement quality of Tai Chi tells a story about self-improvement through returning to simplicity. Tai Chi practice is a quest to discover the efficacy of effortlessness. Tai Chi embodies the history of Daoist methods of spiritual cultivation— sitting and forgetting, *daoyin*, the Golden Elixir, dream—all embodied in a ritual *without* words. It is like the first line of the *Daodejing*, "The Dao which can be spoken is not the true Dao, the words that are used are not the true words." This idea of *wuwei*, of doing without doing, is built into the direct teachings of Tai Chi—it is spoken without being spoken.

Appendix: San Bao Taijian Xia Xiyangji

A big challenge to analyzing the similarities between Tai Chi, the Zhang Sanfeng fight scene in chapter 57 of *Xiyangji*, and the writings of General Qi Jiguang is that each is a different type of writing. A Tai Chi form is simply a list of names. We know each name refers to both movements and postures even if the naming schemes are often cryptic and sometimes imply applications. There are also different Tai Chi forms and different styles with differences in naming. The Qi Jiguang text is a poem with thirty-two verses describing interactive techniques and movements using coded names, it is hard to assess how many movements are in each verse. The play is written in prose which suggest actions on the stage, but in pairs as if one move is a response to another.

Gyves identified eight names from Qi Jiguang in the Yang style Tai Chi form.[164] Tang Hao (1896-1959) identified twenty-five names from Qi Jiguang in the Chen style form. Gu Liuxin (1908-1991) added four making it twenty-nine.[165] Marnix Wells, looking at Chang Naizhou's *Twenty-four Dynamics* text from the mid-1700s found two near variants that match Tai Chi names, eight that match both Qi Jiguang and Tai Chi, and five that match Huang Zongxi's inner school.[166]

Marnix Wells and Douglas Wile have both produced detailed comparisons of theses texts to Qi Jiguang. *Xiyangji* and all the other texts are readily available in searchable Chinese characters on-line, as well as complete facsimiles. The following names from *Xiyangji* were translated by Marnix Wells with a few minor changes by me. The underlined text matches Qi Jiguang. I refer readers to the excellent work of both Wile

---

[164] Gyves 1993.

[165] Wiles 1999, 11.

[166] Wells 2005, 3.

Figure 37. Zhang Sanfeng.

and Wells for detailed comparisons to other similar texts, and I see no reason to repeat their work here.

San Bao Taijian Xia Xiyangji

LVII: Jin Bìfeng zhuân Nánjingchéng, Zhang Sanfeng jiàn Wànsuìyé 733-734:

Here over half of *Xiyangji's* 32 moves are identical or have a close affinity with 18 of Qi Jìguang's 32 Verses (with the named techniques):

1-2 Tàishan yadîng vs. Shénxian duôyîng.

Grand Mountian Crush Peak vs. Fairy Immortal Dodges Shadow.

3-4 Xîquè zhengcháo vs. Wuya bûshí.

Magpies Fight for Nest vs. Crows Feeding

5-6 Mânmiàn hua vs. Cuìdì jîn.

Face Full of Flowers vs. <u>Ground Fallen Brocade</u>.

7-8 Jinji dúlì vs. Fúhû cèshen.

Gold Cock on One Leg vs. Subdue Tiger Oblique Body.

9-10. Gao sì-píng vs. Zhong sì-píng.

High Four Level vs. Mid Four Level.

11-12 Jînglán sìpíng vs. Duijiù sì-píng.

Well Railing Four Level vs. Pound Mortar Four Level.

13-14 Hû bàotóu vs. Lóng xiàn zhâo.

Tiger Holds Head vs. Dragon Displays Claws.

15-16 Shùn luánzhôu vs. Aó luánzhôu.

Standard Phoenix Elbow vs. Reverse Phoenix Elbow.

17-18 Dangtóu bào(=pào?) vs. Cèshen ai.

Aim at Head Cannon vs. Oblique Body Press In.

19-20 Shânruò shengqiáng vs. Jiécháng bûduân.

Evade with Weakness To Generate Strength vs. Cut the Long, Reinforce the Short.

21-22 Yi-tiáo bian vs. Qi-xing jiàn.

One Tail Whip vs. Seven Stars Sword.

23-24 Guî cù jiâo vs. Pào zhulián.

Demon Stamps Leg vs. Cannon Continuous Shots.

25-26 Xià cha shàng vs. Shàng jing xià.

Down Thrusts Up vs. Up Surprises Down.

27-28 Tànjiâo xu vs. Tànmâ kuài.

Scout Leg Feint vs. Scout Horse Fast.

29-30 Mântian xing vs. Zhuadì hû.

Sky Full of Stars vs. Grasp Earth Tiger.

31-32 Huôyàn zuanxin vs. Sahua gàidîng.

Fire Scorches the Heart vs. Scatter Flowers Over Head.

三寶太監下西洋

這個抽門拴的原出於無意，不曾提防，可可的吃他一掌，就打出一個泰山壓頂來。這個手裡也曉得幾下，就還一個神仙躲影，溜過他的這個，說道：「你怎麼打起我來？」那個說道：「我打你？你倒擘頭子溜我一門拴。」一則是兩個人有些宿氣，二則是黑地裡分不得甚麼高低，那個一拳，打個喜雀爭巢；這個一拳，打個烏鴉撲食。那個一拳，打個滿面花；這個一拳，打個萃地錦。那個一拳，打個金雞獨立；這個一拳，打個伏虎側身。那個一拳，打個高四平；這個一拳，打個中四平。那個一拳，打個井欄四平；這個一拳，打個碓臼四平。那個一拳，打個虎抱頭；這個一拳，打個龍獻爪。那個一拳，打個順鸞肘；這個一拳，打個拗鸞肘。那個一拳，打個當頭抱；這個一拳，打個側身挨。那個一拳，打個閃弱生強；這個一拳，打個截長補短。那個一拳，打個一條鞭；這個一拳，打個七星劍。那個一拳，打個鬼蹴腳；這個一拳，打個炮連珠。那個一拳，打個下插上；這個一拳，打個上驚下。那個一拳，打個探腳虛；這個一拳，打個探馬快。那個一拳，打個滿天星；這個一拳，打個抓地虎。那個一拳，打個火燄攢心；這個一拳，打個撒花蓋頂。到其後，你閃我一個空，我閃你一個空；你揪我一揪，我蹴你一蹴。揪做一堆，蹴在一處。眾人只說是打道士，都說道：「不當人子。」哪曉得道士鼾鼾安穩睡，自家人打自家人。吵了一夜，吵到五更三點，宅子裡三聲梆響，開了中門。

Figure 38. Zhang Sanfeng.

Baguazhang

The Dance of an Angry Baby God

Baguazhang literally means eight-trigrams-palm. The word *bagua* refers to the symbol of the eight "gua" or trigrams. The bagua *symbol* represents the *Yijing*, the *Classic of Changes*, an ancient divination system. The bagua symbol is synonymous with talismans because in Chinese cosmology the *Yijing* is used to represent all the possible fates, and talismans are used to change fate.

The *bagua* symbol is everywhere in Chinese culture. For instance, it is on the back of Daoist vestments (see image on next page) to symbolize the world (all possible fates) coming into being. It is in the center of the black flag, which is used by ritual experts for containing the possession states of trance-mediums in Singapore and other places where native Chinese religions still thrive.[167] Thus, an alternate name for the black flag of possession is the *bagua* flag (See figure 8, page 28).

No one knows how the art of Baguazhang got its name. The forced confessions of an 1813 rebel group called *baguajiao* mention the art of

---

[167] A detailed translation of the text and talismans on a working Black Flag can be found in Chan, Margaret 2014, 25-46.

Figure 39. Daoist priest's robe *(daopao)*, with *bagua* on the sleeves. 1821–1850, Silk. Minneapolis Institute of Art, The John R. Van Derlip Fund, 42.8.118.

baguaquan.[168] But that might be a different art than the one we know to-day as Baguazhang, an idea we will explore shortly.

Baguazhang is one of the coolest martial arts ever. For me, it was love at first sight. It is designed to get behind an opponent, and makes extensive use of rotational momentum, spinning around the vertical axis. It is trained with multiple opponents in mind. It has superb leg breaking and sweeping technology. It uses sophisticated whole-body dragon spiraling techniques to grapple, strike and throw. Its unique aesthetic is itself part of the mystery. Why does it look like that? What kind of milieu did it develop in that made it appear so aesthetically different from other Chinese martial arts?

The first time I saw Baguazhang's distinctive low "mud-walking" aesthetic, I thought it looked a lot like the comical walk used by the Marx

---

[168] *Quan* means "fist," *jiao* means "teachings," as in religious teachings.

Brothers and other clowns for carrying suitcases. The first time I saw this aesthetic used, was a video of Bruce Kumar Frantzis facing an opponent and then suddenly dropping him from behind with an inwardly rotating kick to the back of the head.

Granted, there is a strange beast out there, who goes by the name of "the pure martial artist," who is *only* interested in power generation and technique. Looking only at individual techniques, a person might argue that Baguazhang is similar to other styles of martial arts, but looking at the whole system those similarities diminish. Looking at what all Baguazhang schools have in common—not what makes them different—reveals a unique aesthetic. For that reason this section of the book does not focus on my individual training but rather looks at all the lineages of Baguazhang as a cohesive aesthetic tradition with common roots.

A number of experiences in my background led me to identify origins of the Baguazhang aesthetic that others could not see. Allow me to elaborate.

I got into martial arts when I was ten, in 1977, studying with Bing Gong, a senior student of Kuo Lien-ying who taught Baguazhang but did not teach it to Bing. I was introduced to Baguazhang by my second teacher George Xu in 1988, and later in 1993 I studied with Bruce Kumar Frantzis. At the time I was juggling a diverse six to ten hour a day movement discipline and I was part of a group of martial artists I could rough-house with daily. I was also a dancer and a percussionist. At the time I made a living teaching sailing, children's gymnastics, Northern Shaolin, and one summer worked as a fisherman in Alaska.

In my twenties, I had an enormous appetite for new and diverse movement training. I was trying to make it as a modern dancer, and I had the crazy idea that if I studied movement arts from several different cultures it would make me more desirable to choreographers. I was living in San Francisco, which was the world center for ethnic dance, so I took the opportunity to study dance from all over the world.[169] I discovered

---

[169] The yearly Ethnic Dance Festival auditioned hundreds of local companies, performing dances from all over the world. It was a truly extraordinary opportunity for someone like myself who wanted a direct experience of dance as a world-wide cultural phenomenon.

Figure 40. Chitresh Das. Photo: Tom Pitch, 2009. National Endowment for the Arts.

that the connections between dance and martial arts is a world-wide phenomenon, one I could feel because I studied both.

In the late 80s, I became enthralled with a form of North Indian dance called Kathak. My teacher Pandit Chitresh Das was a fantastic improviser who danced with precision, speed, and power. Kathak is a storytelling dance, most often compared to Flamenco or described as "barefoot tap-dance with five pounds of bells on each ankle." Kathak comes from the storytelling traditions of India which recount the great epics, the Mahabharata and the Ramayana, and stretch centuries into the distant past. Kathak's classical lineages originate among Rajput warriors before it entered the Mughal courts of Lucknow, culminating in the great Wajid Ali Shah becoming a dancer. When the British annexed his kingdom in 1856, he moved his court to Calcutta and became a great patron of Indian music and dance. During this period, Kathak dancers accompanied troops on deployment as entertainers. Beginning in the 1930s, my teacher's father, Pranath Das, was the leader of a nationalist campaign to make dance a symbol of Indian strength and character. My teacher Chitresh Das grew up in a dance school that was the social and political center for India's greatest dancers and musicians. Chitresh gave me a broad insider's view of

Indian dance as a whole. This ability to read Indian dance for meaning later became valuable in identifying elements of Baguazhang, because, as we shall see, they have elements in common.

I studied Kathak with Chitresh Das for six years; this overlapped with the time I was studying Baguazhang. It was uncanny how many similarities there were between the two arts. But at the time I had no explanation for it. Some similarities I did not even notice until I solved the puzzle years later. After going to India in 1994-95, in a state of extreme culture shock, I decided to quit Kathak. I quit for two reasons. One, the only people in America who could appreciate Kathak, who could see it and understand it, were the small number of people who had trained in it. Two, my teacher was an order of magnitude better than any Kathak dancers I saw in India, but for reasons of caste and politics he was not appreciated there. Years later he was welcomed back to India as the great artist he was, but at the time I did not see a future for myself in Kathak.

At the time I quit I was looking for depth. I became intrigued with the idea that great art forms are developed not by individuals but by whole milieus. By that I mean: Skills, aesthetics, awareness and intuition all come from interactions with groups of people who share an interest, a way of seeing, and a reason for working together or supporting each other's projects.

I was troubled because the stories I was told by Chinese martial arts teachers about the origins of the arts did not describe a milieu that would have been capable of creating the arts as I knew them. Individuals do not invent full blown aesthetics like Baguazhang. Individuals can make large distinct contributions within a milieu, like Mozart did for classical music. But that specific aesthetic has to be part of a milieu which recognizes, nurtures and supports it. The idea that a pure martial art could generate a complete aesthetic on its own was too implausible. That led me to seeking answers in Daoist studies.

In the Summer of 1996 I started a relationship with Daoist initiate Liu Ming and immersed myself in the practices and view of Orthodox Daoism (Zhengyidao). I also read a stack of books every month and discussed them with Liu Ming and his other students for the next nine years.[170]

This was an ideal time to dive into Daoist studies because the field had just suffered a catastrophe. The push that changed the field was a professor at UC Berkeley named Michel Strickmann, who argued that in order to write intelligently on Daoism one had to be versed in language, religion, and history—and that most scholars simply were not qualified. Shortly afterwards, Strickmann was accused of sexual improprieties and to quote the NY Times, "For what is believed to be the first time in the 123-year history of the nine-campus University of California, a faculty member with tenure has been dismissed."[171] Then in 1994 he died. These dramatic events caused people in the field to talk, and most agreed that he had been right about the problems with Daoist studies.

That same year, Strickmann's PhD advisor, Kristofer Schipper published a landmark book in English called *The Taoist Body*. From that moment forward scholars treated Daoism as a religion, and discredited previous scholarship which treated Daoism as a philosophical lifestyle. That meant I was stepping into the beginning of what was essentially a new field, and for years I was able to keep up with almost all Daoist studies publications in English.

The point of interest for students of Chinese martial arts is that the same thing is about to happen to us. Hopefully not the sexual improprieties or death, but the end of an era is upon us. Daoist studies, up until Strickmann, had been relying on Chinese informants who were anti-Daoist. These informants were reformers with Confucian and Christian biases. They had painted a picture of ancient Daoism as a pure enlightened philosophical tradition, and presented living Daoism as a useless, superstitious, folk culture which had lost touch with its roots. The truth is that Daoism is a continuous religious tradition of extraordinary range and depth. It was never separate from philosophy and it never lost touch with its roots.

---

[170] A full account of my experience is recorded in *The Journal of Daoist Studies 1*—Phillips 2008, 161-176

[171] DePalma 1991.

Similarly, the received histories of Chinese martial arts originated from suspect Twentieth Century informants whose goal was to deny the theatrical and religious origins of martial arts. We have already discussed these informants which were part of what I call the YMCA Consensus, a powerful modernizing movement which swept China in the first few decades of the Twentieth Century, and continues to hold sway today.

Baguazhang, like most Chinese martial arts, is saturated with theatrical and religious content, which, when considered, makes the art richer, weirder, and deeper. As we shall see, there was a period of time in which nearly everyone agreed that theatrical and religious content had to be eliminated from the stories people told about the art. It is precisely because Baguazhang cannot be separated from its own stylized movement, that the stories about the meaning of the movement had to be hidden.

I intuitively knew that something was wrong with the martial arts histories I was being told by my teachers long before I knew why. Early on it occurred to me that if some Chinese informants were willing to misrepresent Daoism so thoroughly—how much worse might they be representing martial arts?

Now let us turn to the question of aesthetics. Students are attracted to Baguazhang because they recognize an efficient, elegant, dynamic, creative and beautiful way of fighting. However, once immersed in it, they face the challenge of making the movements fit some notion of real fighting. They learn and invent applications which reduce the art to minutiae in an attempt to make it "practical." Because of my experience finding extraordinary martial skills embedded in dance, especially African and South Asian dance, I started with the assumption that the creators of Baguazhang were highly skilled fighters. I asked the question, why put those skills in *this* aesthetic? Instead of trying to modify the art to fit my notions of real fighting, I tried to understand what the sources of the Baguazhang aesthetic were so that I might understand it as its creators did, and thus perfect it.

My aim here is to open the door on the mysterious origins of Baguazhang. Once the door is open there will still be plenty of questions unanswered. Existing historical documents have yet to be explored for the origins of this art because people have been asking the wrong questions. Having asked the wrong questions they looked for answers in the wrong places.

My premise is that a hundred and twenty years ago the origins and meaning of Baguazhang were immediately recognizable to someone raised in Chinese culture. The historical and cultural disruptions of the Twentieth Century were so profound that its origins became politically unspeakable, and today even lineage practitioners of the art do not know them.

Before discussing the specific aesthetics of Baguazhang I want to make my position unequivocally clear. Beautiful expressive movement can incorporate martial skills. Refined aesthetics do not necessarily make martial arts less deadly. Worldwide, throughout history, people have infused martial skills with aesthetics and imitated the beautiful movements of predators, both real and imagined.

The art of Baguazhang has a unique and recognizable aesthetic maintained and cherished by practitioners over the last hundred and fifty years. Here is a list of the elements that make up that aesthetic.

Circle walking—All Baguazhang practitioners practice walking in a circle and changing directions on the circle. Some schools also train in lines or on a nine-box grid called the magic square *(luoshu)*.

Whole body spiraling movement associated with dragons or snakes—The continuous use of spirals is characteristic of Baguazhang movement. This movement is referred to by expressions such as swimming dragon or coiling snake body. The tea-cups or spinning-plates exercise is a common expression of this element.

Spinning—Practitioners spin around themselves and each other, more so than in any other Chinese martial art.

Mud-walking—This low-stepping technique is immediately recognizable as Baguazhang. There are numerous Baguazhang stepping techniques, but all schools train some version of the low, smooth walking. (See page 207 for a discussion of baby-stepping).

Open Palm—The *zhang* in Bagua*zhang* means "open palm." Baguazhang uses many hand techniques, including fists, but the open palm with the fingers spread wide is an iconic aesthetic element of the art.

Improvisation—While the ability to improvise is treasured by all martial artists, the structure of Baguazhang is conducive to spontaneous innovation because it uses modular flowing techniques executed while walking a circle, spinning and spiraling. Baguazhang students learn applications, stepping variations, changing direction (called palm-changes), and movement corresponding to natural elements or totemic animals. One demonstrates mastery of these modular elements by the ability to combine them spontaneously. Long forms are later innovations and style specific.

Unusual Weapons—Wind-fire wheels, giant saber, giant double-edge sword, and deer-horn knives are unique to Baguazhang. The double-ended spear is common in opera but otherwise nearly exclusive to Baguazhang.

Despite the clarity of the Baguazhang aesthetic, practitioners disagree about its sources. How could such a clearly defined aesthetic lack a known evolution? The histories of Baguazhang I have heard from teachers or read in books fail to explain that. The art is iconic, easy to recognize, and fully formed. How did that happen?

Here is what people agree on: A man named Dong Haichuan 董海川 began teaching Baguazhang in Beijing sometime before he died around 1882. He had disciples. Nearly everything else about the history of Baguazhang is in contention. After explaining the origins of Baguazhang's unique aesthetic and how those origins became a source of shame and ridicule, I will turn to the engravings on Dong Haichuan's 1883 tombstone and explore the various made-up stories about Baguazhang's origins.

The basic technical and aesthetic elements of Baguazhang mentioned above are tied together into a single art by a religious and cultural milieu that revolves around the god Nezha.

Figure 41. Screen-shot: Nezha Conquers the Dragon King (Shadow-puppet anima-tion). Masters Degree Project by Huang Jiaqi, 2014. https://vimeo.com/101789329

Figure 42. Eight-Armed Nezha.

Who Was the Best Fighter in China?

Nezha was the guardian deity of the city of Beijing, which was colloquially known as Nezha City for hundreds of years.[172] The people of Beijing understood the city as a map of the Eight-Armed Nezha's body, with each of the thirteen gates representing his arms, legs and his three heads. People gave directions around Beijing by referencing Nezha's body parts. Nezha was a god with a wide range of social functions; for instance, he was invoked as the leader of militias and was the patron saint of caravan guards. As explained in the section on Tai Chi, theatrical rituals of canonization dating back hundreds of years established thunder gods as the invisible demonic leadership of fighting forces. Nezha was the leader of the thunder gods, known colloquially as the Third Prince, the Lotus Prince, and the Marshal of the Central Altar. Nezha was the greatest human fighter in China, although he was once bested by the monkey king Sun Wukong.

Nezha's story was as popular as *Cinderella* is in the West, everyone knew it. It is found in the hundred chapter play *Canonization of the Gods (Fengshenyanyi)*, which was one of the most popular and widespread Chinese sacred literary epics before the Twentieth Century, and a leading source of basic knowledge about Daoist religion. The people around Beijing believed *Canonization of the Gods* was written by the same guy who designed the city of Beijing, Liu Bowen.[173]

Nezha, known as The Third Prince, is the third son of the great General Li Jing, whose martial prowess came from cultivating the Golden Elixir. Nezha's mother was pregnant with him for three years, and his father threatened to kill her if she did not give birth within a week. She

---

[172] Chan, Hok-lam 2008.

[173] Liu Bowen was a fengshui architect and advisor to the founder of the Ming Dynasty Zhu Yuangzhang; he is still invoked in spirit-writing as a "folk spirit." Mair & Seaman 2005, 467.

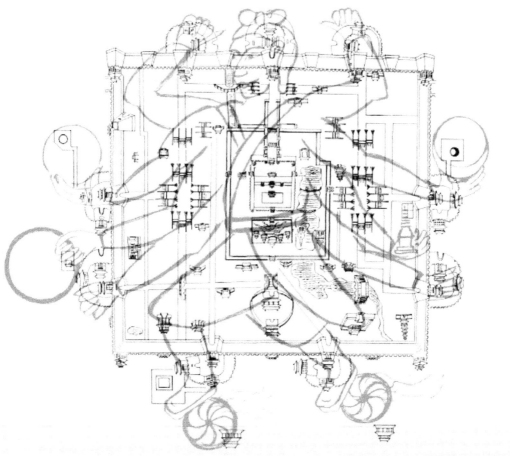

Figure 43. City of Beijing also known as Nezha City. Image from Schinz, A. *The Magic Square: Cities in Ancient China.* 1997, p. 332. Stuttgart: Edition Axel Menges. Used with permission.

did, but she gave birth to a giant spinning blob! Nezha's father General Li Jing thought it was a demon and chopped it with his sword. Nezha popped out of the blob, luminous and happy, already walking and talking. General Li Jing continued to see his son as a freak and a bad omen. After a time, the Immortal Tai Yi descended to earth and told Nezha that he, Tai Yi, was his true "spiritual" father.[174] Tai Yi gave him two magic

---

[174] A mythic explanation for the hatred and degraded status of the acting caste is that they would have sex with local women and then return a few years later for the children. Taiyi is like an outcaste actor returning to a village where he had previously performed and impregnated a local woman, now returning to claim his bastard child (Nezha) for the theater.

weapons, a throwing hoop *(qiankun quan)*, and a red sash used for confounding attackers *(huntian ling)*.[175]

One day, while Nezha is playing on the beach, he kills a dragon. A Dragon Prince is sent to investigate and he confronts Nezha. Nezha dives into the ocean where he has an epic battle and kills the Dragon Prince. He then rips out the Dragon Prince's tendons as a gift for his father. Then, for fun, Nezha wreaks havoc on the palace of the Dragon King, beating up all the shrimp soldiers and crab generals. After several humiliating altercations with Nezha, including one where he sadistically pulls scales off of the Dragon King one by one, all the Dragons have had enough. They decide Nezha is unstoppable and they assemble at Nezha's home and take his family hostage. The Dragon Kings threaten to destroy the entire region with rain and floods. Nezha arrives and offers to sacrifice himself to save his family.

In this famous scene, the Dragons are assembled in a room with Nezha's parents and agree that if Nezha's life is sacrificed they will consider the matter settled. Nezha immediately cuts himself open, splattering the room with blood. Dancing as he cuts, he returns his flesh to his mother and gives his bones to his father. The Dragon Kings are mortified by his impulsiveness, his mother is heart-broken, and his father is happy to be rid of him.

After being visited by Nezha in a dream, his mother secretly builds a temple with a golden statue in it to house her son's disembodied spirit. Because his death was a suicide, Nezha's spirit cannot receive offerings on the family altar. But his temple becomes a popular place of worship for villagers. When his father learns of the temple, many months later, he destroys it. This infuriates the disembodied Nezha, who felt that he had formally severed all ties with his father. The Immortal Taiyi responds by descending from the heavens and giving Nezha a body made out of lotus flowers and a bit of the Golden Elixir. This makes Nezha invincible.[176] He also gets two new weapons, wind-fire wheels, which he rides around

---

[175] *Qiankun quan* 乾坤圈, *huntian ling* 浑天绫.

[176] This is akin to taking a magic pill in other epics.

Figure 44. Portrait of Nezha performer. One hundred portraits of Peking opera characters, late 1800s. Metropolitan Museum of Art, Roger's Fund 1930. Creative Commons 1.0.

on at lightning speed, and a fire-tipped double-ended spear.[177] Nezha then goes on a murderous rampage trying to kill his father. His father barely escapes death in scene after scene. Finally, another immortal intervenes, putting Nezha in a magic pagoda. Once he is trapped in the pagoda, Nezha cannot move, he is frozen in a mediation posture. When let out, Nezha immediately tries to kill his father again. After several timeouts in the pagoda, the immortal roasts Nezha with "true-fire" *(zhenhuo)* to burn away his anger.[178] This requires several roastings. Finally he calms down and agrees not to kill his father. His father keeps the pagoda just in case Nezha has another tantrum. Nezha goes on to fight countless battles as a child hero in the ancient battle of succession between the Shang and Zhou Dynasties. Besides his role in *Canonization of the Gods*, Nezha appears in other epics, short plays, and in countless religious contexts. He was a popular god.

Mud-Walking Wind-Fire Wheels

When he is not swimming with dragons, Nezha's main mode of lo-comotion is wind-fire wheels, which are like cosmic roller skates. Baguazhang's distinct mud-walking mimes Nezha riding wind-fire wheels.

Mud-walking developed out of a centuries old exchange between highly skilled performers and indigenous expressions of martial prowess. For at least five hundred years before the Twentieth Century, Nezha was a popular acrobatic stage role. The role demanded specific virtuosity and expertise, which had a continual influence on amateur and ritual depictions of Nezha.

---

[177] Wind-Fire Wheels (fenghua lun) 風火輪. Fire-tipped Spear (huojian qiang) 火尖槍, also called a Purple Flame Snake Lance—Mair & Seaman 2005, 482.

[178] Magic fire is a way to visualize the Golden Elixir; it is often seen in Tantric Buddhist art surrounding an icon. In the scene there is a blurring of the lines between torture, disciplining a child, and forging enlightenment. Zhenhuo could also mean truth-fire, as in "*tell the truth.*"

Figure 45. Li Ziming as Nezha with wind-fire wheels 風火輪 and Nezha stature for comparison. Photo sources unknown, Fair Use.

In China, everyone knew the story of the Buddha walking through mud and lotus flowers blossoming in his footsteps. Nezha's body was made of lotus flowers. The iconography of Baguazhang conveys the idea of walking through mud to produce an indestructible lotus body. Nezha, like the Buddha, is originally from India. In the Twentieth Century the culture-wide iconographic bond between history, literature, and theater was severed by the YMCA Consensus. This type of self-apparent knowledge became hidden.

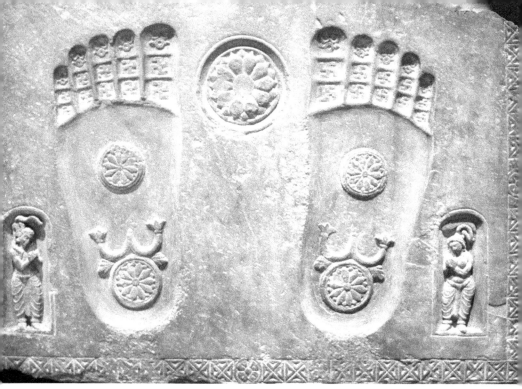

Figure 46. Buddha's Footprints Filled with Lotus Flowers. Gandhara, 2nd Century. Yale University Art Gallery.

Indian Origins

The Indian baby-god Krishna is the original model for the god Nezha. Krishna is a martial deity. He is Arjuna's charioteer in the Bagavadgita, the sacred texts in which Krishna unfolds a vision of non-duality. Like the thunder gods, Krishna and Nezha are both known as killers of snakes and dragons. *Naga,* the Indian word for snake-like water demons, was translated into Chinese as *long,* which is translated into English as dragon. Krishna's other name, Natawar, means Lord of the Dance, and an early version of Nezha's name means "Best Dancer" in Chinese.

According to Meir Shahar, Nezha's name comes from Nalakubar, the son of Yaksha King Kubera and nephew of Ravana (the villain of the Ramayana). Nalakubar's Chinese name, found in Buddhist sutras, was

Naluojiupoluo (那羅鳩婆羅) then changed to Naluojubaluo (捺羅俱跋羅), Nazhajuwaluo (那吒矩韈囉), Nazha (那吒) and finally Nezha (哪吒). In the *Bhagavata Purana* Krishna rescues Nalakubar from imprisonment in a tree. A Tenth Century Tantric Buddhist sutra mentions a child god that is an amalgam of Krishna and Nalakubar called Nana (那拏). In addition, Nalakubar's father Kubera was eventually absorbed into the Buddhist pantheon as the War God Vaiśravaṇa, who then becomes the historical Tang Dynasty general Li Jing, Nezha's father.[179]

Nezha can be depicted as a toddler, a normal child, a big child, or a child with multiple arms and heads who is eighteen feet tall—numerous Indian origin gods are depicted with extra arms and heads. When depicted as a toddler Nezha wears a red bib, when depicted as a guardian he wears gleaming golden armor.

As I mentioned earlier, I studied Kathak dance from North India. Kathak is also called Natawari Nrytia *(Krishna's Dance)*. The most basic footwork comes from the story of Baby Krishna subduing Kalya the king of the Nagas (also called Nachetaka). Krishna was playing on the banks of the River Jamuna when his ball went into the water. He dove after it and had a great underwater battle with Kalya. After defeating and then tormenting Kalya, Krishna emerges victorious dancing on Kalya's head. The sound of the feet slapping the ground in Kathak dance is symbolically the sound of stamping on Kalya's wet head. This story is the prototype for Nezha killing the dragon.[180] It is also the first story that all Kathak dancers learn to dance, because it is the creation story of Kathak. This gives us the mechanism of transmission. Vassal states sent dancers and musicians along with their envoys as gifts to foreign monarchs because it was an inexpensive and effective form of diplomacy. Dancers routinely accompanied envoys to Beijing during the Ming and Qing Dynasties. The known history of Kathak only goes back about two

---

[179] Shahar 2014, 20-45; Shahar 2015, Introduction & 166.

[180] The stamping used in Kathak could also look like a child throwing a tantrum, which we do not see in Baguazhang, at least not in its current form, but it would make an interesting addition and it does supports the Nezha story connection to Kathak.

Figure 47. Krishna dancing on the head of Kalya. Artist unknown.

hundred years, but the Kathak aesthetic comes from the Bhakti movement that was a prominent part of Indian culture by the 1500s. When
these dancers arrived in China, this Krishna-dance creation story would
be their first performance.

Embodying the martial element of Kathak, called *tandiva,* is a re-
quirement of the dance.[181] Most Kathak dancers today do not think in
terms of fighting skills. But to quote my teacher Chitresh's brother Ritesh
Das, "There was an army barracks next to our house, so [Chitresh] tried
boxing with the army guys. He got beaten up the first time. But he practiced until he beat them."[182] When I visited Chitresh's guru-brother
Bachan in Calcutta, his dance studio was filled with photographs of boxers for inspiration. When I performed for him he shed tears of joy ex-
claiming that the true martial spirit of Kathak was still alive. Speed and
power were two of Chitresh's favorite words. Kathak has body technique
that can be used as chops, sweeps and elbow strikes, joint locks, and drop
steps, lots of drop steps. The bronze bells worn for Kathak are strung
tightly together with open facets, they double as armor for the ankles designed to catch blades and as weights for developing speed and power. In
the historic epic, the Mahabharata, the thunderous sound of thousands
of men stamping their feet with ankle bells struck terror in their enemies'
hearts. For the Chinese martial artists who long ago witnessed the envoy-
accompanying performers from India, the martial elements of the dance
would have been apparent, as they were to me.

---

[181] I started studying with Chitreshji when I was twenty. I traveled to India when I was
twenty-six and met up with him there. He was a child prodigy known throughout India,
but because of political favoritism in the Guru system he felt unappreciated, and when
modern dancer Murray Louis offered him a chance to come to America and teach he
took it. For twenty years he did not return. He moved to California where he worked
intimately with Zakir Hussain and Ali Akbar Khan to innovate new forms of rhythmic
mastery. When I was with him in Kolkata (Calcutta) he was mending fences and building
new relationships after 20 years; it was intensely emotional and profoundly gratifying. He
introduced me to a lot of people but sent me alone to visit his Guru brother Bachan Lal
Mishra, who watched me dance in his tiny studio in a dilapidated building.

[182] http://www.theglobeandmail.com/arts/theatre-and-performance/chitresh-das-was-
an-ambassador-of-indian-classical-dance/article22796920/
http://northstarmartialarts.com/blog1/2015/1/5/pandit-chitresh-das-dies-at-70.html

A Rebel

Nezha is a complex and fascinating god who represents a rebellion against the Confucian value of respecting one's father as the basis for subordination and service to the state. He is a rebel. Nezha's character is a playful child who angers easily, is full of bravado, has insatiable enthusiasm, is indestructible, and is unstoppable.[183]

All the aesthetic and technical elements of Baguazhang correspond closely with the Nezha story and cult. We already discussed mud-walking as a depiction of riding wind-fire wheels, now we will look at the other aesthetic elements.

Baguazhang schools use the term swimming dragon and snake coiling to refer to body spiraling techniques which come from the Nezha story. In Asian solo performance styles like Kathak, all the elements of a story are portrayed by a single dancer. Baguazhang seen through this lens depicts both the swimming dragons Nezha fights and Nezha himself. Nezha made his belt from flaying a live dragon. Depictions of Nezha often include a dragon skin floating around his body. Nezha is the leader of the thunder gods who are the arch enemies of snakes and dragons.

Recall from our discussion of Tai Chi that snakes are easily possessed by the homeless ghosts of people killed in battle. Thunder gods hunt them and turn them into ghost-soldiers which are then ritually enlisted in heavenly battles that happen simultaneously with actual battles on the ground.[184] The Nezha performance tradition comically plays with this centuries old cosmology by replacing ghost-soldiers with shrimp-soldiers and crab-generals, who Nezha fights in the palace of the Dragon King.[185] In the corresponding ritual cosmology, sailors and fisherman

---

[183] Nezha is a great defender of his mother, and an icon of hope for women trying to free themselves from the dictates and constraints of family and society. He may also be a fertility god of sorts, because his birth was arduous yet joyful. Nezha has become a character in several popular video games, where he is sometimes depicted as a female.

[184] See sections on Demonic Warfare and Lin Zhao'en as a performer of battlefield rituals (pages 23 and 54).

[185] Some Baguazhang schools use a crab-hand technique to great effect. The Chinese expression "crab generals, shrimp soldiers," which means "useless and ineffective," likely comes from acrobatic scenes of Nezha defeating them in undersea battle.

Figure 48. Shrimp soldier & Crab general. Shadow Puppets from the Museu do Oriente , Lisbon. Creative Commons 1.0.

Figure 49. Nezha at Sea. Block Print. Artist unknown.

who die prematurely at sea cannot be fed on the family altar, so they become wandering ghosts (like suicides and battlefield deaths) who then possess shrimp and crabs. Once they control the bodies of shrimp or crabs, they can make the jump to humans and become the cause of future violence. Because dragons make ocean waves and Nezha kills dragons, images of Nezha were used to protect boats. Were Nezha a little less symbolic of rebellion, one would expect to find Nezha shrines near the ocean for fisherman and sailors who died at sea.[186] The Baguazhang spiraling-body-art is a depiction of water, waves, snakes and dragons, which are all part of the Nezha aesthetic.

Lotus Body

The basic lotus-hands pattern in Kathak is a key movement pattern used to develop spiraling power in Baguazhang. The spinning tea cups exercise is basic training for both Kathak and Baguazhang. When combined, lotus hands and tea cups integrate to become an advanced whole-body movement pattern that underlies all Baguazhang movement. This whole-body integration then becomes the basis for improvisation.[187]

Improvisation is a big part of both Kathak and Baguazhang. Advanced fighters and dancers must be capable improvisors, but both arts are outliers in their respective cultures because of the emphasis they both put on improvisation. No other dance form in India emphasizes improvisation to the extent that Kathak does. Baguazhang is an improvisational

---

[186] However, Nezha shrines were considered rebellious, so they are rare on the Mainland but are more common on islands. No doubt, Nezha was on pirate altars.

[187] Watch the video, "Baguazhang Lotus Body Origins" at https://www.youtube.com/c/NorthStarMartialArtsUSA

martial art, rote forms were later additions. Again, Kathak is Krishna, Krishna is Nezha, Nezha is Bagua.[188]

Spinning

Spinning is a major part of Baguazhang performance and fighting, which makes it unique among Chinese martial arts—no other Chinese martial art uses so much spinning. A characteristic part of Kathak is high-speed continuous rhythmic spinning.[189] As the dance of Lord Krishna, Kathak is the only Indian dance tradition that makes lighting-fast spinning an essential skill. Nezha was born spinning, and like many children he spins for fun. There is a technique in Kathak that makes use of high-speed spinning along with an alternating teacups arm pattern to create the illusion of multiple arms and heads—it is ideally suited for portraying the eight-armed Nezha. Spirit-mediums possessed by Nezha love to spin, and play with spinning toys like tops, hoops, and balls. We will return to this shortly when we discuss spirit-mediums.[190]

---

[188] The barefoot rhythmic stamping used in Kathak might have looked to the Chinese like a child throwing a tantrum, something Nezha does regularly. In China, stamping the ground is a symbol of martial prowess. The stamps used in Kathak are high speed "drop-steps," a common power generation technique used in fighting.
There are other links between Kathak and the Nezha story and Kathak and Baguazhang which would require pages of detail about how the expressive body integrates in motion—easy to feel, hard to explain.

[189] Spinning in Kathak is considered *nritta* or virtuoustic display, but can also be natayam or storytelling. It is used to portray multi-headed beings, and Paverti's sari in the Mahabarahatta epic. When Paverti is given away by her husband in a game of dice, she prays to Krishna to save her. Krishna makes the fabric of her Sari infinite so when they try to strip her, she spins and spins but the Sari never ends.

[190] Watch this video of Kathak spinning "Pandit Chitresh Das' world-renowned Kathak training": https://youtu.be/GHU5PZRyaJY

Weird Weapons

Any cultural explanation of Baguazhang's origins must explain the weird weapons. One of Nezha's weapons, which is mimed in Baguazhang is the chaos and confusion scarf *(huntian ling)*. In Baguazhang's fighting technique, hands become like fast flowing silk, leading and confusing the opponents' attention before tying multiple attackers up in knots. Excellent mime skills can translate directly to martial skills.

A weapon unique to Baguazhang is the giant saber *(dao)*. This weapon is identical to a normal saber except that it is large. As the picture on the next page shows, it makes the person holding it look small and powerful—like Nezha—a child with super-human strength. This visual trick is a common theatrical convention. The same is true of the less common giant straight sword *(jian)*. Not surprisingly, it is sometimes argued that using a giant sword is good strength training. Perhaps, but it is still a theatrical convention, much like the baby pacifiers Nezha spirit-mediums stick in their mouths in Singapore and Taiwan.[191]

Another of Nezha's weapons is called the double-ended fire-tipped spear (火尖槍 *huojianqiang*). In Baguazhang the same weapon is called the two-headed snake spear (雙头蛇槍 *shuangtou sheqiang*).[192] In one translation of the Nezha story it is called a Purple Flame Snake Lance.[193] In both cases the association with snakes points to Nezha's role as the leader of the thunder gods, who are responsible for killing spirit-possessed snakes, as we explained earlier and will elaborate on shortly.

In Chinese Opera, Nezha was played by male acrobats who specialized in female warrior roles. The double-ended spear was primarily a

---

[191] Nezha's Pacifier, Material Culture Analysis of 3 Nezha Rituals: Video https://youtu.be/1g3piFm1Syw   Also: 阿佑電視台 https://youtu.be/yl2syBdA1jo

[192] Szymanski 2000, http://www.chinafrominside.com/ma/bagua/bapanzhangintro.html

[193] Mair & Seaman 2005, 482

Figure 50. Cheng Haiting, Son of Cheng Tinghua.

theatrical weapon used by women warriors. While not the most practical of weapons, the double-ended spear is a symbol of fully committed defiant integrity. It is used to depict a martyr's willingness to fight to the death. Women warriors were emblematic of this self-sacrificing aesthetic. Theatrically, the double-ended spear is an ideal weapon for a romantic face-to-face blood-soaked simultaneous murder suicide. Nezha commits

Figure 51. Nezha spirit-mediums with pacifiers (Youtube screen-shots), see video in footnote 191.

suicide, and afterwards receives the double-ended spear as a symbol of his self-sacrifice and his newly acquired invincibility. Before the Twentieth Century, this is the lens through which Chinese people would have viewed Baguazhang's double-ended spear.

This suicidal aesthetic turns out to be indicative of a large number of secret millennialist organizations which practiced the Golden Elixir and martial arts, one of which happened to be called the Baguajiao (Eight-trigrams Religion). Each of these secret groups had its own name, but the government's eradication strategy lumped them together under the title White Lotus Rebels. What we know about these secret groups comes from two sources, tortured confessions and the sometimes cryptic "trea-sure texts" (*baojuan*) which these groups kept for teaching and chanting. These secret societies saw themselves as children of a goddess, the Eter-nal Mother (Wusheng Laomu), whom they longed to return to. A few of

Figure 52. Screen-shot of Sun Zhijun instructional video for double ended spear.

these groups invoked Nezha chants recounting the act of self-flaying and the return of his flesh to this mother and his bones to his father.[194] They saw themselves as the elect few awaiting the coming of the Maitreya, the Third Buddha, who would bring about mass killings of the wicked and allow the devoted to "return home" to the Eternal Mother. These secret doctrines were complex and varied. Some groups felt they were destined to do the killing themselves. Others thought they would be reborn after dying in battle. Some were preparing to survive an extinction-level event. Some planned to become the new rulers on earth. But for our purposes in understanding the origins of the Baguazhang aesthetic, there were numerous groups of rebels who pursued what looked like suicidal strategies because they believed they were invincible, or that they would be reborn in a better place.[195] This aesthetic was all over northern China—and it was recognizable to everyone.

---

[194] Liu, Kwang-Ching 2004, 291, 292, 309, 316n
For a contemporary example see: 心壇敬 2010, https://youtu.be/mdFr-Qv16Jw

[195] Liu, Kwang-Ching 2004, 281-322

Self-cutting, also called self-mortification, is used by spirit-mediums when possessed by Nezha and other unruly gods to prove the authenticity of the possession. It is also used to demonstrate an impenetrable body in spirit-hitting *(shenda)* cults, where initiates cut themselves and experience either no pain, no bleeding, or no wound—practices that still exist today.[196] A Nezha invulnerability possession is consistent with lots of blood but no pain. Invulnerability cults were common throughout North China and were part and parcel of the Boxer Uprising (1899-1901), which we will return to.

Flaying, called "Death by a Thousand Cuts," was the standard punishment for treason and rebellion in China. For example, some of the captufred Baguajiao rebels were flayed after their confessions were extracted. The practice became a symbol of Chinese barbarity which was roundly rejected in the aftermath of the Boxer Uprising. One reason the Nezha connection to Baguazhang was intentionally severed during the post Boxer period is that Nezha was strongly associated with the practice of flaying—because he flays himself.[197]

The Mystery of the Deer-Horn Knives

The deer-horn knives, with thirteen points and edges, are a mystery. As a famous Baguazhang master said in confidence, "They are completely impractical. You would cut yourself. Anything you might do with them you could do better with two long knives. Maybe they are for swimming?"[198]

---

[196] Amos, 1999.

[197] Shahar 2015, 27-37.

[198] In the past there were many forms of sharpened knuckledusters, and I have heard it claimed that Deer-Horn Sabers were simply giant knuckledusters. That assertion is contradicted by the name, the size of the weapon, and the way it is used in Baguazhang. Although giant knuckledusters could be just another giant weapon designed to make the artist look small.
There are countless defenses of its use in combat, ranging from claims that the weapon has been substantially modified from its original functional form, to claims that it was for swimming assassins to climb aboard boats, to claims that it was for creating a spinning blender effect for massacring a gathered crowd. While each of these is novel, they would require some evidence to consider seriously.

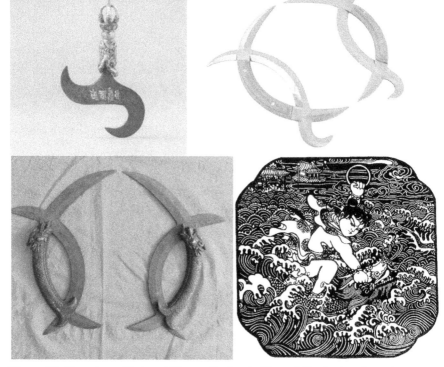

Figure 53. Dear-horn Knives, Tibetan flaying knife, and Nezha beating a dragon.

Lujiao Dao (literally: antler sabers 鹿角刀) are distinctive weapons exclusively associated with Baguazhang, which must have been part of the Nezha performance tradition. When considering this likelihood, keep in mind that there were countless unwritten performance-versions of the Nezha story and Chinese theatrical-religion is diverse at the local level. A weapon created for a theatrical scene in 1750 would not be named or described in a theater text from the 1590s. Deer-horn knives might have evolved as the local weapon of choice for portraying Nezha flaying himself, but other weapons could fill this role.

I suspect the deer-horn knives evolved from magical ritual implements used for flaying. Naturally, it was used in Nezha rituals, and then on the opera stage. Over time, it passed back and forth between different theatrical and ritual contexts. It gradually accumulated new meanings within theatrical-religious culture. Scholars often point to this complete integration of ritual and theater in the Chinese context.

Another point to consider is that, all over Asia, solo performers of theatrical-dance-rituals, like Kathak, will transition between different stage roles and miming elements of the environment, like mountains, trees, or water. The deer-horn knives, and movement in general, may represent more than just Nezha and his weapons. A soloist in Kathak, for instance, would play the snake god Kalya, baby Krishna playing with a ball, and the banks and waves of the River Jamuna using whole-body mime. The range and virtuosity of Baguazhang training is ideally suited for this type of performance.

As we explained in the previous section, Nezha flaying himself was a much beloved scene on the stage. In some versions he cuts off his arm before stabbing himself. Elsewhere he is more obviously shredding his flesh. This scene is still performed—with puppets, in film, in anime, in opera, and by spirit-mediums. But it is much less common than it once was, and we can only imagine what a master solo performer playing Nezha, his parents, and the dragon kings, looked like in Nezha City in 1860. What sort of weapon would he use for the scene? Ideally it would be a versatile prop that could signify other things in the story. One version of the story has Nezha asking the Dragon king for his weapon, but the Dragon king freezes in terror at the thought of witnessing a suicide, so Nezha asks his father, and his father is only too happy to give him his weapon.[199]

Tibet has many flaying weapons used in ritual with long curves for scraping flesh from bones. These curves are found on some Deer Horn knives.

Martial artists might be thinking at this point, "Why would anyone practice martial skills with a self-flaying knife?" But that is exactly the type of commonplace martial practice that was most ridiculed by prominent scholars like Lu Xun in the aftermath of the Boxer Uprising. Lu Xun argued that Ming dynasty literature, like *Fengshenyangyi*, which was part of every village theater tradition, was the source of the Boxer Uprising's irrationality and barbarity. Lu Xun famously argued for separating Chinese culture from its barbaric past because "the Ming

---

[199] Sometimes the weapon is simply a *jian*, (a straight sword); in one case the weapon is called *Kunkun*, a mysterious steel blade which also gets mentioned in *Outlaws of the Marsh*. Thanks to Meir Shahar for clarifying this in an email —Shahar 2015, 70.

Figure 54. Spike Ball, from J.J.M. DeGroot, The Religious System of China, 1892.

Dynasty began and ended with flaying."[200]

It is common for possessed spirit-mediums in Taiwan to cut themselves with a wide variety of magical weapons like shark tooth swords and spike balls. The deer-horn knives are a delightful weapon for a dance about self-flaying.

Yet there is an even better explanation. All Chinese dragons have deer horns, as do demonic snakes.[201] Imagine Nezha is wrestling the dragon in

[200] Lu Xun, 1934.

[201] In Nezha's first battle with the Dragon Prince, he flays the Dragon's skin and makes it into a belt. He is often depicted with the skin around his waist or floating about his shoulders. It would not be out of character for Nezha to take the dragon's horns as a souvenir and do a dance with them.

Figure 55. Two Dragon Kings with Deer-horns.

the water by holding on to its "deer-horns'—with only the horns visible in the Baguazhang performers hands. The dragon would be taking quite a thrashing if the performer were any good. Also, deer-horn knives can be wedged together in the shape of Nezha's magical-hoop *(qiankun quan)*, which he uses to kill dragons.[202] With the right theatrical spinning technique a soloist could use this weapon-prop to switch back and forth between miming wrestling a dragon by the horns, punching it with the unified magical-hoop, and being the dragon reeling from the hit. Later in the story the same weapon-prop can be used for self-flaying. What a perfect stage prop! With narration and music this could be quite a show. It also gives us an idea of how to train with the deer-horn knives—hold onto them as if you have a giant dragon by the horns!

Also, keep in mind that the movements of ritual experts and performers are loaded with symbolism. Audiences for this type of performance know the narrative by heart, just like Americans know *Cinderella*. They do not need or expect the story to be fully enacted, a glass slipper and a pumpkin are enough for a symbolically aware audience to recognize Cinderella. A Nezha performer's audience expected the symbolic movement language of the gods, they did not need

[202] A rarer name for the Deer Horn Knives is *Riyue Qiankun Jian* 日月乾坤劍 Sun-Moon *Qiankun* Swords. *Qiankun Yuan* is the name for Nezha's magic hoop. There is some possibility that the weapons are conflated—*Qiankun* is used generically for outlandish weapons. Baguazhang master Fu Zhensong's nickname was *Qiankun*—his son taught Bow-sim Mark, the mother of movie star Donnie Yen.

Figure 56. Deer-horn knives easily lock together into a thunder hoop.

the whole story. For cultural insiders, the movement of Baguazhang is ideal for telling the story of fighting dragons and snakes inside of flowing ocean waves. Keep this image of a densely symbolic performance in mind, shortly we will be discussing the specific types of rituals popular during this period.[203]

---

[203] None of this precludes the deer-horn knives being a practical weapon. It is just so unusual and we do not have any record of how it was used. Later in this book, I will explain how caravan guards and messengers were connection to Baguazhang. Perhaps they used this weapon for 'opening the road' when blocked by spears. Used as a spear disarm weapon it would not need to be sharpened, and therefore would not be a danger to the user. Thanks to Chad Eisner of the Terra Prime Light Armory for this insight.

Figure 57. *Qiankun Quan* (Thunder Hoops) and *Fenghuo Lun* (Wind-fire wheels)?

Thunder Hoops and Nezha's Qiankun Quan

Thunder hoops are held by thunder gods, and Nezha is a leader of thunder gods, that's why he has one. The empty space inside these hoops represent the sudden vacuum of energy between a thunder clap and a lightning bolt. Like Thor's Hammer, Nezha is the only one who can lift his magical-hoop. These hoops are akin to Sikh throwing rings, called *chakram*, as well as circular knuckle-dusters used in Indian blood-sport wrestling called *vajra-mushti* (lightning fists).[204] Thunder hoops are held up like a *damaru*, which is an Indian drum which makes the sound of thunder. Some Tibetan *damarus* are made out of human skulls. They are used in the self-flaying rituals called Chöd, in which a devotee visualizes offering their flesh and blood as food for demons—as a demonstration of enlightenment. Thunder hoops and *damarus* are common and interchangeable in Buddhist iconography. In Kathak dance, the open palm is the mudra for thunder or, in Sanskrit, vajra.[205] In vernacular Chinese, vajra is the word *"jingang,"* which is an impenetrable diamond-like substance,

---

[204] In India there is a weapon called a *vajramushti* which is used in wrestling matches that are also called *vajramushti*. The weapon is a circle with spikes on the outside. These wrestling matches were bloody fights before the Mughal king. The name means thunderbolt fist, which is a weapon Nezha would wield. It could be the prototype for Nezha's *Qiankun quan* magic throwing ring.

The Chakram, a Sikh throwing ring, is also a good prototype for the *Qiankun quan* because it is a circle and it is a projectile weapon. (See Image)

[205] Also very similar to the mudra for damaru.

Figure 58. Vajramushti (Illustrations of Hindustan, by M. Léger, 1816. Bibliothèque Nationale de France). Chakram (Sikhs with chakram, 1844, Wikimedia).

as well as a description of a deity who has achieved martial impenetrability via the Golden Elixir (see page 79).[206] Nezha's magical-hoop is a form of vajra. In Baguazhang the open palm is a vajra mudra, the magical symbol, and a form of sign language or mime recognizable in both Chinese and Indian cultural milieus.

Nezha's thunder hoop can be depicted by putting together two deer-horn knives, or by holding one wind-fire wheel—which look like thunder-hoops when held in the hand. It is odd that Nezha's wind-fire wheels, which go on his feet, are a hand-held weapon in Baguazhang. However there is a scene in a play called *Journey to the South* where Nezha picks up one of his wind-fire wheels and throws it at an enemy. Furthermore,

---

[206] In the Indian context the acquisition of impenetrability is called a Siddhi, a side-effect of enlightenment or self-cultivation.
Note that I differ slightly with Meir Shahar who argues that Jingang is the Buddhist icon Vajrapani (Thunder Hands). I think it means different things in different contexts.

Nezha has an additional weapon, which doubles as a toy, called the embroidered ball (xiuqiu); naturally it turns into a fireball when thrown at an enemy. There are other stories and accounts of Nezha invoked as an exorcist in rituals, where he wields fireballs and flaming dharma wheels (*falun* or *huolun*).[207]

[207] Shahar 2015, 99-101.

Alternative Theories

In a fascinating online article written by New Zealand martial artist Yan Zhiyuan, he posits that Baguazhang is related to another internal martial art that I practice, Xinyi.[208] Because space is limited, I intend to avoid an in-depth discussion of Xingyiquan, and its close cousin Yinyi—both of which are attributed to General Yue Fei (1103-1143). Nevertheless, Yan Zhiyuan's article does merit an examination of iconographic links.[209]

Yan's elaborate historical theory is based on the observation that Xinyi's chicken-walk is similar to Baguazhang walking. I came to a related conclusion independently, which is that the two arts are similar because they share an aesthetic designed to depict thunder gods riding wind-fire wheels. The main difference is that Baguazhang steps tend to be larger than those of Xinyi. Baguazhang looks more like skating on two wind-fire wheels, while Liuhe Xinyi chicken-walk looks like riding one big one.

The chicken-walk is used modularly with all of the various ten animals of Xinyi. Thunder gods are bird-like, they have wings, claws, and beaks, and ride a single wind-fire wheel. Four of the ten Xinyi animals are birds; eagle, hawk, swallow, chicken.

The other Xinyi animals: snake, dragon, horse, monkey, bear and tiger are animals used in depictions of demon generals—which are a kind of terrestrial version of thunder gods. Demon generals can be de-

---

[208] See Yan Zhiyuan, 2007, http://www.tai-chi.co.nz/EnglishArticleText4.html —He develops a complex theory based on lineages which parallel Dong Haichuan and pre-date him by a hundred years. He ties the practice to the Jindan Baguajiao or similar rebel groups. The lineage calls itself yinyang Baguazhang. Some of it is credible, but impossible to verify. He also invokes the Tombstone inscription to repeat the less than credible idea that Dong Haichuan was a rebel set on assassination and that was why he castrated himself!—(see page 188).

[209] Yinyi's full name is Ten Animal Mind Intent Six Harmony Fist (Xinyi Liuhe 心意六合拳)
See Jarek Szymanski 2002, for a brief history. http://www.chinafrominside.com/ma/xyxy/xylhhistory.html

Figure 59. The author doing Liuhe Xinyi, Chicken Walk with Hawk & Horse.

picted with animal faces and predator feet but otherwise walk upright like humans. In Liuhe Xinyi practice, the terrestrial animals are paired with a bird, for example bear and eagle are practiced together as one moving technique. We train Xinyi in linear stepping patterns as if traveling along roads and paths. My guess is that Xinyi was a local theatrical procession used for training militias, bandits or rebels. In many villages, theatrical processions were conceptualized as armed escort for the gods, just like Song Jiang exorcist dance troops which are currently having a revival in Taiwan.[210] In the case of Xinyi these escort troops were made up of thunder gods and demon generals led by Yue Fei, the incarnation of Garuda (see page 97).[211]

Being an extremely effective form of martial training, Xinyi was adopted by the Chinese Muslim community known as Hui People. Before 1900, Hui communities had their own "talking animals" theater which might have been incorporated into Xinyi cosmology, while keeping

---

[210]Sutton 2003; Boretz 2010; Perry 1980.

[211] On Garuda as the iconic basis for thunder gods see: Meulenbeld 2007.

Figure 60. Thunder Gods. (Sources unknown.)

Figure 61. Thunder God (Leigong), 1542. The Metropolitan Museum of Art. (Opposite page

the training and iconography the same.[212] The Hui communities kept the memory that Xinyi was created by Yue Fei.[213]

Xingyiquan, which is related to Xinyi, also uses the open palm symbolizing the thunder-bolt. Xingyiquan's iconography is a close match for depicting thunder gods. Its stances and movement patterns also look like

---

[212] Because of rules against depiction of icons, stories about anthropomorphic animals were common among Chinese Muslims. Hui were Muslim cavalry garrison communities which became resident over many generations.

[213] Both criminal and legitimate armed escorts in Shanxi, the area Xinyi comes from, were called Red Beards (hongjing) because they dyed their beards red like generals in the theater! This character role type is called a beard (*Jing*). Obviously, the general population identified them with the theater—see Perry 1980, 61. But the beard dying tradition may originally come from Islam.

they are for grabbing and stamping on snakes, as a thunder god would do.[214] As I will show, this iconography fits with the types of temple rituals that were common in and around Beijing.[215]

Riding a wind-fire wheel as an explanation for the aesthetic of chicken-walking is a promising direction for research, as are the theatrical origins of Xingyiquan in depicting the movement of thunder gods. I hope to investigate this more deeply in the future.

As we move on to address other alternate theories, recall that all the unique weapons used in Baguazhang, wind-fire wheels, deer-horn knives, double-ended spear, and giant swords, come from the Nezha story. Wind-fire hoops, however, also come from Buddhist iconography where they represent the dharma wheel.

Chan Buddhist Circle Walking

Baguazhang is a form of moving meditation, like Tai Chi, but based on walking in a circle. Laugh if you must, but walking in circles is considered a path to enlightenment. Before the Twentieth Century, in Chan Buddhist monasteries monks would alternate between periods of sitting and then walking in a circle around eight pillars clustered near the center of the meditation hall. This was done at various speeds, from slow to brisk, numerous times throughout the day. Chan Buddhist Temple meditation halls across China were designed and built specifically for this practice.[216] This is not the direct ancestor of Baguazhang but rather part

---

[214] It is also hard to ignore the iconography of Mongolian wrestling dances as an aesthetic influence, where Garuda is represented by the wrestler doing an eagle dance soaring in a circle with arms outstretched. There are variations of this martial dance, hopping side to side or swinging each other around by the neck. The people of Beijing would have been familiar this dance and there is plenty of wrestling technique in Baguazhang. Is the winner of the match Garuda and the loser a snake? Or is it two eagles, talons locked together, "fight-mating" as they fall thousands of feet through the sky— as I witnessed in Alaska.

[215] Xingyiquan practitioners tend to identify their art as coming from southern Shanxi or northern Henan, which are adjacent territories known for having the highest concentrations of both professional and amateur theater. At the beginning of the Ming Dynasty a large number of loyal ministers (and probably military officers too) were banished to Shanxi and declared actors in perpetuity —Johnson 2009, 219-233.

[216] Prip-Moller 1967, 73-80.

of the Chinese collective unconscious, or the common gene-bank of movement ideas. Rebels and secret society cults freely incorporated elements of Buddhism and Daoism. Rebel groups, practicing enlightenment circle walking on imagined karma resolving fire-wheels, while practicing the Golden Elixir, is a small jump to Baguazhang.[217] Local ritual culture blended Daoist, Buddhist, and millennialist cult practices with layers of cosmological meaning, all of which was stripped from Baguazhang when it was transformed into a "pure martial art" after the Boxer Rebellion.

Daoist Origins

A primary technique used for trapping demons in Daoist ritual is making a magic square inside of a circle.[218] The Chinese character for a water-well *(jing)*, which looks like a tic-tac-toe board, is used to make the magic square. Daoists draw it on the ground surrounded by an expanding spiral, symbolically trapping the demon in a well. In this ritual, ceramic jars are used as miniature storage wells and then sealed with a talisman, much like a pickle jar with an expiration date.[219] The same magic square layout is used in Baguazhang schools to develop footwork and fighting strategies.[220] When square-walking is followed directly by circle-walking, it is an aesthetic match with the Daoist ritual for trapping demons. As with Buddhism, this does not necessarily mean that Baguazhang is Daoist; it means that the aesthetic is Daoist, or that practitioners were copying the Daoist aesthetic because of its powerful associations with having command over the *unseen world*, ideas which everyone gleaned from watching theater. Nezha's play, *Fengshenyanyi*, has countless demon trapping scenes.

---

[217] Nezha is prominent in Chinese Tantric Buddhism, a line of inquiry that has barely been explored—Shahar, 2015.

[218] Chinese coins are often used in exorcisms because they are circles with a square in the middle. "Making a square inside a circle" is also a basic training concept used in Tai Chi.

[219] From a presentation by Mark Meulenbeld and Terry Kleeman at the 9th International Conference on Daoist Studies, 2014.

[220] The magic square is also the standard configuration of a stage, which Jo Riley suggests links all traditional stage production to exorcistic purposes—see Riley 1997.

 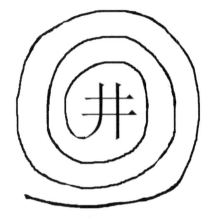

Figure 62. Chinese coin and character *jing* 井 with circles around it for catching demons.

In another close parallel, circumambulation of the altar in Daoist ritual represents the traversing of territory to unify the nine cities of *wuwei* —a concept which spatially represents the self-resolving nature of existence. The nine cities are also represented by the nine boxes of the magic square. In order to distinguish themselves from spirit-mediums who take shamanic journeys, Daoist Priests conceptualize this circumambulation as an anti-journey. They take a journey which goes nowhere, symbolically walking backwards inside of walking forwards, called *nixing*, which is an undifferentiated state of consciousness where Supreme Unity is rediscovered.[221] The iconic representation of Supreme Unity is Taiyi, Nezha's spiritual father who gives him his lotus body (see page134). There just happens to be a Baguazhang circle walking training technique that reverses muscle patterns in the legs so that it feels like one is walking backwards *inside* of walking forwards.[222] The distinct aesthetic elements of Baguazhang are rooted in this theatrical-religious framework. It is a perfect match.

---

[221] Herrou 2012, 91.

[222] Reversing techniques are characteristic of Golden Elixir practices and the definition of *neigong* training (see page 228).

In Chinese opera, a person on stage traveling in a circle means the passage of time or covering a large distance. Embodied as both theater and Daoist ritual, walking the circle represents traveling from temporality, called *houtian*, to atemporality, called *xiantian*.[223] *Xiantian* is the state of potency outside of time, used for ritual action. It is the source of creativity. Simply knowing this basic Daoist cosmology enriches our understanding of the embodied iconography of Baguazhang—the content is vivid and full of potential.

At the risk of repeating myself, strong Daoist influence in the practice of Baguazhang before the Twentieth Century is undeniable. However, the majority of evidence for the Nineteenth Century origins of Baguazhang is found in rituals which exist outside of Daoism.

The Ritual Origins of Baguazhang

During the Qing Dynasty (1644-1911), the Manchu ruled as a foreign ethnic occupation. They needed the Chinese gentry to maintain local order and organize militias. But they also feared that gentry coordination could lead to rebellion or banditry as it did throughout the Nineteenth Century. Adding to the tension was the simple fact that the lines between different types of martial organizations were fuzzy. Secret societies and militias were both organized around religious and theatrical themes. And they both served the mutual-aid needs of a broad part of society. While it is possible to draw lines between small-group defense lineages, family-defense alliances, martial brotherhoods, bandits, militias, crop-guarding farmers, caravan guards, smugglers, and rebels, in practice they overlapped. For the purposes of learning the origins of Baguazhang, we do not need to know which one of these is more original than the others. A

---

[223] These two terms are often confusingly translated pre-Heaven and Post-Heaven—*see* Lee Fongmao 2012, 214.
Baguazhang schools have related meanings for these terms, for example, in Gao style xiantian refer to circular and houtian refers to linear ways of practice. They can also correspond to training vs. improvising.

sub-set of each of those groups practiced martial skills along with the Golden Elixir and ritual chanting infused with millennialist visions of the return of the Maitreya (the third Buddha). All of them knew the Nezha story. Some made offerings to Nezha and chanted Nezha invocations or performed possession rituals. Portrayal of Nezha by these groups had real martial elements. Whatever the finer details of Baguazhang's development, it is a martial art for portraying Nezha while practicing the Golden Elixir. It came out of this general milieu. The Golden Elixir itself will be explored in the final section of this book.

Having laid out the aesthetic origins of Baguazhang, I will now explore some examples of how it fit into Chinese culture by looking at six specific ritual frameworks. Then I will show how it changed after the Boxer Uprising.

Individuals can play pivotal roles in the invention of art forms, but they always happen within a milieu. To reconstruct the milieu Baguazhang emerged from we need a baseline for what normal life was like from roughly 1700 to 1850. Life in China was punctuated with theater. Students studying to take exams in the hope of becoming government officials worked thankless hours immersed in the written word. Farmers worked the fields. Cottage industry craftsmen and women wove silk, made baskets, and produced clothing. Porters carried people, water, fish, and fruit on bamboo poles. Merchants moved goods, travelled, traded, and ran businesses. What they all had in common was participation in theater.

China was a violent place. Almost everyone had direct personal experience with violence. Big and small bandit armies were a continuous part of the landscape for a thousand years. Kidnapping for ransom and human trafficking was a widespread problem everyone had to take precautions against, especially children. Villages fought tit-for-tat wars so often in some regions that no one even bothered to write about it. Famines, floods, droughts, and disease epidemics were a normal part of life—something people expected to happen every few years.

China's religious-theatrical culture was fully immersed in this regular devastation and chaos. The purpose of ritual-theater was to perpetuate love-of-life, a sense of humor and priorities; to teach history, and to transmit morality. It solved real life problems, revolving around a liturgical calendar that gave regularity and order to an otherwise unstable world. Ritualized storytelling cycles perpetuated social coherence and were models for governance.[224] But they also supplied mythic support for the weird and wonderful, an outlet for transgressive tendencies. The people who organized festivals were civic and commercial leaders who used the opportunity to organize everything from communal defense to road repair, and to negotiate shared resources like water rights and rights-of-way. They also used it to organize things like gambling, drinking, and carnival mischief. Around Beijing, eunuchs were the major organizers of temple festival culture. At that time in history, theatrical performances, rituals, and processions fully integrated martial skills. Ritual theater was an intensely physical way of life, a source of meaning between order and chaos—and a way to enlist one's physical body to better purposes in an unstable society. Baguazhang fits seamlessly inside this world.

Rituals played a central role in organizing and ordering society for both the contented and the discontented. Rituals were ways of renewing covenants with the invisible world of gods and spirits while simultaneously establishing commitments in the social-political world. Most rituals contain elements of exorcism, healing, protection, purification, and rectification. There was a culture of martial expression in ritual practice which used swords, symbolic weapons, and talismans as weapons of harm and protection. Everyone used talismans; they were more common than swords.[225]

Ritual experts played many different roles. One thing which distinguishes Daoist ritual experts from other types of ritual experts is that Daoists do not engage in blood sacrifice. Because of this commitment, Daoists at times took a leadership role in managing spirit-mediums and possession cults as a way to ensure that blood sacrifice, and bloodshed in general, was limited. During the Ming and Qing Dynasties, Daoists

---

[224] Chan, Margaret 2009, 109; Yuan 2000, 277-278.

[225] Phillips 2016, 78-82.

served a governance function. Daoists certified cults as orthodox, meaning they monitored and regulated temple cults and festivals to ensure they were not perpetuating rebellious tendencies.[226] The big risks were martyrdom rituals and blood sacrifice. This is important because, to an outsider, Daoist involvement with other cults might make it appear like they were one and the same. A ritual can have Daoist content, without being a Daoist ritual. A Daoist can have an officiating role in a ritual without the ritual itself being Daoist. Nezha does play a role in Daoist rituals as a central guardian who commands spirit-armies, but Nezha plays other roles in non-Daoist rituals as well. In fact, the list is quite long. Nezha served as a locality god *(difeng shen)* for territorial cults. He became a doctor-healer when invoked by a spirit-medium. He was a road-opening god for caravan guards and messenger services, and a tutelary god for martial arts groups.[227] In present day Taiwan, he often lives on the dashboards of taxis and truck drivers where his road-rage clears traffic jams and wards off tickets.[228] He is a good-luck charm for gamblers. A bringer of children to barren mothers. He is an entertainer of children. A heavenly ally for criminal organizations. One who brings loved one's home safely from the seas. A guardian against bandit attacks. A potent granter of martial prowess for secret rebel organizations. And a psychological ally to rebellious teenagers and housewives.[229] None of these roles are based in the historic sacred literature of Daoism. In other words, Daoists would not call it Daoist, but others might.

Below are six examples of ritual culture that included Nezha and represent the cultural origins of Baguazhang. Now that we have the aesthetic overview of those origins, it is easy to see how Baguazhang can fit into any of the following ritual traditions.

---

[226] Schipper 2012, *forward.*

[227] Sangren 2017, 24-33

[228] Shahar 2015, 119.

[229] Shahar 2015, 110-111.

Figure 63. Generals of the Five Directions with Nezha at the center.
These are tongue spears used by possessed spirit-mediums. J.J.M.
DeGroot, The Religious System of China, 1892

1) Daoist Ritual

The official center of a Chinese town is the altar for the generals of the five directions.[230] This altar represents an ancient ritual practiced throughout China that predates written language. The title Marshal of the Central Altar describes Nezha's role as the leader of a heavenly army. He is the commander of the generals of the four directions. For the last five hundred years, Nezha is the most common deity given the role of Marshal of the Central Altar, although there are other gods who play this role too. Before the Twentieth Century, everyone in China would have recognized Nezha as the spirit-center of a village.

During ritual performances, Daoist priests invoke legions of ghost-soldiers *(guibin)* which are visualized and felt as active symbols of chaos and order. Daoists priests issue commands to these invisible armies through a visualized Nezha, along with the generals of the four directions, who all play the role of intermediaries during the ritual. They are intermediaries between the needs of human beings and the Dao. This type of felt-visualization ritual is also an elaborate form of the Golden Elixir. Baguazhang could be used to act out this orthodox Daoist visualization. In that case, scholars and Daoists would accept the proposition that Baguazhang is Daoist. Elements of this basic ritual were on display during the Boxer Uprising.[231] After the Uprising, and then again during the anti-superstition campaigns of the 1920-30s, tens of thousands of rituals were deemed destructive to the social progress of the Chinese

---

[230] The tradition of the four generals is much older than Nezha. There are several other gods given the honor of commander, but Nezha is recognized in many regions. Nezha's canonized names are "Third Lotus Prince" (蓮花三太子) and Marshal of the Central Altar" (中壇元帥). The title Lotus, besides describing Nezha's indestructible body, invokes the image of the lotus heart expanding infinitely in all directions, a practice shared by Indian Dance, Tantric Buddhism (Vajrasatva Invocations for example) and Daoist *Golden Elixir*. The Lotus Elixir *(liandan)* is another name for the Golden Elixir, and was widely practiced in North China by secret societies in the 1800s along with martial arts. As I will explain later, this combination creates a type of skill and invulnerability called the lotus body.

[231] Cohen 1997, 108-109; Doar, 1984.

people and eliminated. Because the link has been severed, we may never know how Baguazhang fit into of these rituals.[232]

2) Spirit Medium Rituals

The mainland Chinese government violently suppressed ritual for several generations. But in Singapore and Taiwan spirit mediums still invoke Nezha outside the front gates of temples dedicated to other gods.

Mediums possessed by Nezha become child-like and are in the habit of initiating silly games or of running off to play! The problem of keeping spirit mediums possessed by Nezha from running off is solved by offering him toys to play with, especially balls, marbles, and tops. The childlike Nezha loves to spin things and spin around himself—just like Baguazhang practitioners.

Nezha rituals in Taiwan and Singapore are part of a growing revival of traditional culture. While they share cosmology and visual iconography, these traditions of depicting Nezha do not involve the kind of in-depth training Baguazhang uses to portray Nezha, and they are from the cultural South, whereas Baguazhang is from the North.

Nezha rituals in northern China around Beijing and Tianjin, where Baguazhang was based, involved spirit possession. As I will explain later, Nezha's role as a vanguard fighter during the Boxer Uprising is proof enough of that. But Nezha operas *(Fengshenyanyi)* were also constantly being offered to the gods by local communities as an integral part of the ritual calendar. These operas were performed by both amateur and professional actors, who were of course martial artists.

---

[232] The answer to the question "is Baguazhang Daoist?" will pivot on the question of whether Nezha is Daoist. He is both Daoist and not Daoist. He has many Tantric Buddhist attributes too. In one story he brings a tooth of the Buddha down to earth, which becomes an imperial rainmaking device. He has a role within Daoism, a role in popular religion, a role in rebel uprisings, a role in the mythology of Beijing, and a major role in theater. Nezha is the hero of the epic *Canonization of the Gods*, which was constantly being performed before the Twentieth Century and was also a great source of popular knowledge about Daoism. Now that we have the basic story of Baguazhang's aesthetic origins sorted out, scholars can begin to poke and prod out the complex religious content of the practice. At the moment, it is accurate to say that Baguazhang embodies a major element of a distinct religious society which has yet to be given a name.

An important piece of this puzzle to understand here is that there were no Nezha temples documented near Beijing because Nezha was considered too dangerous and rebellious to be the subject of temple worship. *In situ* it was his ever present absence that gave him power. That means there is now no material location to base a study. Nezha murals, statues and dramas were everywhere, but Nezha rituals were tied to the practitioner-performers, and those rituals disappeared after the Boxer Uprising. Baguazhang is the only surviving Nezha ritual from northern China.

—Watch these Nezha rituals from Taiwain:

Chiang Mei 2012. 06/19 南嶽宮 小孩與三太子進場. Nezha offering incense, Taiwan. https://youtu.be/mvIiSO6cig4

Showt1993 2011. 马来西亚-[东方花园-佛天公. Nezha's presenting to the altar, Taiwan. https://youtu.be/I6m7LjNUerg

Steve Hau 2011. 哪吒三太子@港口宫. Medium possessed by Nezha, playing games, Taiwan. https://youtu.be/KAM_qSUBbFc

Kunlun Meditation Hozn 2012. 三太子 妹妹 武藝高強 Sister San Taiz. Nezha devoties spinning. https://youtu.be/Q_eQmvNSjOY

3) Sai and other Village-Festival Rituals

There was a well-established pattern of village festival culture in Northern China. The ritual was called a *sai* and it was based on a three-part structure: inviting, welcoming, and seeing off the gods. Ritual could last anywhere from three days to a month. Wherever you happened to be, these rituals were happening nearby every two weeks. A smaller *sai* might have only fifty people officiating and a thousand participants, while a large one might involve hundreds of ritual experts and 100,000 participants. A large ritual could invoke as many as 500 gods, their statues escorted out of temples in massive processions with armed escorts of martial performers that snaked between villages for miles.

According to David Johnson, ritual festivals were so common and so old and so large that they were overwhelmingly the most important influence shaping the symbolic universe of the common people. Regionally they happened about every two weeks and could involve over a hundred villages, with processions that strung on for miles attracting thousands of spectators. "It is quite impossible to understand what villagers…in north China thought and felt about the world of politics, about Chinese history and traditions, about the world of gods and demons, or about any of the grand matters of life and death, without a close familiarity with *sai* [and similar rituals]."[233]

The inviting of the gods entailed a procession which commonly used martial arts. Johnson translates a New Year's ritual manual in which people representing gods circle around eight bagua/trigram altars in preparation for an exorcistic ritual called "collecting disasters." After a procession around the village they then invite hundreds of gods, including Nezha, to the ritual. This is followed by more circling of the altars, dancing, and drumming. There are several blood-letting rituals, songs, and other elements, followed by days of theatricals. Johnson goes on to describe other elaborate rituals with hundred-man martial arts troops and all sorts of ritually potent weapons.[234]

The welcoming of the gods section included ritual dramas, which were wild, diverse, and local, but also based on the large pantheon of gods shared across the region. They could be performed in the home by family members. They could be professional opera troupes, sometimes performing on three simultaneous stages in different parts of a village. They could be ritual specialists *(shenjia)* who inherited the role of embodying specific gods, like Nezha. They could be possessed individuals, like you and me, who suddenly sat bolt upright in bed and ran out to the ritual grounds to perform as the god. The possessed were widely believed to be capable of cutting themselves open without damaging internal organs. Alternately these performers could be *yuehu*, a degraded caste of musicians, actors, slaves, and entertainers, who had only first names, no genealogies, and were referred to as "mean people." Yuehu performers

[233] David Johnson 1997, "Temple Festivals in Southeastern Shanxi" *in* Overmyer 2009, 8.

[234] Johnson 2009, 39-110. Some of the ritual manuals Johnson translates include the Dragon kings—the 5th type of ritual described bellow.

were considered the most efficacious.[235] Theatrical castes were officially outlawed at the beginning of the Twentieth Century.

To further contextualize these village rituals, let us review the social-political cosmology of canonization.

The popular gods, heroes and villains of China's epic theater developed organically and locally for generations before they found their way into standard written texts. Even after the epics were codified, local innovation and improvisation was the norm. Gods like Sun Wukong, Guan Gong, Xuan Wu, and Nezha were the subjects of local cults and theatrical-rituals that, over time, were collected into the enormous epics, *Journey to the West, Three Kingdoms, Journey to the North,* and *Canonization of the Gods* respectively, but they also continued to evolve and change at the local level.

These plays, or parts of these plays, were originally rituals of canonization *(feng),* stories about the transformation of unruly demonic characters into righteous gods.[236] That fact is made explicit in the title of Nezha's epic, *Canonization of the Gods (Fengshenyanyi).*

As explained earlier, these plays had at least three religious-military purposes: to organize militias, to invoke the gods for battle, and to enshrine the battlefield dead. Plays brought whole regions of people together for seasonal festivals. Naturally these were good times to organize village militias as well as small martial alliances and brotherhoods. Martial-theater of this sort echoes massive participatory spectacles, with generals acting out key roles on the stage, at some time in the distant past. The thematic content of these plays entailed the transformation of unruly violent chaos into righteous, ordered martial prowess. In addition, the

[235] Almost all of them were thought to have disappeared until 151 Yuehu families were discovered in 1993 in the Shandang area of Shanxi. Overmyer 2009, 79; Johnson, 2009 219-231.

[236] Nezha as a religious theatrical character was already well established in China during the Yuan Dynasty (1271–1368), even though the codified version of his story in *Fengshenyanyi* is dated to the 1590s. A musical structure called a mode, was named Nezha and noted in Yuan Dynasty Zasu plays. Lines in these plays end with the martial sounding "ha," suggesting it may have been a type of military march (thanks to Marnix Wells for pulling one of these plays off of his shelf and showing me). Nezha's father Vashravana, the god of war, morphed into the Tang General Li Jing—as early as the Tenth Century (found in Dunghua Caves)—see Shahar 2014, 20-45.

cosmological content of these ritual-plays was used as a model for organizing social institutions, not just militias, and provided mechanisms for sharing resources and solving problems.

Theatrical festivals were sites for learning history, codifying ethics, providing mutual aid, and engaging in collective action. Before battle, the powerful gods of the theater were invoked as warriors either fighting up in the sky, running alongside, or actually possessing the individual combatants of a militia.

After battle, the dead were given a kind of collective funeral. These same theatrical-canonization rituals were used in the process of enshrining the battlefield dead so that they would not haunt the living as homeless ghosts. In a nutshell, Chinese culture viewed the causes of violence as cyclical and spatial. The spirits *(ling)* of the battlefield dead would slowly seep into grass, stones, snakes, trees, and animals that travel close to the ground. The fear was that if these animate spirits were not given some way to resolve their lingering grievances, they would possess living people and cause them to commit mayhem and vengeance. Thus, canonization rituals created shrines for the battlefield dead, and promoted the dead leadership of the losing side, making them into righteous heroes and gods. I discussed a national shrine of this sort in the introduction, the war memorial in Nanjing which had an image of Garuda killing snakes over the front entrance (see page 23). *Sai* rituals were large events that contained canonization rituals with in them.

Another large war memorial for the enshrinement of the battlefield dead was the Temple of the Eastern Peak in Beijing. The Eastern Peak was a symbolic entrance to hell; if I understand it correctly, it was also a location for ritual enactments of the epic *Fengshenyanyi* and functioned as a center for territorial cults.[237] The Eastern Peak Temple would have had ritual experts on call to perform the role of Nezha. This is another likely place for expert Baguazhang-Nezha performers to be centered.

---

[237] The best source on the diverse and complex uses of the Eastern Peak Temple is Meulenbeld 2015.

4) Guild Rituals

For modern readers, deity worship and communal ritual might seem like a distinction without a difference. But in the Nineteenth Century, Nezha was the patron saint of caravan-guarding companies. These companies had their own Nezha altars and shared rituals which served to unite them in a patronage network linking the cities where these companies operated. It did not mean they worshiped Nezha. Today, when a truck driver puts a talismanic image of Nezha, that he got from a temple, on his dash-board, he is participating in a communal ritual. Nezha is opening the road, offering protection from accidents, and conferring martial prowess and speed on the driver. It is not an act of worship in the Western sense of subordination and devotion. Rather, it is a type of communal commitment to right-action. Given the sheer number of Baguazhang lineages which claim to have been employed as caravan guards, the art must have been part of the companies' religious practices.

Messenger services and caravan guarding companies maintained altars to Nezha because he was fast on his wind-fire wheels and a great fighter.[238] Nezha, more than any other god, was blamed and punished for the humiliation he brought on China during the Boxer Uprising. That is why Nezha had to be eliminated from any association with Baguazhang for it to survive.

5) Two Kinds of Dragon Rituals

The Nezha story was popular partly because it disrupts the normal cosmology of dragons as rain makers. The "job" of dragons in the Chinese cosmos was to bring the right amount of rain for agriculture. In Northern China, local rituals were performed when it did not rain. First locals would plead with the dragons to make it rain. If that did not work, they would force the dragons to comply. Some of these rituals involved beheading dragons, theatrically spraying symbolic blood. A Nezha performer sent to the Temple of the Dragon King to rough him up,

---

[238] Because Nezha made a belt out of dragon tendons, the belt-making guild in Beijing had a private temple dedicated to him as well—see Shahar, 2015.

maybe pull off a few scales, is exactly that kind of ritual we can imagine Baguazhang being used for. There were sixty temples to the Dragon King in Beijing alone. They were symbolic Courts of the Dragon King under the ocean. A few were symbolic dragon courts up in the sky filled with statues of frightening thunder gods. Sending a Nezha performer to a Dragon Court to punish, torture, or kill the Dragon King would have been a perfect ritual for bringing rain. The Nezha story itself takes the form of this ritual. The cosmology fits. Nezha is a punisher of dragons. This was crystal clear within Chinese culture at the time. Dragons can be fickle about the rain, but Nezha will set them straight.

Dragons are also responsible for floods. To stop a flood, a Nezha performer would symbolically flay himself with (dragon) deer-horn knives as a symbolic sacrificial offering to appease the Dragon Kings. No one knows for certain if this happened—it is an educated guess that captures the explicit ritual significance of the Nezha story in which he flays himself to save his family from the dragon induced floods. It perfectly incorporates the movement and weapons of Baguazhang.

There were more than 4000 temples in Beijing before the Twentieth Century, plus countless business and guild altars. They were all destroyed or converted to other purposes between 1898 and 1977, mostly in those first three decades.[239] The Dragon King was an important cult all over North China because dragons control rain. Statues of thunder gods with beaks, thunder rings, and clawed feet surrounded some Dragon King altars.[240] Rain rituals commonly included an opera as an offering to the Dragon King. The Nezha opera was a common offering because it was acrobatic and martial.[241] Nezha was the leader of these thunder gods. These ritual operas for bringing rain or stopping floods were often

---

[239] Goossaert 2006; Naquin 2000. In recent years a small number of these temples have re-opened but the ritual continuity is mostly lost.

[240] Naquin 2000, 39-40. —Suggesting to me that Xingyiquan might also have been part of these rituals.

[241] Acrobatic Chinese Opera performance of Nezha: Suling Guo 真假哪吒 2011. https://youtu.be/8NgOeyUkrpw

performed by lineage experts. This was another ideal place for the Nezha performing skills of Baguazhang to manifest.

6) Rituals of the Baguajiao Rebellion

In 1793 and again in 1813 there were uprisings by a group called Baguajiao. The word *jiao* means teachings or religion. The government collected numerous forced written confessions from captured participants before executing them. Like similar millennialist rebel groups, they also produced Treasure Texts (Baojuan) which include mythology, chants, Golden Elixir instructions and other teachings. The rebellions arose from secret societies, which were organized into cells named after the different *gua* or trigrams of the *bagua* symbol (ie., *li, xun, kan, zhen*, etc…). Practicing a type of millennialism, participants thought these rebellions would pre-cipitate the coming of the Third Buddha. They secretly practiced the Golden Elixir, which they used to confer martial prowess and otherworld-ly powers on the righteous, just like in the theater.[242] The government found it difficult to eliminate these groups because their practices were easily hidden within the social-religious culture of the time.[243] These rebel groups developed out of a long tradition of charismatic religious rebellions and morphed into new organizations throughout the 1800s.

Followers of the Baguajiao subscribed to a mythology in which the Eternal Venerable Mother (Wusheng Laomu) sent humans to earth rid-ing wind-fire wheels to fulfill their fate. But humans got bored and re-turned home to the Eternal Mother. She then sent them without wind-fire wheels so they could not return.[244] They believed that humans had a

---

[242] They sometimes used an alternate name for the Golden Elixir, *liandan* or lotus elixir. Nezha's body, like the Baguazhang body, is the lotus elixir—*see final section of this book.*

[243] One reason for this is perhaps that there were restrictions on teaching the Golden Elixir within Daoist contexts. For example, a center of Golden Elixir training during the 19th Century was White Cloud Temple in Beijing. Mainly Daoist initiates (monks and priests) studied there, but the training was also available to actors and eunuchs, although closed off to the general public. Eunuchs were politically elevated but socially degraded. Actors were elevated on the stage but degraded everywhere else. Daoists see themselves as the lowest of the low, like water, and so have an affinity with those of degraded status.

[244] Personal communication, Israel Kanner.

longing to return to their Eternal Mother and hoped that they would be reunited with her when the Third Buddha (Maitreya) returned. They were just one of numerous groups organized into secret networks around the teaching of the Golden Elixir, massage, and martial arts. Baguazhang might have been part of the Baguajiao or a similar secret network.[245] The rebellion conceived successive plans to kill key leaders of the Qing Government with the intention of inspiring a rebellion which would bring about a world transforming event in which the evil people would be slaughtered and the followers of the Eternal Venerable Mother would become the new leaders in a world re-imagined. When these groups staged a rebellion they saw themselves as trying to prime the pump of mass slaughter that would bring about the new age.[246]

It is notable that in at least seven cases, sacred chants invoking Nezha were recorded in depositions by other rebel groups in northern China in the 1790s.[247] In 1796, the governor-generals of Shaanxi and Gansu issued a joint declaration in which they mention the problem of Nezha sectarians.

---

[245] Fifty years before Dong Haichuan is purported to have begun teaching Baguazhang in Nezha City, members of the Dong family were implicated in the Baguajiao. Some members did practice *baguaquan*, among other arts, which is described in a single confession as a collection of stepping techniques identified with two of the eight trigrams. Naquin 1976, *bagua* fighting skills 31-32, 87-88, 106-107, on the arrest of Dong family members 187.

[246] It is possible that Baguazhang was transmitted through one of these groups, since they shared the cosmology of the wind-fire wheels with thunder gods and Nezha. The government's forced confessions show uniformly that the coming of the Third Buddha was believed to be the trigger which would bring about full rebellion. But the recording official may have written Third Buddha in place of Third Prince (one of Nezha's names) as a way to ensure that all these rebellious organizations were treated as one giant White Lotus rebellion—in accord with government policy. It was also common for communities to cover up their local powerful deities or spirits by presenting them as doctrinally orthodox deities. For example they might make sacrifices to a statue of Guan Gong, but secretly every villager knew the spirit in that temple was a fox spirit. Perhaps, then, in some sects, the Third Buddha was Nezha, the Third Prince.
Israel Kanner is a researcher currently studying the confessions of Baguajiao members which contain much information about martial arts. *Baguaquan* is a martial art that was mentioned by some Baguajiao members, but, as yet, there is no evidence that it is an early version of Baguazhang.

[247] Liu 2004, 291, 316.

These six types of ritual culture, *Daoist, spirit-medium, sai, guilds, Dragon King, and Baguajiao,* were all common throughout northern China. All six play a part in the Boxer Uprising, as I will show in the next section. They are the sources of the Baguazhang aesthetic and the rich creative milieu that nurtured the martial art into being. Now that we have asked and answered the right questions, we can begin to look for the precise details of Baguazhang creation.

The Nezha Rebellion

Nezha is a difficult deity to figure out. On the one hand he is a military rebel, and a rebel against Confucian ethics, especially the ethic of obedience to one's father. On the other hand, he is the guardian of the capital city Beijing. Is Nezha's presence evidence of rebellion or loyalty? The answer is complex. Nezha performances were everywhere, and he was loved as a theater role, even by the royal family. But crossing into the realm of ritual and sacrifice, Nezha could be the inspiration for a rebellion. That is what happened during the Boxer Uprising. And yet, the Chinese government was polarized over the question, "Are the Boxers loyal or rebellious?"

Understanding the Boxer Uprising sheds light on the religious-theatrical context in which Baguazhang was taught. It is also key because Baguazhang practitioners were entwined in the Uprising and that had a profound effect on the way Baguazhang history was constructed in the Twentieth Century.

The uprising of the Boxers in the north was preceded by the Taiping Rebellion (1850-1864), the largest civil war in history, with an estimated 20 million dead. The Taiping Rebels occupied major parts of Southern and Western China and made major inroads into the North (1853).[248] It was inspired by a native version of Christianity in which the spirit-medium leadership of the Rebellion claimed to have direct access to the family of Jesus and other Biblical figures. The leader, Hong Xiuquan, claimed to be the brother of Jesus. Tai Ping means "Great Peace" and the rebels fought to bring about a "New Kingdom of Heaven on Earth." They sought to abolish class and caste distinctions, and they declared women equal to men.[249]

During the same period there were other rebellions. The Nian bandits rebelled in the North, marshaling hundreds of thousands of troops, and

---

[248] Perry 1980.

[249] Spence 1996.

the Opera Rebellion in the South took control of Foshan, the largest port city.[250] This was a chaotic time. Massive displacement of populations and widespread starvation continued to affect everyone for years after battles died down. British and Americans were involved in training and leading Chinese troops.[251] Western battleships were in the harbors and Christian missionaries were opening schools and hospitals at a rapid pace. In the aftermath of these rebellions, the mutual-aid benefits for people joining secret societies outpaced the dangers. There were strong incentives to make up false back stories in order to hide one's personal experience of the wars, and the lines between loyalty, treachery and cowardice were fluid.

In 1895, China lost a war with Japan that ended in humiliating concessions. In 1899, when the Boxer Uprising (1899-1901) broke out, the trauma of these earlier rebellions shaped people's reactions and behavior, but so did long developing concepts of theater, martial arts and ritual.

The Boxers set out to kill all Chinese Christians and kill or expel all foreigners from the country. They performed martial-invulnerability rituals which they believed made them bullet proof. These rituals involved each individual becoming possessed by a magical deity from Chinese theater. Nezha was a common possessing deity. Other common deities were Yue Fei, Guan Yu, and Sun Wukong, a list of China's greatest fighters. The Boxers also performed rituals to invoke deities fighting up in the sky where they would fly to foreign capitals and burn them to the ground. Boxer rituals contained elements of Daoist thunder rituals, which invoked the spirit armies of the five directions with Nezha at the head. They also paralleled temple-stage canonization rituals and spirit-medium rituals.[252]

When the Boxers entered Beijing, businesses were shut and theaters burned to the ground. Actors, being martial arts masters, were made

---

[250] See Perry, 1980, on the Nian. See Judkins 2015; Lei 2006.
The Opium Wars also took place during this period but were minor skirmishes in comparison to everything else—*see* Platt 2018.

[251] Carr 1992.

[252] Doar 1984; Cohen 1997; Esherick 1987.

leaders of the Boxers and carried on in costume, as did temple performers. Huge crowds of Boxers wearing red headbands set up altars to the deities from *Canonization of the Gods* and other plays. Stately gods like Guan Yu controlled the logistical altars, whereas fighters like Nezha made up the vanguard.[253]

From the outset, journalists, historians, and propagandists hotly contested the origins of the Boxer Uprising. They recounted the Boxer's prowess, heroism, stupidity, weakness, or betrayal to suit the politics of the moment.[254] That said, one theory is that the rebels organized from already existing mutual-aid societies, like the remnants of the Baguajiao, whose rituals and millennialist outlook have much in common with Boxer rituals. Another theory is that Boxer organizations grew out of gentry-led militia and crop guarding groups like the Big Sword Society (Dadaohui), the Red Spears, and the Plum Blossoms.[255] These groups organized using rituals which invoked Nezha and other theatrical characters, particularly those from *Canonization of the Gods*.[256] Both theories are probably correct.

Resentment itself was a cause of the Uprising. Local Christian groups had been refusing to pay local taxes which patronage networks collected in the form of dues for putting on operas. Christians opposed opera because it put pagan gods on the stage. Another source of resentment against Chinese Christians was that they had acquired special access to the Imperial Court through foreign priests and pastors, a power granted as a concession of the Opium Wars (1839–1842 and 1856–1860).[257] This allowed Christians to defy local powers and offer protection to converts who were accused of violating law or custom. In the eyes of the local

---

[253] Doar 1984, 91-118.

[254] Cohen 1997.

[255] Esherick 1987.

[256] Perry 1980, 194, 204, 224.

[257] Esherick, 1987; Clark 2017.

"CANNIBALISM"   LIVING SKELETONS

Figure 64. Starvation in North China. Woodblock, The Graphic, London, July 6, 1887.

population, Christians were seen as evil magicians that harbored and protected bandits.[258]

Hunger and starvation were widespread because of a string of droughts. As mentioned earlier, rituals to end droughts were common in North China. For example, we mentioned in the previous chapter that there was a festival in which a dragon was dramatically beheaded, spraying blood (hidden in the costume) on the assembled crowd.[259] The Boxers referred to foreigners as hairy-men, but Christian missionaries were also called drought-dragons.[260] In hindsight there is a perverse logic to the image of villagers being possessed by Nezha and going on an

---

[258] Esherick, 1987.

[259] Overmyer 2009, 23.

[260] Clark 2017, 47. Foreigners and Christians were thought to be drought-dragons, which of course Nezha would eliminate, and whom he was already fighting up in the sky.

angry rampage to behead drought-dragons. Nezha's intense hatred for his own father was directed at Church Fathers.

Nezha was the tutelary deity of both couriers and caravan guards. These two types of laborers were facing an extinction level event as "Western" trains and telegraph services took their jobs. They eagerly joined the Boxers. The Boxers targeted trains and telegraphs for destruction. The Boxers made extensive use of fire for destruction, but also thought themselves resistant to fire in the form of bullets and canons. Caravan guards, and other ad hoc laborers, possessed by the mythology of Nezha and his thunder-god generals, all riding wind-fire wheels, and burning down trains, telegraph lines and other symbols of foreign power—makes for a tight description of the Boxer Uprising.

The Boxer Uprising was not large in terms of the number of people involved, but it had far reaching consequences.[261] One group of princes, led by Prince Su, opposed the Boxers and initiated efforts to put them down. Other princes, especially Princes Duan and Zhuang, championed the Boxers and teamed up with them to attack foreigners.[262] When government troops along with the Boxers besieged the foreign concessions and embassies in Beijing, threatening all foreigners with death, Eight Allied Countries invaded: The United States, Austria, Germany, France, Russia, Italy, Japan, and Britain. The Dowager Empress and her court fled the capital, which was looted and then occupied by foreign troops for a year.

Recall that the entire city was a map of Nezha's body, with the gates representing his limbs.[263] It was Nezha's job, as the Marshal of the Central Altar and Commander of the Generals of the Five Directions to protect the whole city—and he failed.

---

[261] 20,000 foreign troops, perhaps 12,000 Christians killed, an unknown number of Chinese forces and deaths were a mix of civilians and military. Estimates of total deaths come in around 100,000.

[262] Xiang, 2003; Rhoads, 2001.

[263] Chan, Hok-lam 2008. Ten of the twelve gates had Guandi, the god of war, installed in a temple next to the gate, and the two northern temple-gates were for Zhenwu, the perfected warrior. Remember Nezha was considered too dangerous to have his own temples.

Figure 65. From left to Right: Prince Su, Prince Zhuang, Prince Duan. Wikimedia.

Readers might be inclined to ask whether I have overemphasized the influence of Nezha in my descriptions of the Boxer Uprising. I asked the question: what was Nezha's influence on the Boxer Uprising? It turns out there is a lot of evidence that Nezha played a significant role. Other deities were significant too, and there are other explanations for the Boxer Uprising, but the logic of Boxer cosmology suggests that Baguazhang experts were natural leaders of the Uprising. Perhaps the Boxer Uprising should be renamed the Nezha Uprising?

Creating a New Mythology

The earliest confirmed account of the art of Baguazhang does not mention Baguazhang by name. It is a tombstone for Dong Haichuan, the purported creator of the art, dated 1883. There are three more tombstones, one dated 1904, directly after the Boxer Rebellion, and two from 1930 during the anti-superstition campaigns.[264]

There is no way to determine if the date on the first stone is a forgery or not. As I will explain, there are reasons to suspect it was created after the Boxer Uprising or re-carved at some point to conform to political pressures. Advanced forgery skills were, and still are, widely available in China.

The four Dong Haichuan tombstones are currently displayed next to Dong's tomb, which was built in 1982. Before that, they were buried in an unmarked planted field. We do not know when or why the four stones were buried, along with Dong Haichuan's bones, or whether burying them was an act of destruction, indifference, or preservation in a moment of social chaos. The stones were dug up in 1978 at a moment when China was barely out of the Cultural Revolution (1967-1977). Baguazhang practitioners, like most martial artists, were tortured, beaten, imprisoned and sent to re-education camps during this period.[265] Some accounts say the oldest stones were severely damaged and had to be reconstructed. Others claim that they were fine. Needless to say, authenti-

---

[264] I have been vexed trying to figure out how to present the Dong Haichuan tombstones. At present there are no published authoritative translations to work with. I debated presenting full translations of them, but they are long, and full of problems, especially the 1883 one—it would be a larger collaborative book, without adding significant value. My purpose in examining the tombstones is to respond to the common and fictional claims that have been attributed to them.

[265] The disciples of survivors may know what happened but might be unwilling to discuss it because it is still a thought crime in China, and because personal tragedy is considered too intimate to share. After being dug up the stones were briefly displayed in front of the Beijing Wushu center, suggesting no one knew quite what to do with them.
There is a photograph of the Baguazhang disciple Magui and about thirty of his students in 1930 at Dong Haichuan's previous tomb site. Presumably the stones were buried after that, although the stones are not visible in the photograph and the faces are difficult to make out—see Lee Ying-arng 1972, 24.

cation is a problem because the chain of custody was broken. At the time they were dug up, the show trial and execution of the Gang of Four was still three years off in 1981—this was a watershed event formally ending the Cultural Revolution by assigning blame. This was an Orwellian period in which 2+2 could equal 5 if the government said so. It is still possible to parse eyewitness accounts for credibility, but it is not easy. It is now forty years in the past. It would be a mistake to think that history can be written honestly in China today. It cannot. The risk of being fined, harassed, denied access to jobs, or imprisoned is real. China maintains a list of historic figures who by law cannot be criticized.

Still, the stones are our earliest accounts so let us examine them.

The first stone, dated 1883, is authored by Dong Haichuan's student Yin Fu and states that Dong became a eunuch later in life. Eunuchs were detested. Hardly anyone wants to study eunuchs today because it is such a disturbing thought. Chinese eunuchs had their penis and testicles removed. For the sake of my readers I have done as much research as I could bear. From my informal survey of Baguazhang teachers, about half believe Dong could not have been a eunuch because eunuchs are very weak. In fact, the three later engravings all compensate by protesting that he was very strong, and they do not mention he was a eunuch.

Most eunuchs had their genitals removed before puberty. The tombstone states that Dong Haichuan became a eunuch late in life. The reason a man would become a eunuch late in life in the 1800s was that he was starving to death during one of the many famines. Eunuchs were paid and fed.[266] On the tombstone his birthplace is given as Wen An, which was a traditional place for sourcing eunuchs. Of course there could be reasons other than hunger for becoming a eunuch late in life, but that is the only reason given publicly. Bewilderingly, some claim the

---

[266] I found examples of the children of rebels being forced to become eunuchs after being captured during the Qing Dynasty, but no adults (*Beijing Gazette* is a good source).

back of the first stone states that Dong was serving a secret cause.[267] That
is a strange thing to put on a tombstone. It is too cryptic to decipher, but
perhaps the secret cause was Nezha?

The name Haichuan is probably not Dong's given name, it is a *nom-
de-plume*, and it means "Ocean-Rivers," which is a good name for a
Nezha performer. This expression is used to mean "a whole lot of something'; for example, an "ocean-river of books" is slang for a library.

There is a common story that some people could fake being eunuchs.
I have researched this. The problem is that the penalty for being caught
was death. So we will never know. But it would be hard to fake. Eunuchs
have an unpleasant smell, they lose their beards and eyebrows, and their
voices become high and scratchy like a fishwife. They were excessively
emotional, easy to anger, or reduce to tears. They were required to travel
in quick short steps tilting forwards. If they were well fed, they would
collect something called "hollow fat" in unusual places, distorting their
body's shape. It is worth noting that the voice, emotional instability, lack
of hair, and a more feminine look, could all make a Baguazhang performer appear more child-like, and therefore more Nezha-like. Three-
hundred eunuch actors were kept to entertain the royal family, including
Nezha performers.[268] Eunuch actors may have had a method for making
themselves strong, perhaps a combination of herbal formulas and acrobatic training. Eunuchs were also guards and had access to guns. We do
not know if Dong Haichuan was a eunuch or not, but considering the
low regard most people felt toward eunuchs, it is improbable that anyone
who liked Baguazhang would make that up.

The first tombstone says he was a servant in the Su Palace, and that
he only began teaching martial arts after he was released from service
because he became too old. This first tombstone claims he then gained

---

[267] For example, Yan Zhiyuan, 2007, makes this claim in the essay we discussed earlier
(see page 154). The expression in question here is *yinjunzi* 隐君子, which could mean a
person in hiding, keeping a secret. It also means an opium addict. To dull pain *yintong* 隐
痛 is in the next line. Most likely the whole passage is simply a repetition of his regret at
being a eunuch.

[268] Stent 1877.

hundreds of students. Later tombstones claim he had hundreds of thousands of followers. The back of the first tombstone lists sixty-six students. Even that is a lot of students for a eunuch too old to serve the Prince.

If Dong Haichuan served in the Su Palace, he would have known both Su Princes, because it is a hereditary title. He served the father (Longqin 隆懃; 1840–1898) until sometime in the 1870s, and he would have known the son when he was just a boy. The "boy" Prince Su (Shanqi 善耆; 1866–1922) went on to lead the opposition to the Boxer Uprising as an adult. During the Uprising the same Prince Su gave his fortified palace to the British Embassy, which was next-door.[269] This was so that the British could defend, and house, thousands of Chinese Christians who were streaming into the city, and so that the British could spearhead the defense of the other foreign embassies. After the defeat of the Boxers, Prince Su became the Beijing Chief of Police.[270] The new police force was created to root out the remnants of the Boxers and was made up entirely of Manchu Banner Guards. Baguazhang practitioners were obvious targets for beheading. Perhaps the story on the tombstone was a post-Boxer attempt to associate the embattled art of Baguazhang with a man in power, Prince Su. One way to plausibly associate Dong Haichuan with Prince Su was to make him a eunuch.[271] Politics were thick on the ground and the truth was squirrelly.

On the other hand, the second engraving, dated 1904 and also authored by Yin Fu, does not mention the Su Palace, which inadvertently lends credibility to the accuracy of the first engraving because that would have been the ideal time to make such a claim. The truth may be somewhere in between. Was the purpose of carving a new tombstone to bolster the creation of a new mythology? There is considerable ambiguity

---

[269] Xiang 2003, 272.

[270] Rhoads 2000, 70-71, 86.

[271] This strategy of self-preservation resembles a common practice in the West in which houses of prostitution keep strict records for tax and accounting purposes, but use the names of politicians and members of high society in the place of client names.

here. Did Yin Fu intend to replace the first tombstone in 1904 or add to it? We do not know.

The 1883 engraving explains that before Dong Haichuan became a eunuch he learned his martial art from a "Yellow Crown" he met while traveling. This tells us almost nothing. A Daoist ritual leader, called a Gaogong, literally meaning "high-merit," wears a gold crown. Monks and other Daoists do not. Any Daoist priest (Daoshi) can be called a Yellow Crown as an informal gesture of respect. Or perhaps we are dealing with a linguistic convention used exclusively on tombstones. It is possible Dong studied the Golden Elixir at the White Cloud Temple in Beijing. The temple was a training center for Daoist monastics who made lifelong commitments, but eunuchs and actors were permitted and encouraged to study the Golden Elixir there too. Famous actors were direct students of the abbot.[272] Daoists gave special reverse-status to eunuchs and actors as the lowest of the low, because, as Laozi said, "The Dao is like water, it sinks to low places most people shun." Thus, the teacher referred to on the tombstone could be an actor who specialized in Daoist Immortal roles on the stage and therefore wore a yellow crown! Or a Daoist-actor who played the Nezha role. There is no way of knowing because the engraving is intentionally vague.

The three later tombstone engravings do not help at all. The second engraving mythologizes that he learned the art in a dreamlike place which disappeared into the clouds. It also claims that he was a second rank officer later in life, but without knowing Dong Haichuan's real name there is no way to look that up.

The first tombstone describes an event on the Great Wall in which Dong Haichuan was encircled by men with weapons all trying to attack him, as he spun around like a whirlwind demonstrating his miraculous skills and his invulnerability powers. This is the earliest description of Baguazhang we have and it epitomizes the Nezha aesthetic, a whirlwind.

There are countless tales about Dong Haichuan and his disciples, most of which were probably adopted from fictional radio plays in the

---

[272] Goossaert 2012, 136

1930s.[273] They simply took the stories they heard on the radio and re-placed the hero's name with Dong Haichaun. All in all, the tomb engrav-ings tell us little other than the names of his disciples. These disciples become the focus of future mythologizing too.

Other than the first tombstone, we have nothing written about Baguazhang or Dong Haichuan or his disciples until the second tomb-stone in 1904, twenty-two years after his death. The 1904 tombstone emphasizes his extraordinary strength and it states that he inherited his martial skills from immortals and that no one could defeat him! Hmmm…sounds like Nezha.

Lineage

We began by connecting Baguazhang to the aesthetics of Nezha. Next we connected Nezha to various theatrical and religious rituals. Then we showed how those rituals were part of the Boxer Uprising. Now we will connect the Boxer Uprising to Baguazhang lineages.

Every Baguazhang lineage has stories about being involved in the Boxer Uprising. Most Baguazhang lineages claim to have come from Dong Haichuan, whose 1883 tombstone lists sixty-six of his students. I do not possess a complete list of Baguazhang practitioners killed during the Uprising, but it is reasonable to assume that most of them were. That is not surprising, since they were based in Beijing and Tianjin, where the largest battles took place.

The Boxer Uprising was a mass hysteria that appealed directly to the sentiments and worldview of Baguazhang practitioners. They were asso-ciated with it, and it was associated with them.[274]

---

[273] Zhang Gehao, in a personal communication at Second International Martial Arts Conference, Cardiff, 2017.

[274] The Sha family Baguazhang lineage has a form (*taolu*) called "Soul Kill Spear" (Hun-sha qiang), which happens to be the title of a short story by Lao She (1899-1966). The story is an ambiguous analogy which does a good job of relaying how martial arts changed under the YMCA consensus. I read it as being about the unspeakable connec-tion between Baguazhang as Nezha, read it and decide for yourself—Lao She 1985, 149-164.

Dong Haichuan's Students

The stories about Dong Haichuan, his students, and the origins of Baguazhang were created to cover up the Nezha origins of Baguazhang and its connections to the Boxer Uprising.

The myth of Dong's student Yin Fu, is worth repeating. Yin Fu was a donut seller who became so good at martial arts that he became the bodyguard of the Dowager Empress and was responsible for spiriting her out of the city during the Boxer Uprising.[275] Then he taught in the palace until he died in 1909. This story is not true. I suspect that, like many of the second generation's stories, it was meant to shield practitioners from the backlashes of the post-Boxer era.

Cheng Tinghua was shot and killed in 1901 fighting German soldiers, but the story is that this was a kind of accident, he was not a willing participant in the Boxer Uprising, even though he used his giant saber in the attack.[276] This is the kind of improbable story that might satisfy a policeman who was looking for declarations of obedience, rather than facts, in the immediate aftermath of the Uprising.

Another of Dong Haichuan's students, Li Cunyi, did not hide his participating in the Boxer Uprising. He was covered with blood while killing foreign troops with his giant saber and continued to pridefully wear his bloodstained shirts until his death in 1927.[277] This story is extreme, but understood as an artifact of the anti-superstition era it becomes coherent. Temples were allowed to exist if they were national memorials for state heroes. The same standard was applied to martial artists. The story makes him patriotic. Only after successfully suppressing Baguazhang's association with Nezha and invulnerability could this myth could have arisen.

---

[275] Lee, Ying-arng 1972, 26-27.

[276] Lee, Ying-arng 1972, 28—says he used two daggers, I have also seen barehanded, but the Bagua Dao makes a better story. Obviously it is a story told without witnesses and any weapon would have been confiscated, not returned.

[277] Allen & Zhang 2007, 136-7—is the best collection of Baguazhang stories in English.

Li Cunyi's father owned a caravan guarding company and was made a leader of the Boxers. His mother fought with the Red Lanterns, the female Boxers, whose performances of circle-walking around bronze vessels magically allowed them to fly through the sky at night and set foreign capitals on fire.[278] I suspect this story came to light at a time when the Boxers were in political favor as patriots, perhaps during the Cultural Revolution.[279] Because the politics of remembering the Boxer Uprising swung back and forth, so do the stories.

Some stories are just weird. Zhang Zhaodong strangled a horse to death with one hand.[280] Imperial guard Gong Baotian led an Imperial army through Fujian (far away from the fighting) during the Boxer Uprising, and then started a security company. Ma Weiqi was poisoned by the relatives of a man he killed using the five-fingers of death, a technique made famous in the film Kill Bill.[281]

Another of Dong Haichuan's students, Fan Zhiyong (1840-1922), was a Manchu Bannerman, Everyone called him "Fan the Madman." This could be a reference to his portrayal of Nezha throwing a tantrum.

There are quite a few alternate myths about Dong Haichuan as well. The one most often repeated is that when he was a waiter in Prince Su's Palace, there was a dish that had to be served to the Prince's table at a crowded party, but none of the other waiters could get through the crowd. Naturally, there was a death penalty for serving food cold, and the waiters were starting to worry. Suddenly Dong Haichuan took up the platter and walked sideways on the walls, then stepping from table to table, swirling and flying through the crowd, he re-appeared at the Prince's table. This revealed him as a great martial artist and he became the in-house martial arts expert for the Prince.

---

[278] They also practiced Daoyin (yoga?) at home during the day—Xiang 2003, 277.

[279] Cohen 1997, 119-145—for details of Red Lantern magic and how stories about the Boxers were transformed for political purposes in different eras.

[280] Allen & Zhang 2007, 23.

[281] Allen & Zhang 2007.

Another story has Dong Haichuan as a tax collector for the Prince, mud-walking delinquent tax payers into compliance.

There are stories of Dong Haichuan being able to walk through walls, walk up walls, float boulders with one finger, become invisible, fight in his sleep, and move people without touching them.

In some myths about Dong Haichuan, he lived with Prince Duan instead of Prince Su. Prince Duan was the most prominent advocate for the Boxer cause at Court and led Imperial troops in support of the Boxers. The Bapanzhuang lineage claims to have lived in Prince Zhuang's palace.[282] Zhuang's palace was the headquarters for the Boxer forces in Beijing. Both princes lost large numbers of men in battle and after the Rebellion they were disgraced. When the two princes were in control of Beijing, everyone out on the street was forced to wear a red headband in support of the Boxers. Prince Zhuang was so humiliated at the end of the Uprising that he committed suicide. Prince Duan fled the capital and was in hiding for twenty years.

One intriguing thing about the mythologizing of Dong Haichuan's students is the pervasiveness of strange body types in their descriptions. As a eunuch Dong Haichuan would have had a weird body. His student Yin Fu was extremely thin and was missing his two front teeth. The portrait of his student Chen Tinghua's son appears to intentionally make him look like a child (see page 147). Ma Gui was a dwarf. Gong Baotian's arms reached his knees (matching a description of the Buddha). Most lineages have a story about strange body types. When the art was openly associated with Nezha, childlike attributes would have enhanced its theatricality.

Both pro- and anti-Boxer stories distract from the real story; as do stories about martial prowess which are devoid of religious or theatrical content. The real story is that Baguazhang was a form of Nezha fighting that invoked the magic of invulnerability. The members of the Baguazhang community fought in the vanguard of the Boxer Uprising possessed by Nezha and other characters from the Nezha stories.

----

282 Szymanski 2000, http://www.chinafrominside.com/ma/bagua/bapanzhangin-tro.html

Figure 66. Xie Peiqi and Fu Zhensong.

Baguazhang After the Boxers

As explained in part one of this book, the aftermath of the Boxer Uprising had profound effects on the way we understand the relationship between martial skills, religion and theater. In the first forty years of the Twentieth Century as the YMCA Consensus was taking shape and new governments were coming in and out of focus, Baguazhang practitioners struggled to redefine themselves. The Consensus produced a number of divergent voices which shed light on the way martial arts are practiced today.

Just before the Boxer Uprising, an advisor to the Emperor named Kang Youwei (1858–1927) wrote a proposal known today by the slogan "turn-temples-into-schools." Kang Youwei, under the influence of Christian Missionaries, imagined a China in which people would attend a Confucian-Temple on Sundays and sit in pews to hear the ancient Confucian Classics preached aloud. In 1898 the Emperor made Kang's proposal an official edict, however, it is unclear to what degree they intended to implement it, especially given that it was a description of an experiment. Kang's vision of Sunday sermons was never tried, but his slogan "turn-temples-into-schools" was used by successive Chinese governments to bolster their anti-superstition campaigns. It seems unlikely that Kang's vision would have led to the destruction of half a million temples—that was only possible after the passions and humiliations of the Boxer Uprising had been unleashed in 1901.

By 1904, Chen Duxiu, who went on to found the Chinese Communist Party, began calling for drastic changes to the theater, festival culture, opera, and literature.[283] By 1918 he increasingly invoked the Boxer Uprising to attack religion and martial arts which had by that time, under great pressure, begun to function as separate categories.

Chen argued that Chinese theater could be a powerful tool for propaganda and moral education if it were to become more like Western theater. Plays about immortals, gods, ghosts and anything sexy should be

---

[283] Li Tsiao t'i 1996, 50.

gotten rid of and replaced with loyal and righteous heroes. Eventually, leftist intellectuals argued for replacing the gods with the Communist party.[284] In 1918 Chen argued that nothing had changed, all the elements which had caused the Boxer Uprising were still in play and should be destroyed. He blamed Buddhism, Daoism, Confucianism, Opera, Opera-gods, and of course, superstitious martial arts.[285]

The literary elite's position is best represented by Lu Xun, who attacked literature for its connections to festival and temple culture. He attacked the martial arts directly too, but it is more accurate to say he was attacking the whole of Chinese culture for the sin of being saturated with martial-religious beliefs. All writers in this period agreed that theatrical martial rituals of invulnerability were a major source of humiliation. Such criticisms were already being expressed in the press during the Boxer Uprising. During the late Qing Dynasty, China was called the "Sick Man of Asia" by Westerners. Then, in the first decades of the Twentieth Century the expression was spread by Chinese reform advocates. The three main reasons for this insult were eunuchs, foot-binding, and opium addiction. Both Chinese and Westerners quickly added the Boxer's mix of theater and religion to the list of "sicknesses." Chinese writers of this period were increasingly vitriolic towards their own culture.[286] Writers like Lu Xun specifically targeted Nezha's classic, *Canonization of the Gods*, as the source of the crazy ideas that fostered the Boxer Uprising. These reformist writers, of which there were many, saw temple and festival culture as mass public spaces for the expression of this shameful theatrical-literature. This vitriol led to the destruction of more than four thousand temples in Beijing alone. Think of it this way, back in the 1800s festival

---

[284] Li Tsiao t'i 1996, 60-72.

[285] Cohen 1997, 227-234—includes Chen Duxiu's later views and details of a sarcastic public debate between Lu Xun and a certain Chen Tiecheng, a man with some military background—about whether there exists such a thing as non-superstitious Chinese martial arts.

[286] Meulenbeld's (2015) Chapter One, "Invention of the Novel," is dedicated to showing the way in which theatrical-literature was blamed for China's humiliation. These reformist writers insisted that martial arts combined with *Canonization of the Gods* (Nezha), as a "sacred text," must be removed from Chinese culture.

culture was so widespread and common that if you were reading this book in a village back then you would be hearing the sounds of a festival in background right now. These reformist writers unleashed a pointed attack on Chinese culture itself.[287]

The YMCA Consensus was a sort of salve on the perceived wounds of humiliation. If martial arts, theater, and religion could be completely separated, China could reclaim its greatness. This is what Chiang Kai-shek, the Nationalist (KMT) leader, and Christian convert, had in mind when he wrote, "Avenge Humiliation," on the top of every page of his diary for twenty years.[288]

In hindsight, the only well organized dissenters from the YMCA Consensus were isolated and remote gentry-led militia groups, known collectively as Red Spears.[289] These groups continued to use *Canonization of the Gods* rituals to induce martial prowess for battle against any and all invaders of their local territories until after 1949, when the Communists completely wiped them out.

There is no better example of what the Nationalist anti-superstition movement wanted to rid the country of than martial artists who believed their prowess came from the gods. Scholars of religion have recently produced excellent, narrowly focussed, studies of how Chinese people responded to the anti-superstition campaigns.[290] These studies mostly focus on religion and/or politics. By including the religious theatricality

---

[287] What happened to theater during this time? Censorship, detention, and public ridicule, were a constant throughout the Twentieth Century. While defanging the martial prowess of actors, theater began a torturous process of re-writing and purging traditional plays and generations of treasured performance skills to fit fickle political purposes. At the same time actors began to experiment with transforming exorcistic rituals and plays with great religious significance into commercial entertainment. Then, after 1949, the Communist goal of completely eliminating human nature and replacing it with rationalist patriotism (and idealistic propaganda) did irreparable damage to artistic values.

[288] Platt 2017.

[289] Perry 1980.

[290] On religion see Katz 2014; Goossaert 2006; on religion and politics see Nedostup 2009; On film and politics see Zhang 2005, and Bao 2015; on literature and religion see Meulenbeld 2016; on athletics and politics see Morris 2004; and on theater and politics Li Hsiao-t'i 1996.

of martial arts in our accounts of history, we make it easier to understand what the anti-superstition movement was about. For most of us, understanding what people were doing with their bodies makes history more meaningful.[291]

Religious scholars call the YMCA Consensus "the Christian-Secular Normative Model."[292] Within this framing, there is a dichotomy between 1) the movement to "de-spiritualize" and 2) the movement to "secularize," both of which apply to our discussion of martial arts.[293]

The YMCA Consensus is an information filter; it is like a pair of glasses that only allows us to see things in "pure martial" or "pure religious" terms. Once those glasses are removed a great deal of theatricality and religious culture is visible in the martial arts we practice today.

Three modernizing visions emerged from within the YMCA Consensus; 1) Pure Martial, 2) Knight Errant, and 3) Martial Virtue. Each of the three visions agreed that the martial arts had to be cleansed of old-rituals, mythologies, and the festival culture which had previously defined them. Each of these visions changed over time.

The first vision, Pure Martial (Jingwu) is represented by Huo Yuanjia, who founded the Jingwu Society in 1907.[294] He died in 1911 but his organization continued to grow. He envisioned YMCA-type Physical Education classes open to men and women together, a place where a healthy mind-body would build morally upright citizens. This was the secularization model where theater and religion were completely separate from martial arts. A similar vision was implemented in Christian-run schools, especially girls' schools where martial arts as physical education was a tool in the anti-footbinding campaigns.

---

[291] Little scholarship in English has been done on the cultural pressures and changes that happened in theater other than Li Hsiao-t'i 1996, dissertation (2019 forthcoming). Although trained actors consistently point out that martial arts is infused with master level performing skills—see Mroz 2011; Riley 1997.

[292] Goossaert & Palmer 2011, 68, 73-75, 83, 89.

[293] Katz 2014, 10-11.

[294] Kennedy & Guo, 2010.

This Pure Martial vision was coopted by the state and became the Guoshu (Nation Arts) movement in the 1920s. "A strong body produces a strong nation," became the new motto under the influence of what was elsewhere called fascism. The Chinese government created "institutes" which fostered national competitions, and even rewarded winners with military rank. But things soured at the institutes after an alleged sexual impropriety, and women were summarily kicked out of the movement.[295] In the early 1930s violations of censorship rules became punishable by execution. Martial arts movies were banned, and our hero Zhang San-feng was written out of the history of Tai Chi. The Nationalists were fearful that the sudden popularity of martial arts in movies was rekindling deeply held religious traditions. After 1949 the movement was called Wushu. The Communists' stated goal with regard to martial arts and theater was to eliminate human nature and replace it with rationality.[296]

The second YMCA Consensus vision, Knight Errant (Wuxia) is exemplified by Xiang Kairan. His idea was that martial arts are fun. He was a Baguazhang teacher. His vision was to re-mythologize the martial arts. He started writing new stories about martial arts and popularized the idea of Wuxia Jianghu (Righteous Heroes of the Rivers and Lakes). He wrote a fictional account of the founder of Jingwu, Huo Yuanjia, in which he is a martial arts champion who saves China's national pride from humiliation by the Japanese.[297] Xiang Kairan wrote two kinds of fiction, one where heroes are men and women of extraordinary talent

---

[295] "Nationalists and Communists competed to legitimize the body codes that emerged from their differing versions of female citizenry. The Nationalists attacked the Communists as politically illegitimate partly on the grounds that the physical appearance of Communist women did not fit into the shifting state codes. This could have dire consequences: during the coup against the Communists in 1927, Nationalist forces killed thousands of "modern" women accused of "free love," sometimes simply because they had bobbed hair or unbound feet, or because they had a local reputation for opposing familial authority (Duara 2003, 137). Although the Nationalist government used laws and regulations to control the Shanghai film industry during the 1930s, leftist filmmakers, were allowed to make films which espoused educational values, social responsibility, and the patriotic struggle against Japanese imperialism. See Gao 2010, 97; Zhang 2005.

[296] Yang 1969; Li Ruru 2010.

[297] Portrayed in film six times, including Jet Li, in Fearless (2006).

and discipline. The other where they can fly and wield magical weapons. His brilliant innovation was to replace religion with fantasy. This is an example of de-spiritualization rather than secularization. His stories were massive hits. His vision became the Shanghai film industry, which produced an astronomical 240 films between 1928 and 1932. Films based on Xiang Kairan's books were blockbusters. There was a seemingly insatiable appetite for martial arts films. "Some people were so enthralled by the superhuman power and freedom embodied in the image of the knight-errant *(xiake)* that they went to the mountains to become disciples of martial arts or Daoist masters."[298] Controversy swirled around a 1928 film called the *Birth of Nezha (Nezha chushi)*. It was frequently cited in film magazines of the time that film goers were burning incense in the theater and throwing themselves to the ground in awe when Nezha appeared on the screen. Critics also complained that the destruction of huge numbers of temples was not enough to stem peoples' religiosity because temples were often featured in these films, and people were attending the theater *en masse* as if it were a temple. All that contributed to the Nationalists banning Kung Fu movies. None of those 240 films survive.[299]

Fortunately the film industry moved to Hong Kong where it was outside the Nationalists' reach, and later the Communists'. In British protected Hong Kong, Xiang Kairan's vision was blended with Chinese opera talent and flourished in film. Bruce Lee, the son of a famous opera performer, helped spread it around the world.

Xiang Kairan's vision dovetailed with so called "redemptive societies." These universalist religious groups incorporated martial arts with meditation, and new versions of spirit-writing, under the rubric of religion and science together.[300] Xiang Kairan joined a redemptive society called the Society of the Gentle Fist in Shanghai, which was a charity

---

[298] Zhang 2005, 199.

[299] Zhang 2005, 199, 235-243, 388n4-5.

[300] Yiguandao is a good example, it grew so large it was considered a threat to the state and was outlawed by the Nationalists in Taiwan from 1952-1987. Another example is Daoyuan which was the parent organization for the Red Swastika a successful Daoist charity.

and meditation group that practiced Tai Chi as healing and celebrated Zhang Sanfeng's birthday. Redemptive societies are a fascinating innovation because although clearly modeled on the YMCA, the Red Cross, and other Christian Charity groups, they managed to preserve elements of Chinese temple and festival culture in de-localized institutions.[301] They attracted millions of followers, so the Nationalist banned them as well.[302]

Martial Virtue (Wude), The third YMCA vision, is best represented by Baguazhang teacher Sun Lutang.[303] His contribution to the YMCA Consensus was to re-imagine the concept of Wude or traditional martial virtue. He envisioned marital arts as lineage transmissions of a higher moral tradition rooted not in theater but instead in Confucianism. Confucius, by this point, had been secularized as a "great teacher," he was no longer the founder of a great religion. There are echos of Lin Zhao'en in Sun Lutang's early writing (see page 54). Sun Lutang's student Chen Weiming was the founder of The Society of the Gentle Fist that Xiang Kairan joined.[304] These two different YMCA Consensus views overlapped where they shared the goal of preserving the internal martial arts.

Sun Lutang agreed that that the old mythology had to go, but he saw some traditional mythology and culture as indispensable. He published a book on Xingyiquan in 1915 which starts right in explaining that the Golden Elixir is what makes Xingyiquan work. Then, in 1917, he published a Baguazhang book in which the last two sections explain that the key to making Baguazhang work is achieving the Golden Elixir. In the 1917 book he mentioned that his teacher Cheng Tinghua studied with Dong Haichuan, but is ambiguous about where the art came from. Neither book has any biographies. His vision is constructed around the idea of real fighting skills. Then he shifts. In a 1923 book, he includes a biog-

[301] Katz 2014.

[302] Duara 2003, 109-122.

[303] Sun Lutang's complete writings have been translated by Paul Brennan: https://brennantranslation.wordpress.com/category/complete-works-of-sun-lutang/

[304] Katz, 2014.

raphy of Dong Haichuan as the creator of Baguazhang; he mentions the tombstone engraving but says Dong lived with Prince Rui. Perhaps this is because in 1912 Prince Su was involved in a failed Royalist coup and was still a Royalist when he died in 1922. By 1923, the Republican government's anti-superstition propaganda campaign was picking up steam.

Sun Lutang's 1923 book is about internal martial arts in general and he includes numerous biographies and emphasizes lineages. This change corresponds with the rhetoric of the anti-temple movement. To avoid the charge of superstition all martial arts had to come from real people, not gods or immortals. Dong Haichuan gets a biography. Zhang Sanfeng is also presented in the book, as a real person, and his detailed "lineage" is traced down to the present.

Sun Lutang continued to publish books and articles but as time went by he became more vague about the connection of internal martial arts to the Golden Elixir. His later works show an attempt to scientize the Golden Elixir following the Shanghai Daoist communities' self-protectionist innovations during the same period.[305] His scientization of the practice may have been motivated by the fact that he became a high profile teacher for the Guoshu Institute. However, his students did not do well in competitions and his later articles make it clear that he sees health as more important than fighting.

Sun Lutang sets the stage for Wang Xiangzhai's strange scientizing. Wang Xiangzhai created a new-composite martial art called Yiquan (Intention Fist), which I practice. He made an effort to describe the Golden Elixir as science, but without naming it. A subset of his students emphasize magic tricks, like moving an opponent without touching them. He promoted standing still as a powerful force for healing. He promoted the idea of fighting skill as an open-public discourse rather than secret lineages.

Chen Man-ching, the famous Tai Chi "Professor" who taught New York hippies to go-with-the-flow, also owes his "self-cultivation as moral virtue" image to Sun Lutang.

---

[305] Liu Xun 2009.

All three of these YMCA filtered visions helped the martial arts survive by hiding their origins.[306]

The Current Official Story

Baguazhang was among the first martial arts to be rehabilitated in the late 1970s, after the Cultural Revolution. During the Cultural Revolution it was normal to stand up on a chair and shout the party line. Those who questioned it were tortured until they themselves would stand up and shout the party line and accuse someone else of being a class enemy. This happened every day for ten years.

Resurrecting Baguazhang from its premature grave required that it conform to the party line. It needed a backstory that was politically acceptable and could effectively cover up the real story. The standard of plausibility for revisionism was low because no one anticipated Baguazhang would ever be of interest to people outside of China.

To fill this need, Chinese historian Kang Gewu (1948-) theorized that Dong Haichuan learned circle walking from an obscure Quanzhen Daoist monastery and then combined it with martial arts from his home village. He was attempting to rationalize circle-walking and reconcile it with the mysterious "Yellow Crown" mentioned on Dong Haichuan's tombstone. This theory was shared throughout the English speaking world by *Pa Kua Chang Journal* (1994, Vol 4, No. 6, p. 3-22).

Kang Gewu came of age during the Cultural Revolution, so he knew next to nothing about Daoism. He incorporated Monastic Quanzhen Daoists into his theory, because at the time that was the only form of

---

[306] The Wudang Mountain Daoist culture that appeared in the 1990s is a composite of these three YMCA visions. No doubt, there was Daoist culture on Wudang Mountain for seven hundred years before the Twentieth Century, and something of that culture survived and returned to the mountain—but how much of it? The personalized inner cultivation Daoism of the Shanghai innovators is now taught there. They have the pure martial arts of the Jingwu movement. They have the invention of lineages similar to Sun Lutang, just more recent. And they have a fantasy past which owes much to Xiang Kairan and the film industry. They are also functioning something like a redemptive society, with satellites and networks round the world teaching martial arts as a path to enlightenment. I find Wudang's delightful embrace of commercial and filmic culture the most promising, yet counterintuitive, route to authenticity and re-connecting with the past.

Daoism recognized by the government. It would be another twenty years before a handful of Daoist ritual masters came out of hiding. At the time Kang Gewu proposed his theory, Quanzhen initiates were walking a tightrope. The possibility of being tricked out into the open in preparation for another round of executions was a recent memory. Because at the time both asking and answering questions about Daoism was risky, whatever he was told is unreliable. Kang Gewu's theory also does not have any Daoism in it. The monastic circle-walking he described was probably adapted from Buddhism (see page 163). And it does not even try to explain the coherence of the Baguazhang aesthetic or its variations.

The Kang Gewu dissertation ties into another origin theory in which Baguazhang was originally called *Bapanzhang* or eight spinning-dishes palm (八盘掌).[307] All Baguazhang lineages teach the spinning tea cups, which is also found in many dance and clowning traditions. The name hints at acrobatics or street performance.

In this alternate origin theory, Xiao Haibo (1863-1954) taught *Bapanzhang* in Prince Zhuang's mansion (the Prince who committed suicide at the end of the Boxer Uprising). Xiao Haibo learned the art from a lineage brother of Dong Haichuan, this is part of yet another theory that two other people studied with Dong's mysterious "teacher." In this theory Bapanzhang is the native art of Dong's hometown, Wen An, and is still practiced there.[308] Kang Gewu argued that the only surviving lineage of Xiao Haibo comes through a student who also studied with Dong Haichuan. I do not see a way to sort through this mess except to reiterate that fully realized aesthetic art forms come from milieus of people who can see, understand and appreciate them. They do not come from individuals. But take note of this clue: Bapanzhang has a different name for Baguazhang's signature mud-walking, they call it Xiao

[307] https://www.plumpub.com/kaimen/the-mystery-of-bagua/

[308] For Wen An as a source of eunuchs see—Haar 2006, 228.

Cai Bu (baby steps).[309] This matches the aesthetic of portraying Nezha as a toddler.[310]

Room For Future Research

Now that we have removed the YMCA filter, the possibilities for Baguazhang research are wide open.

The British Consulate was next door to the Prince Su Palace. British officials were collecting intelligence and sending regular reports back home. Has anyone looked into those archives? G. Carter Stent wrote about eunuchs in Beijing in the 1870s.[311] His writings are informative but casual, making extensive use of novelty and anecdote to paint a complete picture. If he had noticed a eunuch living next door with extraordinary martial or performing skills there is a good chance he would have noted it. Has anyone looked for his diaries or the diaries of people he associated with? If not him, then surely Dr. John Dudgeon (1837-1901) would have noted it. For forty years (1863-1901) Dr. Dudgeon treated the princes and their families in his clinic. He also ran the clinic at the British Consulate, right next door to the Prince Su Palace. Dudgeon studied Daoyin for years, and published the first book in English on Daoyin in 1895. It is an impressive book.[312] How could he miss the Baguazhang master next door? He also wrote the first "how to" book on photography in Chinese, and took lots of pictures.[313] He died days after the Boxer ceasefire in 1901. It is crazy that we do not have any verifiable information about

---

[309] http://www.chinafrominside.com/ma/bagua/bapanzhangintro.html

[310] In Chinese opera, comic low walking techniques hidden by a long coat are used to depict children. Nezha is a child. In the cold Beijing winter anyone practicing Baguazhang outdoors wearing a long coat would look like a comic child from the stage.

[311] https://people.well.com/user/aquarius/stent-chineseeunuchs.htm —Stent 1877.

[312] John Dudgeon, *The Beverages of the Chinese: Kung-fu; or, Tauist Medical Gymnastics; The Population of China; A Modern Chinese Anatomist; and Chinese Surgery.* Tientsin Press, 1895 (Daoyin section originally published in Chinese Recorder 1870).

[313] John Dudgeon, *Tuoying qiguan* (1873) 脱影奇观 On the Principles and Practice of Photography.

Baguazhang before 1904. For every Stent and Dudgeon making notes and taking photographs, hundreds of Chinese were also making notes and taking pictures.

Here are the possibilities: 1) Baguazhang was practiced in total secrecy (that would contradict the first tombstone which says that Dong Haichuan had hundreds of students). 2) It was too boring, weird, common, or incomprehensible to be of note (unlikely). 3) Documentation did exist, but much of it was destroyed, lost, or hidden (probable). 4) Twentieth Century practitioners were so effective at removing the Nezha connections, that everyone who has subsequently gone looking for evidence of Baguazhang's origins has looked in the wrong places (that's why I wrote this book). 5) Perhaps people have found documents concerning Baguazhang before the Twentieth Century but felt it was too politically dangerous to publish them (we will not know unless the situation changes).

Now that we know to look for a ritual-theater skill based on the god Nezha, the search for evidence can begin.

Having seen that Baguazhang is Nezha, some people will protest that Baguazhang culture has changed! We should not try to change it back. But has it changed? Nezha never disappeared from Taiwan, and now he is growing in popularity. He may travel back to the mainland at some point, and there is nothing stopping him from visiting the rest of the world.

Perhaps it has changed. Many of us love Baguazhang and its naturalness, body puzzles, and spontaneity. We love fighting, spinning, spiraling, slapping and throwing. Does understanding the mythology, after being in the dark, constitute some sort of betrayal? Mythology opens up new ways of seeing physicality and methods. But it will also cause us to re-evaluate. Acknowledging the history and mythology might cause us to abandon certain parts of our practice. Do you have a superhuman angry baby inside? Would you dive to the bottom of the ocean to fight dragons? Could the deep process of remaking all the flesh and bones of your body help you come to terms with your parents or your ancestors?

Baguazhang is an embodied myth, a daily theatrical ritual. It is an ongoing practice of re-imagining what matters. It is a reference point for those constituents of being which we can continuously improve. It is a pathway back to our original nature, whatever that turns out to be. It can be done empty of myth, but the reality is that once the Nezha story was taken away, it was replaced with other stories. Is there such a thing as a martial art without its myths? Now that we know the truth what should we do? Should we teach the Nezha story? We could replace the myths with science, or our own made up stories, whatever they may be. Perhaps the mythology can be replaced with crystal clear emptiness? That is the very tool that gives Daoist exorcism its power.

If you find yourself metaphorically diving into the ocean to fight dragons, you will be in the company of shrimp soldiers and crab generals, whether you know it or not! I think we should whole-heartedly take on this traditional mythology because it is potent. It has the power of the collective unconscious. To "dive into the ocean" was an expression used to describe amateur literati actors who went professional later in life!

The story of Nezha having both a birth father and a spiritual father is full of meaning. One anthropological theory about why actors were a hated-caste is that they were extremely handsome and when they came to a village they would knock-up the local ladies. Fear of that is why they were not allowed to sleep inside the village walls. This also explains why they had to be good at fighting. After finishing their performances in the village, they would continue on their itinerant journey. After a few years they would return to that village, to perform again, and to collect their bastard children and train them. It is just a theory, but it parallels the Nezha story. Nezha's father hates him because his spiritual father (Taiyi) is an actor. And Nezha takes heart in knowing that his difficulties will resolve when he meets his spiritual father and gets a new body—from training Baguazhang.

Figure 67. From: *Kung-fu*; or *Tauist Medical Gymnastics*, 1870, by John Dudgeon. Internet Archive.

The Golden Elixir

Internal martial arts are a combination of the Golden Elixir *(jindan)* and martial skills. This final section of the book is a meandering essay about the Golden Elixir. There is no other way to discuss this subject—it is meandering. Were it otherwise, demons would be able to practice it.

Throughout this book, I have referred to the Golden Elixir as the most significant defining element of internal martial arts. In both metaphor and practice the Golden Elixir is central to the definition of both Tai Chi and Baguazhang.

If you ask an American kid, "What do monkeys like?" he will say, "Bananas." If you ask a Chinese kid the same question, she will say, "Peaches." These are self-evident facts, first-thoughts, embedded in our respective languages and cultures. If you quiz the Chinese kid further about what sort of peach a Monkey would like, she would tell you, "The Immortals' Peach," because everyone knows Sun Wukong, the Monkey King, steals the Immortals' Peach. In the story, Sun Wukong already has powers of invincibility and is already destined to become enlightened, but eating that peach takes him over the top. The Immortals' Peach only comes to fruition once every thousand years and only one bite is enough to confer immortality; however, Sun Wukong ate the whole thing, and the immortals gathered at the feast of the Queen Mother of the West are pretty mad. They try to kill Sun Wukong by pressure-cooking him, which he enjoys as a refreshing sauna. The Twentieth Century did real damage to the transmission of Chinese culture, but even today, if you asked a sophisticated kid, "What does the peach represent?" she would say it represents "The Golden Elixir, a Daoist meditation practice."[314]

In the first two sections of this book I explained that in the theater the Golden Elixir conferred martial prowess. This was partly due to the association of the Golden Elixir with invulnerability.

Jindan (Golden Elixir) meant different things in different places at different times and has overlapping meanings with other terms like *neidan* (inner elixir), *liandan* (lotus elixir), *neigong* (inward strength), *neijin* (hidden power) and even *qigong* (breath work). I am going to describe what I practice, and how it confers martial prowess. Then I will explain the ways in which my definition is both the same and different from other definitions, thus providing a greater framework for understanding these sorts of practices.

After sages like Lin Zhao'en popularized the Golden Elixir in the 1500s, non-Daoist teachers of the Golden Elixir became numerous, and non-Daoist texts, including plays, became vehicles for teaching the Golden Elixir. Long before that, Daoists infused Golden Elixir rituals into meditation and from there into painting, literature, poetry, ceramics, ar-

---

[314] Alchemy is primitive chemistry and herbology framed within a religious cosmology. Inner-alchemy is a type of meditation with visualization techniques. It is called inner-alchemy, *neidan*, because it uses concepts from alchemy or metallurgy as metaphors for transformation. What I term here Golden Elixir is a literal rendering of *"jindan,"* a term roughly interchangeable with *"neidan."*
Qigong, literally qi-labor, has become a catch-all which simply serves to obscure distinctions, promote the ignorant and diminish expertise. But it overlaps with *jindan*. As a teacher I need to be able to distinguish between any old exercise which might be an ancillary part of the practice, say a posture, or a breathing pattern, and the complete practice as defined by its fruition. For the complete practice I use the term *jindan*. Without the fruition as a reference, the practice becomes a method only. One of the reasons I wrote this book is because people have a tendency to get lost in method, a tendency which is made ten times worse when we abstract the practice from its religious and theatrical roots.

chitecture, and *daoyin*. That is the reason the Golden Elixir has meant different things at different times, and yet remains a central teaching of religious Daoism.

I am going out on a limb here. My Daoist teacher Liu Ming did not think it wise to introduce the Golden Elixir to students with less than a year of consistent non-conceptual stillness meditation practice. He was not a martial artist and his teachings did not reflect an understanding of the connection between internal martial arts and the Golden Elixir.[315] I put this together by reversing everything my teachers taught me. I doubt that I can teach or transmit the Golden Elixir here, but I have a greater purpose, I want people to understand that the Golden Elixir is a necessary element of internal martial arts.

I am going to go further out on the same limb and say that existing texts on the Golden Elixir range from incomprehensibly complex to unusably simple. The incomprehensible texts are missing the esoteric transmission. The unusable texts are too simplistic to have viable fruition, often focusing on health. Scholarly works are of some help, they provide thorough and detailed context, examples and analysis. But the scholarly appetite to investigate something do-able without doing it puzzles me.[316] The crux of of this section of the book is that there is a direct connection between the Golden Elixir, theater, and internal martial arts—which I began to notice because I was practicing all three.

The Golden Elixir is a practice of turning the world upside-down, inside-out and backwards. Zhang Sanfeng and Nezha are backwards characters. Nezha is the antithesis of Confucian ethics, he wants to kill his Dad and he commits suicide (yet he does not die). Zhang Sanfeng had the audacity to reverse Shaolin, to fight without fighting, and to make the Perpetual Happiness Emperor angry. A slow-motion martial art is about as upside down and backwards as it gets. A martial art based on an angry baby god who flays himself is a good demonstration of the word "crazy."

---

[315] On the other hand he did teach a few students a *daoyin* practice for distilling *jing* and *qi* which is a great preliminary to the Golden Elixir.

[316] The practitioners vs. scholars debate consistently comes to the ridiculous conclusion that each think the other one is like a virgin giving advice about sex.

Figure 68. Rabbit in the moon, a depiction of the Golden Elixir. Author's personal collection

The practice of the Golden Elixir is a strange combination of contrariness and extreme openness. It is also an invitation to have a sense of humor. While I am out here on this limb I might as well add that I do not think a person can learn internal martial arts without all three: contrariness, openness, and humor.

The fact that such a practice was widely thought to have extraordinary healing powers is worth contemplating, but I will only touch on it briefly to say that the Golden Elixir reveals how things self-arise and self-resolve.

Grokking the Golden Elixir on the front end requires some symbolic abstraction, in addition to the experience of practicing it. The Golden Elixir satisfies a human appetite, like building a home, winning a competition, or writing a book. It is a disciplined habit that requires getting inside the loop of self-conditioning. That is why it is a major subject of Chinese art, both as a source of creativity and as an experience worthy of representation. It is an act of creativity, like fighting or mathematics. The Golden Elixir is a big subject. It was incorporated into many forms of religious expression in China, and because of that, it sometimes served odd purposes such as the spread of apocalyptic visions.

Falling out of the tree into the boiling caldron of the Golden Elixir is to land somewhere between Rococo and Minimalism. Putting it into words is to negotiate between infinite complexity and trite simplicity—the Golden Elixir is both, simultaneously. Any simplifying I do should not be taken as a negation of the complex. Because I want readers to understand, I will frame some things scientifically, and thereby risk scientizing the subject. Because I want readers to follow what I am saying, I offer the practice in a do-able framework. But this path resists explication precisely because it has to be travelled in darkness, with intimacy. In other words, this is not a "how to" book—you are on your own.

The first Golden Elixir I learned was a visualization of the god Zhenwu, the Perfected Warrior. I was taught to visualize:

- The god wearing armor that gleams infinitely out in all directions.
- His skin as black as the night sky, infinitely deep, dark and inward.
- His hair cast about his shoulders and loosely braided with chain and silk as armor for his neck.
- A silk scarf floating around his shoulders.
- Bare feet symbolizing his readiness to act.
- Standing atop a turtle and a snake.

In addition to visualizing myself as the deity, I was taught to visualize Zhenwu facing me, above me, and inside me. It is easier to imagine being an entity, than it is to visualize all the details of an entity outside oneself.[317] After the image of the deity has been visualized daily for a year, the visualization itself can become a conditioned response—it can then be animated like a puppet. Notice that both the armor and the infinite skin are descriptions of invulnerability.[318]

The question of how Daoism and martial arts meet in the swirl of history and culture is not easy to sort out. If we use narrow definitions of both Daoism and martial arts, they do not intersect, if we use broad definitions of either one, they do. Looking at the 5300 scrolls of the Daoist Canon (Daozang), we find no martial arts. There are Daoist precepts against owning rare or sharp weapons and against serving in the military. *Wuwei*, the precept of non-aggression, is central to the Daoist worldview. Earlier in this book I tried to give some depth to the idea of an immortal *(xian)*. In the Daoist canon there are methods for becoming immortal, as well as descriptions of immortals. The Golden Elixir is a primary path to becoming an immortal. But it is also hard to dismiss that a significant part of society saw becoming an immortal as a type of invulnerability and thus a type of martial power. Daoist rituals to establish peace by resolving the claims of the aggrieved dead, or to protect the living from unseen forces, can be classified as war magic, and thus in some ways were akin to invulnerability practices.

The Golden Elixir comes from the Daoist religion, but it has long had an existence outside of Daoism in the ambiguous margins of temple cults, secret cults, martial arts, and theater.

The Daoist practice called Sitting-and-Forgetting, Zuowang, is a prerequisite for learning the Golden Elixir because the elixir spontaneously arises out of it. Zuowang contains the conditions for beginning the elixir and for completing it. Zuowang is also the base or fundamental experi-

---

[317] See Elaine Scary, *Dreaming by the Book*, 2001, for a discussion of the common limitations of the imagination.

[318] Also note that I have not provided the complete instructions for visualization because it requires one-to-one mentoring over several years.

ence underlying a long list of Daoist practices.[319] There are many different types of meditation. They are not the same, and they are not interchangeable. Sitting and forgetting is a posture. The fruition of holding
this posture is a non-conceptual experience of stillness. It is the grand-
parent of the Zazen practice of the Soto School of Zen Buddhism,
which Suzuki Roshi called "Beginners Mind." By putting this non-conceptual experience into words, I am limiting it, defining it, constraining
it, and shaping it. That points away from the experience itself, so I will
not try to explain it further. This type of non-conceptual stillness practice
is highly accessible. It requires being still, and the *Daodejing*, with commentary, can be studied and chanted as a guide to experiencing its
fruition.

To practice the Golden Elixir, one must first establish emptiness *(xu)*,
both as a spatial experience and as a physiological one. This type of
emptiness is an indirect, self-arising fruition of Zuowang practice (not the
purpose of Zuowang). Then, as if on a stage, the solidity *(jing)* of the felt
body is smelted *(lian)* and transformed *(hua)* until it feels like a cloud *(qi)*.
The cloud feeling is simultaneously visualized, and it can be visualized as
anything with infinite attributes, for example colored light, a floating
scarf, infinite darkness, water moving in ten directions at once, or a deity
with those qualities. In the ritual versions of the Golden Elixir, a deity
with infinite attributes is used for the visualization. For integrating the
practice with martial arts it is the mechanism that matters, not the
specifics of the visualization. Next, the cloud-like body is smelted and
transformed at its periphery into a larger sense of felt space *(shen)*. Felt
space can also be visualized as rainbows, clouds, mountains, or a vast net
made of the stars in the sky. With this order established (body/clouds/
space), it then reverses (space/clouds/body). The felt-space sensation
moves the cloud-like body, which moves the substantive body. Finally, the

---

[319] This is an idea contested by some scholars, who for complex reasons do not see the
practice of *zuowang* in the original meanings of the *Daodejing*, Daoism's most sacred text.
Suggesting they might try practicing *zuowang* and see for themselves is a real conversation
ender. On the other hand, scholars universally acknowledge that lineage Daoists use the
Daodejing to transmit *zuowang* and *jindan*.

whole experience is returned (還 *huan*) to emptiness.[320]   Golden elixir practices are endless loops, cycles, beginning in emptiness, taking form, and then returning to emptiness. They are processions of spatial order and simultaneous action.

Kinesthetic Synesthesia

To access the mechanism of felt space, look at an actual mountain from a distance close enough to see details. Then imagine the weight of that mountain as a felt sensation. Or imagine the weight of a nearby object, like a coffee cup on the table. Or look at a tree and imagine the tactile feeling of bark. These experiments move the mechanism of touch off of the body. The perception-of-touch mechanism is always operative when we use tools, because our brain tricks us into experiencing the working tip of the tool as our sense of touch. This is highly functional, we use it for everything from open-heart surgery to screwing in a lightbulb. It is a tangible property of the imagination. It is immediately accessible, although generally unconscious. The assumption here is that with practice the mechanism of perceiving kinesthetically outside the body can be improved. With practice, space felt outside the body can be moved around without the use of a tool. I believe this is a type of functional synesthesia, like feeling color, or seeing sound, in this case moving felt-space.

Opposite of Chinese Medicine

This whole affair is different from the common Chinese medical cosmology most martial artists are familiar with. In that realm *qi*, defined as the nutritive elements of breath and food, produces the physical form called *jing*.[321] But the Golden Elixir reverses that. Stillness becomes a catalyst for releasing *qi* from *jing* so that it surrounds the body. The common

---

[320] Here is the standard phrasing: *Lian jing hua qi, lian qi hua shen, lian shen huan xu* 煉精化氣，煉氣化神，煉神還虛—*see* Lee Fongmao 2012, 208

[321] Jing, in the medical context, is not just the physical form, it is raw potency which is reproducible and reproduces itself.

ideas of "storing *qi* in the dantian" or "circulating *qi* up the back and down the front," are simply descriptions of a normal healthy person, not the developed practice of Tai Chi or Baguazhang. The Golden Elixir reverses what is common, distilling *jing* and *qi* so that *qi* can surround the body as a protective barrier. *Qi* protects us from our own imagination.

At some point, most people who stick their head into the deep well of Chinese martial arts find themselves trying to figure out what *qi* is. The most common route is to study the mislabeled Traditional Chinese Medicine (TCM). This is usually a dead end because the subject they encounter is full of sloppy scientism, lack of historic context, a hodgepodge of mutually incoherent lineages, polysemous terms that have been defined rigidly, and the insufficient cultural grounding of whoever is teaching them. Way back in the Ming Dynasty, the first two years of Chinese medical training included the study of the Golden Elixir.[322]

Intensity as the Source

It is possible that the Golden Elixir can spontaneously arise from certain types of intensity, like violence for example. The aftermath of intense encounters can pull us in positive directions, making us stronger and smarter. Positive changes are the normal adaptive response to surviving violent encounters. Traumatization is the exception, not the rule. We are innate predators. Each encounter with violence changes us because it brings out potentialities which are already there. The mind, the body, emotions, feelings, strategies, spatial perceptions, how fear and danger are managed—the ways you see and move—are all changed by encounters with violence. Surviving a violent encounter triggers automatic training and conditioning through play. If you survive a life-threatening encounter, afterwards, your imagination will automatically re-play it repeatedly so that you can learn from it. It will change the ways you move, see, feel, what you pay attention to, and who you trust.

---

[322] This gave doctors an extraordinary background for understanding the mundane basis of health. The Golden Elixir, with *qi* outside the body as our original state of being, was the framework for understanding basic health as: the mixing of *jing* and *qi* in the body, the flow of *qi* around the meridians, and the production of *jing* as the material basis of self-reproduction.

A great deal of myth-making worldwide has revolved around people with a hundred or more positive-growth experiences with violence. The positive influence of these people as teachers and leaders is embedded in historic martial arts. The automatic types of training that spontaneously arise from experiences with violence are latent in the martial arts too, along with psycho-emotional and motor-perceptive adaptations. We have access to these insights because, as humans, we are highly evolved predators. It is possible that the reverse ordering of perception-action was developed by people who survived extreme environments and then went on to develop creative strategies for safely stimulating and transmitting the positive adaptations of those experiences to others.

The deep adaptations that intensity brings to our perceptions and our capacity to orient is the same mechanism the creators of the Golden Elixir recognized as our original nature, our immortal selves.

The Tangible Imagination

The Golden Elixir comes with a recognition that there are states of being which are like gates or doorways to change, forms of cultivation that can change the way we interact with the world, the thresholds of identity.[323] Regardless of whether the process of change is automatic or cultivated, the imagination leads these changes of identity. This is a key idea. Even in times of safety, joy, and relaxation, our automatic imagination is operating. It continues to sense what is around the next corner, what is inside that wedding cake, and what holds up the house. If you open a door that you have never opened before and suddenly realize you are much higher or lower than you thought, or facing a different direction, your automatic imagination will instantly re-configure. This func-

---

[323] This capacity to self-change is called *xing* (性) in Daoist language. The circumstances that create the change are called *ming* (命), meaning fate or destiny. In the play *Xiyangji*, the question of legitimacy of the dynasty is discussed in terms of *ming*, the mandate to rule, and *xing*, the finesse to rule. Obviously *xing* and *ming* are reversed in *jindan* practice— we become our own puppet master, which is another definition of *xian* (immortal).

tion of the imagination is sometimes called body mapping. This constant neurological process links the Golden Elixir to martial arts.[324]

Play is the most effective form of learning because it utilizes this same mechanism. All play entails imagining a world into being. But, for the same reason, play has the potential to disrupt order. Systems of training will discourage play when the objective of training includes preserving an established hierarchy. This is why mythology and theatricality are so vital. Sacred stories carry around the re-making of the world. They contain re-visioning which has the capacity to bring down tyranny and free people from mass delusion.

The word *shen* in Chinese means the realm of the imagination—both automatic and intentional.[325] As noted earlier, it also means a god, a character on the stage, or a puppet. Chinese cosmology does not make a strong distinction between the automatic and the intentional, or between an imagined realm that people share and a unique individual experience. In this cosmology, gods and ghosts can be true or not true—even at the same time—because both are part of the tangible imaginary realm called *shen*.

The Chinese word for visualization (*cun* 存) carries the meaning "to actualize." It means to make it real, or to bring it into being.[326] In practice, the Golden Elixir creates fertile ground for working-questions with no definitive answers. Such as, "Does precise visualization trigger a more active, automatic imagination? Does vividness improve efficacy? Are automatic imagination and intentional imagination interchangeable, and which is more efficacious? How does a visualization change the effectiveness of an action? Does ritualization improve actualization? Can group visualization stimulate or support group action?"

––––––––––––––––––––

[324] Rory Miller calls this mechanism "plastic mind," which is a hat tip to the term neuro-plasticity (personal communication).

[325] For a discussion of this issue in Chinese Medical diagnosis see: Kuriyama 2002.

[326] Kohn 2008, 287-289.

Internal Strategies

A common martial arts strategy is to force the opponent's mind into his body by causing pain, which will sometimes limit their capacity to respond. Another strategy is to create an opening using confusion or distraction—which can trigger a disorientation freeze. Similarly, drawing out the opponent's attention in order to get in range and then suddenly forcing the opponent's attention back to his body using pain or damage, will again force the opponent to waste time reorienting. Internal martial arts work with the attention. Keeping one's mind outside the body is key to creating internal martial arts illusions. These illusions have to do with creating a misread of social and asocial cues by the opponent, particularly those related to balance and orientation. The internal martial arts make use of a body organization that acts and responds in unexpected ways because it is oriented differently—creating real and fake power at the same time.

Are the Gods Real?

Mary Douglass, in *How Institutions Think*, explains that institutions are defined by common dreams or shared visions.[327] Daoism as an institution shares a vision of what a human being is in relationship to the cosmos. In that vision, the imagination is capable of changing reality. This is radical materialism in the sense that imagination is understood to be substantive. Translating *shen* as "spirit" is misleading to the extent that it coincides with imagining a separation between our experience and the divine. "Are the gods real?" "Are immortals real?" are the sorts of questions that arise from the pseudo-rational assumption of separateness. They are not important questions from a practice point of view. When accessing the mechanism of intuition, the gods become images which create order. The gods are also intermediaries that disintegrate into emptiness. The extent to which we insist that belief matters, is the extent to which we have been indoctrinated into the YMCA Consensus. Or as Mary Douglass would put it, the YMCA's shared dreams.

---

[327] Douglass 1986.

The term *xian* is most often translated as immortal. The term is important for understanding the Golden Elixir because it is the ultimate, yet elusive, fruition of the Golden Elixir. Lately scholars have been translating *xian* as transcendent. Zhang Sanfeng is a trickster of time and space. The terms "immortal" and "transcendent" both miss this meaning. *Xian* might mean, in the Western sense, to live forever in this body like a vampire. Or it might mean to die and take your body with you. Or to make a new body and leave the old one behind. Or to attain a rank in an afterlife bureaucracy. Or to travel to a liminal dimension of spacetime where one can influence the world, yet not be harmed by it. It is also used as a term of reverence. Or even to mean someone who lived a long time, or had a lasting positive influence. *Xian* does not have a fixed meaning. It is reversible. It is polysemous. Its layers of meaning are multiple and simultaneous. It is both divine and mundane, tangible and empty. And yet, in the theater, it conferred awesome fighting skills.

The Definition of Golden Elixir for Martial Arts

The Golden Elixir is a re-ordering of perception-action. Perception and action can never be separated. They always exist together. But the way they are ordered can change. The Golden Elixir is a process for leading action with imagination and integrating that experience so that it becomes automatic. All movement is led by the imagination. An animal's need to move around is the evolutionary niche imagination evolved to fill. There was a survival advantage in being able to imagine what was around the next corner or on the other side of the log, but most functions of the imagination are unconscious processes. In the West, we have developed the notion that the mind commands the body with an electrical feedback loop, such that kinesthetic experiences are continuously informing the mind. Instead of this two-part system, the Chinese systems uses three parts. Mind-body is replaced with *jing-qi-shen*. In the simplest explanation, *jing* is the gross material substance of the body, *qi* is an invisible force that animates it, and *shen* is the imagination.

One of the primary images of the Golden Elixir is that of a cosmic egg. In this idealized Golden Elixir perception-action ordering, *jing* is the egg yolk, *qi* is the egg-white, and *shen* is the shell radiating out in all directions. In this re-ordering of perception-action the imagination outside of the body leads the action. *Qi* is a buffer in between the imagination and the gross physical body.

The cosmic egg is a key concept for putting the Golden Elixir into martial arts practice. Again, before even attempting to produce the egg, one needs at least a year of one-hour-a-day, non-conceptual stillness practice. Gradually the body *(jing)* and what animates it *(qi)* separate through effortless stillness, through giving up control and letting go of all agendas.[328]

We can give scientistic definitions of *jing*, *qi*, and *shen* and still maintain some coherence across paradigms. In stillness there is movement. That assumption is the most reducible and accessible explanation of the Golden Elixir. The more still you become, the more obvious it is that stuff is still moving. In Chinese cosmology *jing* and *qi* are normally mixed together because *shen* is unconsciously moving qi all around, inside and outside the body. In clearer English, the automatic imagination keeps the physical body and what animates it mixed together. If the spatial imagination stays outside the body and achieves relative stillness, the physical body *(jing)* and what animates it *(qi)* distill from one another. Then the feeling of the body becomes less solid and less distinct. Hence, awareness of the body starts to float on the surface of the skin. In this metaphorical egg, the yolk and the white separate. Once this happens, the body *(jing)* can be moved indirectly by moving the spatial imagination, on the outside of the egg.

Notice I have defined *qi* as "what animates." It is a finger pointed simultaneously at the unknown and the known.

When *jing* and *qi* have completely separated, the physical body *(jing)* is pure, quiet, empty—like a puppet.[329] This immortal embryo might take

---

[328] There are an infinite number of preliminary steps to cultivating the immortal egg, for example, recognizing qi flow in the body, particularly the du/ren channels up the back and down the front. This intermittent awareness is a consequence of doing-nothing *(wuwei)*. Some teachers claim this is the whole practice. In the search for power, others have created hybrids by cross fertilizing it with other practices.

[329] In teaching this I often describe the *jing*/body as lifeless or dead-weight.

years of practice to produce. Self-arising, it might seem fleeting or delicate. But implicit in the notion of the Golden Elixir is that it can also be instantaneous, constant, and robust. Like a puppet or an actor on the stage, the distillation of *jing* and *qi* can be maintained in movement if the spatial imagination does not break the *qi*-egg. That is, the imagination must stay outside the body. Changes in the spatial imagination will move the entire egg, as a whole unit, maintaining oneness. Should one's intent go into the body, into the hand for instance, the *qi*-egg will be broken and the *jing* and *qi* will remix. The egg will no longer move as a whole. The immortal embryo is temporarily destroyed by focused intent or desire. Thus, one must fight without the intent to fight. That is the internal martial arts challenge, should you choose to accept it.

For the actor or the dancer the challenge is the same. To move without effort or self-consciousness, as the great dancer Vaslav Nijinsky said when asked how he was able to jump so high, "I step off of one foot into the air, pause there for a moment, and then come down on the other foot."

An image that some students find helpful is that the qi is like fluffed up parrot feathers surrounding the body. Parrots preen themselves every morning with fluffed up feathers, internal martial artists preen themselves everyday by standing still.

The process of making a new internal martial arts body, done properly, is a form of the Golden Elixir. That process has different names depending on one's perspective. *Neigong* is a description of a particular golden-elixir fruition—strength which moves in towards the center. That process can also be called *purifying jing* because once there is no longer any intent in the body there is also no *qi* mixed with *jing*, so it is pure. In stillness it is sometimes called *congealing jing*. It is also called making the immortal embryo because the yolk *(jing)* is distinct from the white *(qi)*. There are many other ways to describe it, which is part of the reason people get confused.

That was simple enough, right? With one-on-one instruction, and practice, the explanations and conceptualizations sometimes get more complex and specific—and they also reverse.

This is the basic mechanism that drives the movements of Tai Chi and Baguazhang. The word Tai Chi *(taiji)* itself has been used in Golden Elixir texts for a thousand years and describes a part of Daoist ritual. In Daoist ritual, Tai Chi refers to the alchemy-of-being which is not yet differentiated from chaos—where patterns are tangible but not in high enough resolution to distinguish up or down, in or out, warm or cold, dark or light.

The eight trigrams of the *bagua* are also used in Daoist literature to help make the reversal process of the Golden Elixir visual. Visual aids are better communicators than analogies.

Muscles

For many people, the way they think about muscles is a sticking point of confusion. Fast action is normally motivated from outside the body, like when dodging a ball. The source of confusion comes from the mistaken idea that muscles are normally motivated from inside the body. Muscles can be moved by intent inside the body or by perceptions outside the body. These are the same muscles, but perceived and activated differently. When the whole body is controlled by the cosmic egg the perception of one's own muscles changes in several ways. First, all muscles are perceived as moving inwards, even as limbs move away from the center. This is what *neigong* means. Second, muscles feel empty as if they were dead or hollow, controlled from the outside. The body is puppet-like, although not on strings like a marionette, but instead moved by visualizing water, clouds, light, or crystal clear emptiness.[330]

The Perception of Balance

Try carrying a pole with weighted baskets swinging from each end, which is the way everything used to be carried in China. The weights feel

---

[330] Automatons, or puppets with the strings inside, which were popular in the Tang Dynasty, function by pulling the string towards the center, like real muscles.

like ghosts because the mind unconsciously tracks their location, yet they can only be felt indirectly. To move them around consciously, you must move your center of mass, and then by trial and error track the patterns of pendular movement. Similarly, a man balancing on a tightrope must put his mind out on the tips of a long horizontal pole and keep his eyes fixed straight ahead. The Golden Elixir is a way of formalizing these experiences such that one's attention does not come back to one's body. It stays out—even under high stress stimulus like shoving, hitting, slapping, or tickling.

Martial artists often condition their bodies to be immune from the shock of heavy stimulus and hard forces, and are surprised when light or soft touches disrupt their ability to resist, organize, or re-orient. The internal martial arts make use of these reversals of perception to deceive.

Neigong, Reversing Everything

In the famous *Neijia Quan (Internal Martial Arts)* epitaph for Wang Zhengnan (1676), Huang Baijia writes:

> "Shaolin is the peak of refinement for the external arts. Zhang Sanfeng was a Shaolin expert, but he turned the art on its head and thereby created the internal school. Obtaining just a little bit of it is enough to defeat Shaolin."—from Brennan Translations

Meir Shahar translates this, "…having mastered Shaolin, he reversed its principles…" (p. 176, 2008). However one translates this, the meanings are similar to renowned improvisational theater teacher, Keith Johnstone, who commented that his method of teaching came from reversing everything his teachers taught him. In the theater, the audience wants to see you "leap before you look," exactly the opposite of what we do in normal life.[331] In that sense, improvised theater is a physically safe place to take the big risks of reversing normal life. Chinese theater in the 16th-18th Centuries contained a great deal of improvisation and was thematically based on role reversals and inverting dichotomies from

---

[331] Johnstone 1979.

External Martial Arts (Shaolin)	Internal Martial Arts
normal rooting	reverse rooting
normal breathing	reverse breathing
organs (muscle, tendon, bone)	immortal embryo
structure	five element dynamics
full	hollow-empty (*xu* 虚)
fighting	fighting without fighting (dancing)
acting *(wei)*	non-action *(wuwei)*
straight	bent
tangible *(wei)*	intangible *(wuwei)*
use real and fake	make fake real, and make real fake
outward strength (waigong)	inward strength (neigong)
balance	counterbalance
inner breath	breath outside the body
sinking *qi*	fluffing *qi*
technical know-how (意)	spatial-aliveness (神靈)
direct intent	spherical intent —six directions *(liuhe)*
focused	expansive
listening	ignoring
social	asocial
feeling	trusting (not feeling)
calm mind	predator mind
gather and release	constant (unbroken)
jin (directed power, *fajin*)	*shi* (potential power)
knowing	not-knowing (chaos)

everyday life.[332] After practicing the Golden Elixir with martial arts for about ten years, everything I thought I knew started reversing. (See list on the opposite page.)

Internal martial arts are about what happens outside the body, because with the Golden Elixir everything is reversed. Neigong is a method for refining *jing* from an inverted perspective—that is, once the immortal egg has been established.

When we re-orient internal martial arts back into their proper historical and cultural context, an enormous amount of meaning and value re-appears. It was never gone, it was just obscured.

The Dynamics of Visualization

The elements of the Nezha story are potential visualizations for the Golden Elixir, which in this case can be called the Lotus Elixir *(liandan)*. Nezha's flesh is returned to his mother, and his bones are returned to his father. As visualized-actualization, the practitioner of the lotus elixir empties his body of the feeling of flesh and bones. The body is then replaced with a body made of lotus expanding in all directions. This Nezha body is visualized standing on wind-fire wheels. Nezha's confusion silk *(hunyuan)* floats around one's body, with multiple arms used to fight dragons surrounded by ocean currents moving in ten directions at once. These are all infinite motion visualizations. This is not disembodied fantasy, nor is it additive. It is a different way of orienting.

Likewise, in all weather Zhang Sanfeng wears a big straw hat and a fluffy raincoat made from reeds. He is imagined surrounded by clouds and rainbows.

The options for what to visualize, and thus manifest, during Golden Elixir practice are infinite. The tradition gives us a rich set of stories pre-loaded with good ideas about what sorts of things to visualize and how to move. While the mechanism is universal, the characteristics are cultural.

---

[332] See Sophie Volpp 2011—dichotomies such as: substance and emptiness were major elements of the theater.

How one expresses the Golden Elixir in motion can be context specific. It is also possible to use the same mechanism to experience space as crystal clear emptiness, but that too is a tangible manifest visualization. It is a felt expression of the plasticity of mind and body working together, with a *qi* buffer in between.

Invulnerability

In popular culture there was an overlap between the Golden Elixir and invulnerability practices. After the Boxer Uprising, the Boxers and anyone who practiced martial arts were ridiculed by the New Life Movement and the beginnings of the Anti-Superstition Movement. Initially that ridicule was accompanied by executions, but the forms of repression became more insidious as the discourse of ridicule spread through all strata of society, eventually decimating temple culture. State power and policy for the entire first half of the Twentieth Century was unstable, but the trend was to see state power in opposition to popular religious practice, especially to the extent that popular religion was oriented or organized around festivals, theater, and martial arts. Only martial arts which were re-conceptualized as pure were acceptable to the state. The Nationalists later used martial arts as tools for producing national unity.

The core criticism of the Boxers was that they used martial arts invulnerability rituals to make themselves bullet proof. Before that, invulnerability was an integral part of acquired martial prowess. Meir Shahar (2012) describes two types of immortal bodies, one associated with Buddhism and the other Daoism, and traces them both back to origins in India. The first is the impenetrable body, called diamond body, vajra body *(jingang), or iron body.* Sun Wukong (Monkey King) has this type of body and he is a Buddhist, so it became a component of popular Buddhism practiced at Shaolin Monastery.[333] The second type is the insubstantial body, associated with becoming a Daoist immortal *(xian).* It is a cloud-like emptiness, a body which cannot be touched, which blades pass

---

[333] The full name of the Sun Wukong stories is, *Journey to the Western Paradise in Search of the Words of the Buddha.*

through without meeting any resistance. The sky is the limit here, what other kinds of invulnerability are there? Nezha's indestructible lotus-body seems to be a compromise between Buddhist and Daoist imagery, both insubstantial and impenetrable, but following the narrative, also regenerable.[334]

In this blend of the Golden Elixir, invulnerability, and actualization, one becomes Nezha through a process of visualization and invocation. During the transformation process, Nezha "returns" his flesh to his mother and his bones to his father as he walks a circle returning *(nixing)* to Taiyi, supreme unity, his spiritual father (see page 165). The imagery also conjures the Tibetan Buddhist practice of Chöd; where one visualizes offering one's flesh and bones to hungry demons as an offering.[335] Chöd is conceptualized as a way of dealing with intense karma—like Nezha's anger at his father—by psychically re-producing and feeding the experience until it self-resolves. One gives it so much energy that it burns itself out.

Prominent in discussions of the iconography of Nezha is mention of the Chinese tradition of resolving karma by cutting the flesh, called "cutting the thigh" (to feed the family).[336] People would cut out a piece of themselves and feed it to a sick loved-one because this self-sacrifice was widely believed to have healing powers. The practice was illegal but widespread nonetheless. Nezha's self sacrifice was an extreme example of this practice. It was a form of healing that traded on loyalty, on one's willingness to sacrifice for family—a perversion of the Confucian ethic of filial piety *(xiao)*. While this may seem strange, knowing that it was widespread puts invulnerability practices that involve visualizing or actually cutting the flesh in context.

---

[334] The narrative structure of the Tai Chi form (see page 78) goes from shamanic power to *jingang* (Buddhist impenetrable) to Zhang Sanfeng (Daoist insubstantial), suggesting a popular conception of the history of invulnerability in warfare—as well as the possibility that one type of invulnerability can transform into another.

[335] Interestingly, Chöd is divided into "mother" and "father" lineages.

[336] Shahar 2015, 30-34.

In the Nezha story, his body is replaced with a lotus body. In Tantric Buddhist practice, deities like Vajrasatva are visualized inside an infinite lotus flower. Likewise, in the Golden Elixir, the feeling of the heart opening infinitely in all directions, like a lotus flower, is a common image represented in art. The basic Nezha body creation story is a version of the Golden Elixir whereby a systematic emotional release of the flesh and bones transforms into an indestructible lotus body. Thus ritual-theater becomes a dark path to martial enlightenment. Nezha turns his own body inside-out and achieves invulnerability through the Golden Elixir.

Golden Elixir practices, like internal martial arts, are endless loops of perception-action. The Nezha story loops. When Nezha, now in an indestructible lotus body, becomes possessed by anger and attempts to kill his father, Immortals intervene by placing him in a Buddhist Pagoda. This forces him to transform again, first by forced stillness, then by true-fire *(zhenhuo).*[337] Finally his anger is burned away, resolving his karma with his birth father, only to start from the beginning again the next time the story is told (or ritually enacted).

A similar process is involved in the theatrical creation of the iron-body. Iron-body training is an external version of the inner elixir. This type of invulnerability is symbolized, as mentioned earlier, by the Monkey Sun Wukong, who is born from a stone egg in the epic *Journey to the West*. The Chinese understood Sun Wukong as a yoga master. In Indian yogic terms, this elixir begins by making and firing the body as if it were a clay vessel. Through forming and heating, the body becomes impenetrable. Clay is a metaphor for a perfect mix of the highest quality *jing* and *qi*. In the story, Sun Wukong's body is a vessel containing the possessed monkey demon. As he accumulates merit, his *gongfu* (Kung Fu), sets up an eventual reversal of perception-action ordering which produces the emptiness of enlightenment. Sun Wukong becomes self-reflective, a reversal within a reversal.

---

[337] For discussion of the Nezha pagoda see—Shahar 2015, 94-99. Zhenhuo is also used in the epic *Journey to the North*, as a transformative substance which produces immortals *(xian)*, and can be turned into *jindan* pills!

When the Golden Elixir creates the immortal embryo or egg, the body radiates out in all directions like a bell being rung. When referring to its invulnerability properties it is called golden-bell.[338] The metaphoric vibration of the bell represents the body becoming insubstantial, such that weapons cannot harm it. This is the type of invulnerability Zhang Sanfeng has.[339] But in practice, Golden Bell and Iron Body are both metal and can represent either impenetrability or insubstantiality. In the theater, perhaps the most common form of invulnerability is conceptual. Plays on the stage are already written in heaven and have fixed, known endings. Simply being fated to return to the stage again the next time the play is staged is a kind of invulnerability which is an integral part of the martial-theatrical tradition.

We do not know enough about Zhang Sanfeng to fully re-mythologize Tai Chi yet. Although, for example, the Tai Chi movement, snake creeps down, is probably Xuanwu standing on a giant snake and turtle which are sinking into the mud. This is another narrative version of the Golden Elixir. Snake and turtle are demons Xuanwu is attempting to capture. They originally grew from his stomach and intestines which he cut out and buried in an attempt to make himself empty.[340]

The indestructible lotus body has its own Golden Elixir story of self-repair. Lotus flowers arise spontaneously from the footsteps of the Buddha walking through mud. The mud is the mix of *jing* and *qi*, which in stillness becomes clear water and settled earth. The lotus flowers then take root in the mud, grow up through the clear water, and blossom out in all directions on the water's mirror surface. A common Daoist talisman of protection is made by painting the four thunder gods with a lotus in

---

[338] Practitioners often conflate iron-shirt and golden bell because they are both metal.

[339] The word for diamond in Chinese is "strong-gold" or *jingang*, which is considered a form of Buddhist enlightenment. It is also the Chinese name for the Indian origin god Vajrapani (Diamond-Hands). Vajra is Sanskrit for thunder, diamond, and an impenetrable and indestructible substance. So the term *jingang* used in the Tai Chi form-name "Jingang Pounds the Mortar," is a reference to all these possibilities.

[340] This story comes from *Journey to the North*.

the center, representing both Nezha and the Golden Elixir's capacity to make the imagination manifest.

Real Fighting

It would be easy to misunderstand me here, so allow me to reiterate my position. There is no way any of this martial prowess is real unless you make it real. That means gaining the ability to use physics, deception, emotional clarity, adaptive mindsets, and agility through your physical body. This requires games, training, operant conditioning, conceptual learning, scenario enactment (or a large amount of experience with real violence). You also have to be able to take a hit. Great treasures were lost when the hard-body conditioning of invulnerability training was abandoned, but the idea that invulnerability could trump the physics of bullets and blades was a delusion that needed to die. On the upside, some invulnerability conditioning survived in Chinese opera which has now filtered into contortion, acrobatics and circus. These types of extreme conditioning were also preserved in secret society initiation rituals. They can also be found among martial traditions in Cambodia, Indonesia, Vietnam, the Philippines, and Malaysia. We have the capacity and intelligence to re-discover these treasures.

Stage Combat

Tai Chi and Baguazhang are not personal fighting styles, they are characters being performed. Like most Chinese martial arts, these arts have extensive stage combat skills built into them. Two-person routines are ready-made stage combat which can be jazzed up with assaultive dialog and improved using sound effects like body slaps, stamps, or opera percussion. Many martial artists are good at improvising live fight scenes because the rhythmic action of fighting combined with the telegraphing and movement illusions embedded in forms *(taolu)* are the bread and butter of choreography.

When experts are choreographing a fight scene, they often start with slow-motion movement. In fact, nowadays it is often called Tai Chi speed —a safe speed used for perfecting distance and form. That is not a coincidence, it has always had that purpose. Once the pieces are in place, fight choreography can go up to seventy percent of fight speed. Anything faster is invisible to most audiences. Shaolin has the "fast-freeze-fast-freeze" aesthetic for the same reason, it is easy to see. The popularity of popping and locking in dance follows the same logic. Baguazhang is a great choreography tool because it emphasizes rotational movement around two peoples" centerlines, also a major tool for orienting the action so that an audience can see it. Spirals, spinning, and waves are all effective ways of manifesting power visually.

The biggest problem individual martial artists have transitioning to stage combat is that they tend to fight like themselves. Being yourself on stage is unconvincing. On the stage, fights happen in character, and each character has unique elements of style. Before the Twentieth Century, martial artists could easily transition between real and fake because Tai Chi and Baguazhang were not personal fighting styles, they were characters to be embodied and performed.

In Chinese opera, the costumes of martial roles often depict the Golden Elixir. They show the world coming into being out of the ocean of chaos *(hundun)*. They sometimes include the story arc of the character. Clothing floats on the surface of the skin as an intermediary between the physical body of the performer and the space flowing out around them. The clothing is *qi*. *Qi* in the Chinese theater is used much the way we use the word "presence" in English. These martial costumes represent the limitless martial prowess of the Golden Elixir.[341]

Magic Tricks

Martial arts are context and execution dependent. Internal martial arts are complex illusions which require a lot of practice. Like

---

[341] Daoist Dream practice is called "Day and Night the Same." It is another way to access infinite emptiness, and limitless visualization. One feels an infinitely empty physical body that is then moved by the space around it. The location of a dream and one's body are made of the same stuff. There is no separation. This is why Zhang Sanfeng learned Tai Chi from Xuanwu in a dream. Tai Chi is a way to take the experience of dreaming into the movement in the waking body.

magic, they make use of mis-direction and whole-body sleight-of-hand. They do not always work, and the potential for self-delusion is high.

Tricks are a big part of internal martial arts, they can be used for fighting as well as entertainment. They are also teaching tools for transmitting the Golden Elixir. Many teachers play a trick in which the student can see, feel, or hear an explanation of what the trick is, but are then left to figure out how to do it on their own. These magic tricks are fun body puzzles. They should not be confused with self-defense, which requires us to transmit practical skills and awareness quickly. I can take this further and say it is immoral to teach in a way that confuses magic tricks with self-defense. I put the blame for this problem on the YMCA Consensus. By claiming that martial arts are purely for fighting, they leave no room for magic to be magic!

Daoist Ritual and the Golden Elixir (Jindan)

The Golden Elixir continues to exist as a practice unto itself both inside and outside of Daoist lineages. However, an elaborate form of the Golden Elixir is part of Daoist ritual. In other words, Daoist ritual is normally performed as an "external" visual spectacle while simultaneously it is performed "internally" as a meditation and visualization practice. Some Daoist rituals can be performed entirely in the stillness of meditation as fully visualized spectacles. This internal-external simultaneity, incidentally, is the most likely origin of the notion of internal and external in popular notions of Chinese martial arts. Note that this traditional use of the term internal or inner *(nei)* does not mean inside the body in the biomedical sense. It means both visualized outside the body and inside the body as an established field of emptiness. These fields of emptiness are called caverns *(guan)* or platforms, which are synonymous with the term *dantian* (elixir field).

Visualizations inside the body are a source of confusion in both scholarly and popular writings about the Golden Elixir so I will elaborate. When the felt body (as opposed to the biomedical body) becomes empty of intent, it becomes pure *jing*. It is then possible to visualize deities inside the space of the body without breaking the *qi*-egg. For this to work, the deity is first visualized outside the body in crystal clear detail before being installed in the body, which must first be established and felt as an infinitely empty palace or cavern. Emptiness of this sort arises spontaneously from well established stillness.

Daoist ritual gets potency from two sources. 1) Emptiness, which is the basis for action without pretense or aggression. 2) The capacity of the imagination to create infinite layers of meaning for even the smallest gesture. If you practice Tai Chi you will immediately recognize these two qualities as essential aspects of the art.

The outer edges of emptiness, and the infinite reaches of inner emptiness, along with infinite layers of meaning—merge into a single feeling—continuously giving birth to the immortal embryo which is a model for cosmic renewal, the fruition of Daoist ritual. This Daoist concept of cosmic renewal was accessible to Baguazhang or Tai Chi practitioners in the 1800s.

It is hard to tie internal martial arts directly to Daoism if we limit the definition to what is in the Daoist Canon, Orthodox Daoist Ritual experts, or Quanzhen monasticism. But the Golden Elixir was part of popular culture; *precious scriptures*, called *baojuan*, were particularly widespread in North China. This is a rich and varied category of texts, which includes the sacred texts of heterodox or secret cults. Many of them sketch a millennialist vision followed by a return to the Eternal Mother along with Golden Elixir instruction. These were chanted communally and transmitted though established teacher student relationships, as well as assemblies of the devoted. These texts reveal a vibrant and diverse field of Golden Elixir experimentation along with an odd mix of religious fanaticism and inspiration stretching back to the Ming Dynasty. Some of these cults integrated a martial arts component. They are one of the origins of internal martial arts, but how they might be connected to Tai Chi and Baguazhang is still an open question.

Martial artists may have been self-identified as Daoist, part of an obscure Daoist lineage, or more likely, they created the arts in a milieu where the ideas of cosmic renewal and the Golden Elixir were in the air.

Conclusion: The Golden Elixir Had to Be Separated From the Martial Arts of Zhang Sanfeng and Nezha

If you practice Tai Chi, you have been visibly performing a type of physical theater which ritually enacts the story of a sexy, dirty, generous, comic, hermit, trickster becoming an immortal, while claiming that it is an esoteric, slow-motion fighting skill and/or a spiritual healing exercise.

If you practice Baguazhang, you have been running around in circles doing the self-sacrificing rebellious dance of an angry baby god fighting dragons. while claiming it is about self-defense and/or a kind of Cross-fit for weirdos.

The anti-religious, anti-theater, YMCA Consensus is a filter that stops us from seeing mime, ritual, storytelling, symbolism, the meaning of names, and mythology, as well as redemptive, instructive, and transformative movement-based insights. This book is about what I saw when I took of the YMCA colored glasses. Now that you have taken them off, what do you see?

In hindsight, the belief that martial arts could make a person bulletproof had to go. The wholesale destruction of Chinese temple and festival culture happened quickly, and I dare say, thoughtlessly. When you find yourself in need of a modern army, and what you have instead is a militia organized around an angry baby god, something has to change. Knowing this, we have a duty to honor the choices our teacher's teachers made when they put on the YMCA glasses. But we can take them off. In fact, I believe, we have a duty to take them off and use our clear vision to figure out which discarded treasures should be revived.

In hindsight, the movement to "scientize" the Golden Elixir was a good survival strategy. In the early part of the Twentieth Century, people were associating it with false claims of invulnerability and deceptive rituals. I see the Golden Elixir practice as a treasure-house of conceptualizations and innovative experiments around the experience of having a body and a mind. To surgically remove it from the rituals and cosmology that created it would likely kill it. In fact, a more gentle and gradual evolution is called for. An evolution that takes us back to the original inspiration found in Laozi's *Daodejing*.

In 1952, having escaped the Communists, Long Zixiang authored an essay titled *A Study of Taiji Boxing*, which contains thirteen references to Zhang Sanfeng. One reference points vaguely to the Golden Elixir as the source of the art, another to the Golden Elixir as a source of confusion, the other eleven are seemingly irony-free attempts to establish the biographical Zhang Sanfeng.[342] Long Zixiang was a Nationalist refugee in Hong Kong wondering what the future held in a moment of chaos. His book exemplifies a transitional moment of confusion about which Tai Chi story was "politically correct," a confusion which continues to haunt us today.

When I look at the image of Li Ziming *(page 137)*, taken just after the Cultural Revolution, with wind-fire wheels, and posing like Nezha, I can not help but think he knew what had been hidden. I think he was leaving a clue, hoping for freer times when you and I could re-enchant the art. What do you see?

The first non-theatrical mention of internal martial arts comes from the epitaph for Wang Zhengnan *(see page 76)*. In it, the author Huang Zongxi tells us that internal martial arts were created when Zhang Sanfeng did us the favor of reversing Shaolin. Reversing, inverting, or "flipping something on its head" is a primary characteristic of Golden Elixir techniques. Huang Zongxi was familiar with the Golden Elixir tradition of the Sage Lin Zhao'en, and he knew that Sage Lin claimed to have learned it from the Immortal Zhang Sanfeng and that he taught it to General Qi Jiguang. Nationalist and Communist propagandists obscured this Golden Elixir connection to Tai Chi and other internal martial arts, in order to purify, rationalize, and disenchant them. I have used my Tai Chi writing skills to flip that idea on its head. What will you do?

The attempt to separate the Golden Elixir from martial arts in the early Twentieth Century was successful, but not completely. The survival of countless secret methods within today's martial arts is proof of that. On the other hand, the movement succeeded in creating mountains of confusion; even a single word like *qi* or *dantian* can stir up a hornet's nest.

---

[342] https://brennantranslation.wordpress.com/2018/03/30/the-taiji-manual-of-long-zixiang/

Once the Golden Elixir orientation was lost, methods become supreme. To teach without an accurate, evolutionary, creative orientation and overview of the arts, is to be polarized between the idiosyncrasies of a progressive-cumulative approach to knowledge, and a "do it exactly this way, I don't know why" approach. In that situation what chance do students have to even think of reversing everything they have been taught and flipping what they think they know on its head? It risks cutting students off from the very crux of the practice—the embodiment of spontaneity.

I wish I could write an ending to this book, but that is not how the story ends. We are actually at the beginning. The road is open.

.

Acknowledgements

The dedication and integrity of a great number of individuals made this book possible. First I would like to thank Bing Gong, my first martial arts teacher, who got me started on this journey. Zhang Xuexin, Ye Xiaolong, and Bruce Kumar Frantzis challenged me a great deal. George Xu more than anyone, influenced the way I move, and the way I think about movement. He is a genius whom I have been banging heads with for three decades.

I wish to thank all of my Dance teachers, but first of all Chitresh Das, who taught me what classical learning is, and Malonga Casquelourd, whose enormous talent and generosity was never contained by limited categories like "dance." Both were exquisite improvisors. Alonzo King was a great encouragement. CG Seville, Alicia Pierce, Alberta Rose, Robin Sedgwick, and the whole San Francisco Dance Community in the late 80s to early 90s, which at the time was the center of the world, I thank.

I want to thank Rebecca Haseltine, who for twenty years, has carried on a world class conversation with me about what a body can do. I want to thank Keith Johnstone for teaching me the skills of improvisation and for showing me the easy, terrifying, yet exhilarating access we all have to our collective unconscious. Thanks to Liu Ming, who for ten years, was a constant mentor in the study of Daoism.

Thanks to all my teachers, and to thousands of students over the years for inspiring me.

The martial arts studies community has been outstanding, gratitude to all. Daniel Mroz read an early draft and has long been a supportive collaborator. Ben Judkins has been a foil for ideas, and a continuous source of sources. Paul Bowman for his audacity in putting on the Martial Arts Studies Conferences and its publications. And there are many more people, too many to name, who participated in those conferences and gave me ideas and encouragement.

Throughout this project, Rory Miller and Maija Söderholm were on speed dial and shared their genius and insight. I want to thank the SOJA crew (in Oakland) and Portland Shaolin for giving me a creative outlet to push the boundaries of what can be taught. Thanks to Michael DeAgro for being an awesome collaborator, and to Marnix Wells for being a charming host in London and translating the key *Xiyangji* text for me.

I wish to thank Livia Kohn, who gave me superb and detailed advice about my writing, and published my academic articles in the *Journal of Daoist Studies*. Sabina Knight turned me on to Mo Yan, and carried on a great conversation about Chinese literature with me for several months. Thanks to Katherine Alexander for teaching me about *baojuan*. Georges Favraud and Adeline Herrou for their big hearts, hospitality, and constant encouragement. Dorothy Ko for her thoughts on Tai Chi and the YMCA. Christopher Hamm for his insights into Xiang Kairan and for pointing out that worship and incense burning during the first ever Nezha film was used to justify destroying the martial arts film industry. I want to thank Paul Katz, Chang Hsun, and especially Yeh Chuen-rong, for their help with my research in Taiwan.

Mark Meulenbeld's book *Demonic Warfare* was a watershed event; it gave me great confidence that what I see about the culture and history of Chinese martial arts can be seen by others too. Meir Shahar's book, *Oedipal God* (about Nezha), was a huge inspiration. He kindly invited me into his *Journey to the West* class in Tel Aviv, and listened with great encouragement to an outline of this book. His students Israel Kanner and Eric Kozen (and Eric's puppet-master wife Gili) offered wonderful insights and encouragement.

I'd like to thank Greg Moonie and Patrick Bath, my two favorite people to perform with. Chris Pearce for his incredible video and animation work. Nam Singh for modeling the perfect gentleman and teaching me to cook all the weird stuff. Paulie Zink for embodying the Dao, and Damon Honeycutt for opening a door into Paulie's world. And Joan Mankin, master of physical theater, for being such an inspiring student. Also to

Joseph Svinth, who is the world's leading expert on historical marital arts images, is relentlessly open minded, and regularly sent me awesome images for the book.

Thanks to all the people who read or edited a draft of the book, Mike Sutherland, Paul Menair, Brian Buttrick, Chris Hellman, Rob Schaecter, Bogdan Heretoiu, Shawn Hickey, and Chad Eisner.

Thanks to all the people who were attracted to my blog and took the extra step of starting up a conversation. To my wife Sarah Halverstadt for editing, encouragement, support, and her immortal patience. And finally to my mom and dad.

Bibliography

Allen, Frank, and Tina Chunna Zhang. 2007. *The Whirling Circles of Bagua Zhang: The Art and Legends of the Eight Trigram Palm*. Berkeley, Calif: Blue Snake Books.

Amos, Daniel M. 1983. "Marginality and the Hero's Art: Martial Artists in Hong Kong and Guangzhou Canton." Ph. D. diss., University of California, Los Angeles.

Amos, Daniel M. 1999. "Spirit Boxing in Hong Kong: Two Observers, Native and Foreign." *Journal of Asian Martial Arts* 8.4.

Antony, Robert J. 2012. "Bloodthirsty Pirates? Violence and Terror on the South China Sea in Early Modern Times 1." *Journal of Early Modern History* 16, no. 6,481–501.

_____. 2003. *Like Froth Floating on the Sea: The World of Pirates and Seafarers in Late Imperial South China*. Berkeley: Institute of East Asian Studies.

Barton-Wright, E.W. 1899. "How to Pose as a Strong Man."*Pearson's Magazine Vol 7*, 59-66.

Bao, Weihong. 2016. *Fiery Cinema: The Emergence of an Affective Medium in China, 1915-1945*. Minneapolis: University of Minnesota Press.

Berling, Judith A. 1980. *The Syncretic Religion of Lin Chao-En*. New York: Columbia University Press.

Bhandari, Aparita. "Chitresh Das was an Ambassador of Indian Classical Dance." *The Globe and Mail*, Feb. 4, 2015. https://www.theglobe-andmail.com/arts/theatre-and-performance/chitresh-das-was-an-ambassador-of-indian-classical-dance/article22796920/

Blakeslee, Sandra, and Matthew Blakeslee. 2007. *The Body Has a Mind of its Own: How Body Maps in Your Brain Help You Do (Almost) Everything Better*. New York: Random House.

Brennan, Paul. 2011-2018 This personal project is the largest collection of Chinese martial arts texts in translation. https://brennantranslation.wordpress.com/

_____. 2013. "Boxing Concepts Explained Authentically, by Sun Lu-tang (1924)." http://brennantranslation.wordpress.com/2013/04/29/the-voices-of-sun-lutangs-teachers/

_____l. 2014. 王征南墓誌銘　己酉 Memorial Inscription for Wang Zhangnan (1669), by 黄宗羲 Huang Zongxi, & 王征南先生傳 Biography of Wang Zhangnan (also known in abridged form as 內家拳法 Boxing Methods of the Internal School)黃百家 by Huang Baijia (1676) https://brennantranslation.wordpress.com/2014/08/29/boxing-methods-of-the-internal-school-nei-jia-quan-fa/

_____. 2016. "My Experience of Practicing Taiji Boxing" by Xiang Kairan 1929. Published in Wu Zhiqing's 太極正宗 *Authentic Taiji,* 1936). Translation by Paul Brennan. https://brennantranslation.wordpress.com/2016/07/31/xiang-kairans-taiji-experience/

Brook, Timothy. 1999. *The Confusions of Pleasure: Commerce and culture in Ming China.* Berkeley: Univ of California Press.

Boretz, Avron. 2010. *Gods, Ghosts, and Gangsters: Ritual Violence, Martial Arts, and Masculinity on the Margins of Chinese Society.* Honolulu: University of Hawai'i Press.

_____. 2011. "Ritual Violence and Violent Ritual in Chinese Popular Religion," *Case Studies: Religion and Violence, Past and Present; The Blackwell Companion to Religion and Violence,* 473-484; Oxford: Wiley-Blackwell, 472-484.

Carlitz, Katherine. 2005. "Printing as Performance." *Printing and Book Culture in Late Imperial China,* by Cynthia J. Brokaw (Editor), Kai-Wing Chow (Editor). Berkeley: University of California Press, 267-303.

Cass, Victoria. 1999. *Dangerous Women: Warriors, Grannies, and Geishas of the Ming.* Lanham: Rowman & Littlefield.

Chan, Hok-lam. 2008. *Legends of the Building of Old Peking.* Hong Kong: Chinese University Press.

_____. 1990. "A Mongolian Legend of the Building of Peking." *Asia Major* 3 (Third Series) (2): 63–93.

Chan, Margaret 2009. "Chinese New Year in West Kalimantan: Ritual Theatre and Political Circus." *Chinese Southern Diaspora Studies,* 3, 106-142.

_____. 2012. "Bodies for the Gods: Image Worship in Chinese Popular Religion." In *The Spirit of Things: Materiality and Religious Diversity in Southeast Asia*, edited by Julius Bautista, 197-215. Ithaca, NY: Southeast Asia Program, Cornell University.

_____. 2014 "Tangki War Magic The Virtuality of Spirit Warfare and the Actuality of Peace." *Social Analysis*, Volume 58, Issue 1, Spring, 25–46 Berghahn Journals.

_____. 2016. "Tangki War Magic: Spirit Warfare in Singapore," 2016. *War Magic - Religion, Sorcery, and Performance*. New York: Berghahn Books, 25-46.

Chao, Shin-yi. 2011. *Daoist Rituals, State Religion, and Popular Practices: Zhenwu Worship from Song to Ming* (960-1644). London: Routledge.

Chao, Wei-pang. 1944. "Games at the Mid-autumn Festival in Kuang-tung." *Folklore Studies*. 1-16.

Carr, Caleb 1992. The Devil Soldier: The American Soldier of Fortune Who Became a God in China. New York: Random House.

Chen, Fan Pen Li. 2007. *Chinese Shadow Theatre: History, Popular Religion, and Women Warriors*. Montreal: McGill-Queen's Press.

Clark, Anthony E. 2017. *Heaven in Conflict: Franciscans and the Boxer Uprising in Shanxi.*Seattle: University of Washington Press.

Clart, Philip. 2003. "Confucius and the Mediums: Is There a "Popular Confucianism?" *T'oung Pao, Second Series*, Vol. 89, Fasc. 1/3, pp. 1-38.

Cohen, Paul A. 1997. *History in Three Keys: The Boxers as Event, Experience, and Myth*. New York: Columbia University Press.

Dean, Kenneth. 1998. *Lord of the Three in One: The Spread of a Cult in Southeast China*. Princeton, N.J: Princeton University Press.

DePalma, Anthony 1991. Rare Dismissal on California Faculty, http://www.nytimes.com/1991/08/14/news/rare-dismissal-on-california-faculty.html August 14. *New York Times.*

Doar, Bruce. 1984. "The Boxers and Chinese Drama: Questions of Interaction." *Papers on Far Eastern History*. (29): 91-118.

Docherty, Dan. 2014. *Complete Tai Chi Chuan*. Ramsbury: Crowood Press.

Douglas, Mary. 1986. *How Institutions Think*. Syracuse, N.Y.: Syracuse University Press.

Dreyer, Edward L. 2007. *Zheng He: China and the Oceans in the Early Ming Dynasty, 1405-1433.* New York: Pearson Longman.

Du Lifang. 1959. "Lun Longyan za xi." In *Puju shinian.* Linfen: n.p.

Duara, Prasenjit. 2003. *Sovereignty and Authenticity: Manchukuo and the East Asian Modern.* Lanham: Rowman & Littlefield Publishers.

Dudgeon, John. 1873. *Tuoying qiguan* 脱影奇观 *(On the Principles and Practice of Photography) publisher unknown.*

_____. 1895. *The beverages of the Chinese: Kung-fu; or, Tauist medical gymnastics; the population of China; a modern Chinese anatomist; and a chapter in Chinese surgery.* Tientsin Press (Daoyin section originally published in Chinese Recorder 1870.)

Duyvendak, J. J. L. 1953. "Desultory Notes on the Hsi-yang chi," *T'oung Pao*, Second Series, Vol. 42, Livr. 1/2. Brill, 1-35.

Esherick, Joseph. 1987. *The Origins of the Boxer Uprising.* Berkeley: Univ of California Press.

Eskildsen, Stephen. 2008. "Do Immortals Kill?: The Controversy Surrounding Lü Dongbin." *Journal of Daoist Studies* 1.

Esposito, Monica. 2004. "Sun-worship in China-The Roots of Shangqing Taoist Practices of Light." *Cahiers d'Extrême-Asie,14*1, 345-402.

Farrer, D. S. 2016. "Introduction." *War Magic: Religion, Sorcery, and Performance*, Edited by D. S. Farrer. New York: Berghahn Books, 1-24.

Favraud, Georges. 2008. Adam D. Frank, "Taijiquan and the Search for the Little Old Chinese Man: Understanding Identity through Martial Arts." *Perspectives Chinoises, 1054*, 114-118.

Frank, Adam. 2007. *Taijiquan and the Search for the Little Old Chinese Man: Understanding Identity through Martial Arts.* New York: Palgrave Macmillan.

Gamble, Sidney David. 1954. *Ting Hsien: A North China Rural Community.* Stanford University Press.

Gao, Yunxiang. 2010. "Sex, Sports, and China's National Crisis, 1931-1945: The "Athletic Movie Star" Li Lili (1915- 2005)." *Modern Chinese Literature and Culture*, Vol. 22, No. 1 (Spring). Foreign Language Publications, 96-161.

Ge, Liangyan. 2001. *Out of the Margins: The Rise of Chinese Vernacular Fiction*. Honolulu: University of Hawai'i Press.

Goode, Walter. 1976. "On the *Sanbao taijian xia xiyang-ji* and Some of Its Sources." Canberra: Australian National University, unpublished dissertation.

Goossaert, Vincent. 2006. "1898: The beginning of the end for Chinese religion?" *The Journal of Asian Studies*, 652, p. 307-335.

_____ & David A. Palmer. 2011. *The Religious Question in Modern China*. Chicago: University of Chicago Press.

_____. 2012. "Daoists in the Modern Chinese Self-Cultivation Market." In *Daoism in the Twentieth Century, Between Eternity and Modernity*. Berkeley: University of California Press.

Gregory, Scott W. 2014. "Daydreaming Dynasty: The Eunuch Sanbao's Journeys in the Western Seas and 'Present-Dynasty' Fiction of the Ming." Ming Studies 70, 10-28.

Grossman, David. 1995. *On Killing: The Psychological Cost of Learning to Kill in War*. New York: Little, Brown & Co.

Gyves, Clifford M. 1993. *An English Translation of General Qi Jiguang's "Quanjing Jieyao Pian": (chapter on the Fist Canon and the Essentials of Nimbleness) from the 'Jixiao Xinshu' (New Treatise on Disciplined Service)*. Wright-Patterson AFB, OH: Air Force Institute of Technology.

Haar, Barend J. ter. 2006. *Telling Stories: Witchcraft and Scapegoating in Chinese History*. Leiden: Brill.

Hansson, Anders. Chinese Outcasts: Discrimination and Emancipation in Late Imperial China. Leiden: Brill, 1996.

Henning, Stanley E. 1999. "Academia Encounters the Chinese Martial Arts." *China Review International*, 319-332.

Herrou, Adeline. 2012. "Daoist Monasticism at the Turn of the Twenty-First Century." *Daoism in the Twentieth Century: Between Eternity and Modernity*. Berkeley: University of California Press.

Hinton, David. 2009. *Chuang Tzu: The Inner Chapters*. Translation. Washington, D.C: Counterpoint.

Hong Jeehee. 2016. *Theater of the Dead: A Social Turn in Chinese Funerary Art, 1000-1400*. Honolulu: University of Hawaii Press.

Hsia, C.T. 2004. *On Chinese Literature*. New York: Columbia University.

Hsiao-t'i Li. 1996. "Opera, society and politics : Chinese intellectuals and popular culture, 1901-1937." Dissertation: Ph. D. Harvard University.

Hsu, Adam. 1998. *The Sword Polisher's Record: The Way of Kung-Fu*. North Clarendon: Tuttle Publishing.

Huang, Ray. 1982. *1587, A Year of No Significance: The Ming Dynasty in Decline*. Yale University Press.

Israel, Jonathan. 2006. *Enlightenment Contested: Philosophy, Modernity, and the Emancipation of Man 1670-1752*. Oxford.

Johnson, David George. 1989. "Actions speak louder than words: the cultural significance of Chinese ritual opera." In *Ritual Opera, Operatic Ritual: "Mu-lien Rescues His Mother" in Chinese Popular Culture*. Edited by David Johnson 1-45. Berkeley: Publication of the Chinese Popular Culture Project.

_____. 2009. *Spectacle and Sacrifice: the Ritual Foundations of Village Life in North China*. Cambridge: Harvard University Asia Center.

_____. 1997. "Confucian' Elements In the Great Temple Festivals of Southeastern Shansi in Late Imperial Times." *T'oung Pao ; Vol. 83, Fasc. 1-3*.

Judkins, Benjamin N., and Jon Nielson. 2015. *The Creation of Wing Chun: A Social History of the Southern Chinese Martial Arts*. SUNY Press.

_____. 2018. "Zhang Zhijiang Father of the Guoshu Movement." https://chinesemartialstudies.com/2018/04/16/lives-of-chinese-martial-artists-21-zhang-zhijiang-father-of-the-guoshu-movement/

Kang, Xiaofei. 2006. *The Cult of the Fox: Power, Gender, and Popular Religion in Late Imperial and Modern China*. New York: Columbia University Press.

Katz, Paul. R. 2014. *Religion in China and Its Modern Fate*. Lebanon: Brandeis University Press.

Kennedy, Brian, and Elizabeth Guo. 2010. *Jingwu: The School that Saved Kung Fu*. Berkeley: Blue Snake.

Keulemans, Paize. 2007. "Listening to the Printed Martial Arts Scene: Onomatopoeia and the Qing Dynasty Storyteller's Voice." *Harvard journal of Asiatic studies*, 51-87.

Kleeman, Terry F. 1994. *A God's Own Tale: The Book of Transformations of Wenchang, the Divine Lord of Zitong.* SUNY.

———. 2016. *Celestial Masters, History and Ritual in Early Daoist Communities.* Harvard University Press.

Kohn, Livia. 2008. "Cun." The Encyclopedia of Taoism 2, 2. London: Routledge, 287-289.

Kuriyama, Shigehisa. 2002. *The Expressiveness of the Body and the Divergence of Greek and Chinese Medicine.* Cambridge, London: Zone Books.

Lagerwey, John. 1987. *Taoist Ritual in Chinese Society and History.* New York: Macmillan Publishing Company.

———. 2010. *China: A Religious State.* Hong Kong: Hong Kong University Press.

Lao She. 1985. *Crescent Moon and Other Stories.* Beijing, China: Chinese Literature.

Lee Fongmao. 2012. "Modernization of Daoist Inner Alchemy." *Daoism in the Twentieth Century.* Berkeley: Univ of California Press.

Lee Ying-arng 1972, *Pa-Kua Chang for Self-Defense.* Hong Kong, Unicorn Press.

Lei, Daphne Pi-Wei. 2006. *Operatic China: Staging Chinese Identity Across the Pacific.* New York: Palgrave Macmillan.

Li Ruru. 2010. "Commemorations of the Theatrical Careers of Cao Yu and Li Yuru." *CHINOPERL Papers* No. 29. University of Leeds, Conference on Chinese Oral and Performing Literature.

Liu, Kwang-Ching, and Richard H.-C. Shek. 2004. *Heterodoxy in Late Imperial China.* Honolulu: University of Hawai'i Press.

Liu Ts'un Yan. 1966. *Daoism in History*, ed. Benjamin Penny—series of essays beginning with 1966 study of Lu Xixing the author of *Fengshen yanyi*.

Liu, Xun. 2009. *Daoist Modern: Innovation, Lay Practice, and the Community of Inner Alchemy in Republican Shanghai.* Cambridge, Mass: Harvard University Press.

Lorge, Peter A. 2012. *Chinese Martial Arts: From Antiquity to the Twenty-first Century.* Cambridge: Cambridge University Press.

Lu Xun. 1959. A Brief History of Chinese Fiction. Translated by Glady
    Yang; Yang Hsienyi. Peking: Foreign Languages Press.

_____. 1934. 鲁迅. 且介亭雜文 病後雜談.

Lui Ts'un-yan. 1976. "Lin Chao-en." *Selected Papers from the Hall of Harmo-
    nious Wind.* Leiden: Brill, 149-174.

羅, 懋登; 三山道人: 三寶太監西洋記通俗演義 20 卷, 100 回, 1597
    http://digital.staatsbibliothek-berlin.de/

Mackerras, Colin. 1997. *Peking Opera.* Hong Kong: Oxford University
    Press,.

Mair, Victor H., Nancy Shatzman Steinhardt, and Paul Rakita Goldin,
    eds. 2005. *Hawai'i Reader in Traditional Chinese Culture.* Honolulu: Uni-
    versity of Hawaii Press.

Mark, Lindy Li. 2015. "Yangzhou Village Theater, The Play Pi Fifth
    Celebrates New Year (Pi Wu guo nian, 1999) in Wei Ren's
    Redaction," *Yangzhou A Place in Literature   The local in Chinese Cultural
    History*, ed. Roland Altenburger; Margaret B Wan; Vibeke Børdahl.
    Honolulu: University of Hawai'i Press. 407.

Melvin, Sheila. 2012. "Late Ming Drama: The Peony Pavilion in Per-
    formance." In *China: The Power and Glory of the Ming Dynasty.* Lecture
    at Herbst Theater, San Francisco.

Merkel-Hess, Kate. 2016. *The Rural Modern: Reconstructing the Self and State
    in Republican China.* Chicago: The University of Chicago Press.

Meulenbeld, Mark R. 2007. *Civilized Demons: Ming Thunder Gods from Ritual
    to Literature* Doctoral dissertation, Princeton: Princeton University.

_____. 2015. *Demonic Warfare: Daoism, Territorial Networks, and the History of
    a Ming Novel.* Honolulu: University of Hawaii Press.

Miller, Dan. 1994. "The Circle Walk Practice of Ba Gua Zhang," *Pa Kua
    Chang Journal*, Vol 4, No. 6, 3-22.

Miller, Rory. 2008. *Meditations on Violence.* Boston: YMAA Publication
    Center.

_____. 2012. *Force Decisions, A Citizen's Guide Understanding How Police De-
    termine Appropriate Use of Force.* Boston: YMAA Publication Center.

Miracle, Jared. 2016. *Now with Kung Fu Grip! How Bodybuilders, Soldiers and a Hairdresser Reinvented Martial Arts for America*. Jefferson: McFarland & Company, Inc.

Morris, Andrew. D. 2004. *Marrow of the Nation: A History of Sport and Physical Culture in Republican China* Vol. 10. Berkeley: Univ of California Press.

Morris, Meaghan, Siu Leung Li, and Stephen Ching-kiu Chan. 2006. *Hong Kong connections: Transnational imagination in action cinema.* Vol. 1. Hong Kong: Hong Kong University Press.

Mroz, Daniel. 2011. *The Dancing Word : An Embodied Approach to the Preparation of Performers and the Composition of Performances.* Amsterdam : Rodopi.

Naquin, Susan. 1976. *Millenarian Rebellion in China: the Eight Trigrams Uprising of 1813.* New Haven: Yale University Press.

_____. 2000. *Peking: Temples and City Life, 1400-1900.* Univ of California Press.

_____. 1985. "The Transmission of White Lotus Sectarianism in Late Imperial China." *Popular Culture in Late Imperial China*, ed. David Johnson, Andrew J. Nathan, and Evelyn S. Rawski. Berkeley: University of California Press.

Nedostup, Rebecca. 2009. *Superstitious Regimes: Religion and the Politics of Chinese Modernity.* Cambridge: Harvard University Asia Center.

Ng, Pei-San. 2016. "Strength From Within: the Chinese Internal Martial Arts as Discourse, Aesthetics, and Cultural Trope (1850-1940)." *Unpublished dissertation.*

Overmyer, Daniel L. 2009. *Local Religion in North China in the Twentieth Century: The Structure and Organization of Community Rituals and Beliefs.* Boston: Brill.

Ownby, David. 2002. "Approximations of Chinese Bandits: Perverse Rebels, Romantic Heroes, or Frustrated Bachelors?" *Chinese Femininities / Chinese Masculinities.* Berkeley: University of California Press, 226-250.

Palmer, David A. 2007. *Qigong Fever: Body, Science and Utopia in China.* New York: Columbia University Press.

_____. (Editor), Glenn Shive (Editor), Philip L. Wickeri (Editor). 2011. *Chinese Religious Life.* New York: Oxford University Press.

Paper, Jordan. 1995. *The Spirits are Drunk.* Albany: SUNY.

Perry, Elizabeth J. 1980. *Rebels and Revolutionaries in North China.* Stanford: Stanford University Press.

Phillips, Scott Park. 2008. "Portrait of an American Daoist: Charles Belyea/Liu Ming." *Journal of Daoist Studies 1.*

_____. 2016. *"The Cultural History of Tai Chi,"* https://youtu.be/CAK-BqB5vUeE

_____. 2016. *Possible Origins, a Cultural History of Chinese Martial Arts, Theater, and Religion.* Boulder: Angry Baby Books.

_____. 2019. "The Zhang Sanfeng Conundrum: Taijiquan and Ritual Theater," *Journal of Daoist Studies 12*: 96-122.

Platt, Stephen R. 2018. *Imperial Twilight: the Opium War and the End of China's Last Golden Age.* London: Atlantic Books.

_____. 2017. "The Chip on China's Shoulder," *Wall Street Journal,* March 24.

Plowright, Poh Sim. 2002. *Mediums, Puppets, and the Human Actor in the Theatres of the East.* Lewiston, NY: The E. Mellen Press.

Prip-Møller, Johannes. 1967. *Chinese Buddhist Monasteries: Their Plan and Function as a Setting for Buddhist Monastic Life.* Hong Kong University Press.

Ptak, Roderich, 1985. "Hsi-yang chi – An Interpretation and a Comparison with Hsi-yu chi." Chinese Literature: Essays, Articles, Reviews 8, 117-141.

Raz, Gil. 2012. *The Emergence of Daoism: Creation of Tradition.* London: Routledge Press.

Rea, Christopher. 2015. *The Age of Irreverence: A New History of Laughter in China.* Berkeley: University of California Press.

Reid, Anthony. 2010. "Violence at Sea," Robert J. Antony ed. Elusive Pirates, Pervasive Smugglers, Violence and Clandestine Trade in the Greater China Seas. Hong Kong University Press, 16-17.

Riley, Jo. 1997. *Chinese Theatre and the Actor in Performance.* Vol. 3. Cambridge: Cambridge University Press.

Robinet, Isabelle. 1992. "Le monde a l'enverse dans l'alchimie interieure taoïste." *Revue d l'Histoire des Religions* 209.3:239-57.

_____. 1993. *Taoist Meditation: the Mao-shan Tradition of Great Purity*. Albany: SUNY Press.

_____. 2011. *The World Upside Down: An Essay on Taoist Internal Alchemy*. Edited and Translated by Fabrizio Pregadio. Mountain View: Golden Elixir Press.

Rubiés, Joan-Pau, and Manel Ollé. 2016. "The Comparative History of a Genre: The Production and Circulation of Books on Travel and Ethnographies in Early Modern Europe and China." *Modern Asian Studies* 50, no. 1: 259-309.

Sangren, P. Steven. 2017. *Filial Obsessions*. Cham: Springer International Publishing.

Scarry, Elaine. 2001. *Dreaming by the Book*. Princeton: Princeton University Press.

Schinz, Alfred. 1997. The Magic Square: Cities in Ancient China. Stuttgart: Edition Axel Menges.

Schonebaum, Andrew. 2016. *Novel Medicine, Healing, Literature and Popular Knowledge in Early Modern China*. Seattle: University or Washington.

Scott, A C. 1982. *Actors Are Madmen: Notebook of a Theatregoer in China*. Madison: University of Wisconsin Press.

Seaman, Gary. 1987. *Journey to the North: An Ethnohistorical Analysis and Annotated Translation of the Chinese Folk Novel Pei-Yu Chi*. Berkeley: University of California.

Shahar, Meir. 2015. *Oedipal God: The Chinese Nezha and his Indian Origins*. Honolulu: University of Hawaii Press.

_____. 2008. *The Shaolin Monastery: History, Religion, and the Chinese Martial Arts*. Honolulu: University of Hawaii Press.

_____. 2012. "Diamond Body: The Origins of Invulnerability in the Chinese Martial Arts," *Perfect Bodies: Sports Medicine and Immortality*. Edited by Vivienne Lo. London; British Museum Press.

_____. 2009. "Indian Mythology and the Chinese Imagination: Nezha, Nalakuūbara, and Kṛṣṇa." In conference on Indian Mythology and the Chinese Imagination, Tel Aviv, Israel, 25-26.

Shahar, Meir, and Robert Paul Weller, eds. 1996 *Unruly Gods: Divinity and Society in China*. Honolulu: University of Hawaii Press.

Schipper, Kristorfer M. 2012. "Forward." *Daoism in the Twentieth Century*. Ed. David A.Palmer, Kenneth Dean, Fan Guangchun, and Adeline Herrou. Berkeley. Univ of California Press.

_____.1993.*The Taoist Body*. Berkeley: University of California.

_____. 2000. "Forward," *Taoism and the Arts of China*. By Stephen Little (Author), (Author), Wu Hung (Author), Nancy Steinhardt (Author). Chicago: Art Institute of Chicago.

Seidel, Anna. 1970. "A Taoist Immortal of the Ming Dynasty: Chang San-feng." *Self and society in Ming Thought*. New York: Columbia University Press 483-531.

Sommer, Matthew H. 2000. *Sex, Law, and Society in Late Imperial China*. Stanford: Stanford University Press.

Spence, Jonathan D. 1996. God's Chinese Son: The Taiping Heavenly Kingdom of Hong Xiuquan. London: HarperCollins.

Stent, Carter G. 1876. "Chinese Eunuchs." Journal of the North China Branch of the Royal AsiaticSociety, new series 11, 143–84.

Sutton, Donald S. 2003. *Steps of Perfection: Exorcistic Performers and Chinese Religion in Twentieth-Century Taiwan*. Cambridge, Mass: Harvard University Press.

Swaim, Louis. 1999. *Fu Zhongwen: Mastering Yang style Taijiquan*. Berkeley: North Atlantic Books.

Szymanski, Jarek 2000. "Brief Introduction to Yin Yang Bapanzhang" *China From Inside*. http://www.chinafrominside.com/ma/bagua/bapanzhangintro.html

Taubes, Hannibal. 2016. "Illustrating Gootaers, or, the Principle Gods of Rural Xuan-Da and their Iconographies"— http://twosmall.ipower.com/blog/?p=3876

Thorpe, Ashley. 2005. "Only Joking? The Relationship Between the Clown and Percussion in Jingju." *Asian Theatre Journal*, *222*, 269-292.

Ward, Barbara E. 1979. Not Merely Players: Drama, Art and Ritual in Traditional China. *Man* New Series, Vol. 14, No. 1, pp. 18-39.

Wegner, Daniel M. 2002. *The Illusion of the Conscious Will*. Cambridge: The MIT Press.

Wells, Marnix. 2005. *Scholar Boxer: Chang Naizhou's Theory of Internal Martial Arts and the Evolution of Taijiquan*. Berkeley: North Atlantic Books.

Wile, Douglas. 1992. *Art of the Bedchamber: The Chinese Sexual Yoga Classics Including Women's Solo Meditation Texts.* Albany: SUNY Press.

_____. 1996. *Lost T'ai-chi Classics from the Late Ch'ing Dynasty.* Albany: SUNY Press.

_____. 1999. *T'ai-chi's Ancestors: the Making of an Internal Martial Art.* New York: Sweet Chi Press.

_____. 2007. "Taijiquan and Daoism." *Journal of Asian Martial Arts* 16.4.

_____. 2016. "Fighting Words: Four New Document Finds Reignite Old Debates
in Taijiquan Historiography," *Martial Arts Studies* 4, 17-35.

Witt, Barbara 2015. "Sanbao taijian xiyang ji tongsu yanyi: An Annotated Bibliography." *Special Issue, Crossroads, Studies on the History of Exchange Relations in the East Asian World* OSTASIEN Verlag Vol. 12 Oct.

Wong, Shiu-hon. 1993. Mortal or Immortal: A Study of Chang San-feng the Taoist. Hong-Kong: Calvarden.

Verellen, Franciscus. 2006. "The Dynamic of Design, Ritual and Contemplative Graphics in Daoist Scriptures." *Liu, Cunren, and Benjamin Penny. Daoism in history: essays in honour of Liu Ts'un-yan.* London: Routledge, 159-186.

Volpp, Sophie 2011. *Worldly Stage: Theatricality in Seventeenth-Century China.* Harvard University Asia Center.

Xiang, Lanxin. 2003. *The Origins of the Boxer War: A Multinational Study.* London: Routledge Curzon.

Yan Zhiyuan. 2007 "The Connection Between Yinyang Baguazhang, Baguazhang, and Xinyi Liuhequan." Translated by Joshua Capitanio. Wellington, New Zealand. http://www.tai-chi.co.nz/English-ArticleText4.html

Yang, Richard F. S. 1969. "Behind the Bamboo Curtain: What the Communists Did to the Peking Opera."
Educational Theatre Journal, Vol. 21, No. 1, March. Baltimore: Johns Hopkins University Press, 60-66.

Ye Xiaoqing. 2003. The Legal and Social Status of Theatrical Performers in Beijing During the Qing." *East Asian History.* Vol. 25/26, Jun/Dec, 69-84.

Yuan, Bingling 2000. "Chinese Democracies: A Study of the Kongsis of West Borneo (1776-1884)." *No. 79. Research School of Asian, African, and Amerindian Studies.* Universiteit Leiden.

Zhang, Zhen. 2005. *An Amorous History of the Silver Screen: Shanghai Cinema, 1896-1937.* Chicago: Univ. of Chicago Press.

Additional References:

Nezha Song 1: 心壇敬 2010, https://youtu.be/mdFr-Qv16Jw

Nezha Song 2: 小法咒-請神-13-哪吒三太子 https://youtu.be/3RmeFMOV8pQ

Sidney Gamble http://library.duke.edu/digitalcollections/gamble (Introductory text by The China Institute in NY): Between 1924-1927, Sidney D. Gamble made three trips to Miao Feng Shan (Marvelous Peak Mountain), a popular Daoist pilgrimage site. Film https://youtu.be/RFtpjR6uYnI

Chinese Hell Scrolls (Updated 2019): http://people.reed.edu/~brashiek/scrolls/index.html

Chiang Mei 2012. 06/19 南嶽宮 小孩與三太子進場. Nezha offering incense, Taiwan. https://youtu.be/mvIiSO6cig4

Showt1993 2011. 马来西亚-[东方花园-佛天公. Nezha's presenting to the altar, Taiwan. https://youtu.be/I6m7LjNUerg

Steve Hau 2011. 哪吒三太子@港口宮. Medium possessed by Nezha, playing games, Taiwan. https://youtu.be/KAM_qSUBbFc

Kunlun Meditation Hozn 2012. 三太子 妹妹 武藝高強 Sister San Taiz. Nezha devoties spinning. https://youtu.be/Q_eQmvNSjOY

Suling Guo 真假哪吒 2011. https://youtu.be/8NgOeyUkrpw Acrobatic Chinese Opera performance of Nezha.

傳藝小. 站 民權歌劇團 三太子李哪吒 2011. https://youtu.be/y3HC8xHWUDg Amateur Nezha opera performance of self-flaying.

Opera film: "哪吒出世" 導演: 黃鶴聲 "Nezha's Birth," Directed by Huang Hesheng 1962. https://www.youtube.com/watch?v=J6m6OYfVFro

Jiaqi Huang. "Nezha Conquers the Dragon King" (a shadow-puppet-inspired animation): https://vimeo.com/101789329

Chhandam. "Pandit Chitresh Das' world-renowned kathak training" spinning: https://youtu.be/GHU5PZRyaJY

Baguazhang
   aesthetic elements of 129-130
Bagua jiao (teachings, religion, uprising) 148-150, 159n208, 179-181,
   184,

Baguaquan 123, 180n245-246,
Bagua Symbol 122-123
   Yijing as symbol of Golden Elixir
   101, 101n149
   See Black Flag

baojuan 148, 179, 238

Bapanzhang 196, 196n282, 207,
   208n309

black flag (deity Command
   Flag,)26-29, 43-45, 88, 123
   also called Bagua Flag 113-114

Boxer Uprising 4-6
   possession 18, 196
   YMCA 33-38
   invulnerability 150, 152, 231
   rituals used in 27, 171-181
   Nezha's role 182-187
   opposition to from Prince Su 191
   Princely support for 103, 196
   Baguazhang Lineage stories of
   193-196
   as justification for anti-supersti-
   tion198-207

Buddhism
   Chan 163-164
   Lin Zhao'en 54, 57-58,
   Tibetan 232
   The Buddha in Theater 43, 45,
   114, 172n232
   The Buddah and Yue Fei 97-99
   Third Buddha (Maitreya) 149,
   167, 179-180, 180n246,
   Mud-Walking 137-138, 234

canonization *(feng* 封*)* 23-29, 49, 88,
   115, 132, 175-176, 183

Chang Naizhou 93n135, 95-96,
   96n141, 117

Cheng Tinghua 147, 194, 204

Chinese Literature (epic plays) 175
   *Xiyangji (San Bao Taijian Xia
   Xiyangji)(ZhengHe's Journey to the
   West in a Boat)* 28, 41-63
   Translation 117-120

   Xiyouji (Journey to the West) 25, 46
   Sun Wukong (Monkey) 88, 132,
   175, 183, 212-213, 231-233

   Beiyouji (Journey to the North) 27-28,
   88, 234

Chinese Literature *(continued)*
  Fengshen yanyi (Fengshen Bang)
  (Canonization of the Gods) 27, 232,
  152, 164, 172, 175-176

Christian-Secular Normative Model
  201
  (See YMCA)

Chitresh Das 82n125, 125-126, 141,
  141n181-182, 145n190

Crab Generals and Shrimp Soldiers
  142-144, 210

Cultural Revolution 4-5, 109-110,
  188-189, 206-207

damaru 156

danbian (single whip) (elixir change) 86,
  87n127

dance 124-126

Daodejing (Laozi) 8, 45, 51, 57, 69-70,
  116, 192, 218

Daoism
  vestments 122-123
  Immortals *(xian) 64-74, 231*
  hermits 71
  monastic (Quanzhen) 71, 109,
  115, 192, 238
  Yellow Crowns 192
  Zhengyi (Orthodox) 115, 238
  Kang Gewu on 206, 207
  Golden Elixir 212-241

Daoyin 106, 112, 116, 195n278, 208,
  214n315

Dong Haichuan 130, 159n208,
  188-193, 204-209
  various disciples of 194-196
  Ocean-Rivers 190
  Dong family 180n245
  eunuch 189-191

Door Gods: Xu and Lu 88

Douglas, Mary 223

Dragon Kings 88, 131-134, 142, 152-
  154, 177-179, 261

Dudgeon, John 208-209, 211

emptiness 22, 24, 91-92, 210, 115,
  218-219, 223-238

exorcism 10, 15, 21-23, 55, 57, 88,
  105, 115, 164-168

film 107, 202n295, 203, 206n306

Garuda *(see Yue Fei)*

ghosts *gui, mo, shenmo, guishen, guibing*
  19, 66, 56n79, 88

Golden Elixir *(jindan) 22-23, 112-114,*
  212-241
  in Theater 90-99
  in the Nezha story 130-136
  millennialist uses 148, 164,
  179-180
  martial rituals 166-167, 171
  actors 192
  Sun Lutang 204-205
  Healing reputation 105-106
  separating from Tai Chi 100-103
  in the Tai Chi form 81-83
  Zhang Sanfeng story 67-69,
  76-77
  Qi Jiguang 56
  Lin Zhao'en 54-58

Golden Cock 44, 88, 119

Guoshu (National Art) 4-5, 37,
  96n142, 105, 106n158, 108, 202,
  205

Henning, Stanley 67n102

hundun (chaos) 78-81, 236

improvisation 27, 43-44, 61, 71-73, 89, 125, 130, 144, 166, 175, 228, 235

Immortals 64-74

Jingang
pounds the mortar 79, 87
Vajrapani 157n206
Invulnerability 232n334, 234n339

jindan (see Golden Elixir)

Jingwu Hui (Pure Martial Society) 6, 37, 101, 107-108, 201-202, 206n306,

jiaoben (Prompt Books) 89

Kang Gewu 206-207

Kenneth Dean 67

Krishna 83, 138-145 152

Kathak (Natawari Nritya) 82-85, 125-126, 139-141, 139n180, 145, 145n188-190, 152, 156

Li Jing (Nezha's father) 132-133, 139, 175n236,

Lin Zhao'en 48-64, 75, 93-95, 114, 204, 213

Long Zixiang 240

Lorge, Peter 67n102

Lu Xun 49, 152, 199, 199n285

medicine 105-106, 96n141
missionaries and 23, 35

mime 40, 70, 78-89, 114-115, 136, 146, 152-157

mudra 156-157

Naga(s), Nachetaka (Kalya) 138-134, 152

neidan (see Golden Elixir)

Neijia (Inner School) 91-95, 228

Nezha (Third Prince, Marshal of the Central Altar)
story 131-136
as Krishna 138-141
as rebel 142-144
lotus body 144-145
spinning 145
weapons 146-158
in Daoist ritual 168-172
videos 173

Nezha City 132-133, 152

nixing (reverse path) 165, 232

opium 184, 190n267, 199

performers
Mean People 13-16, 174
yuehu 174
imperial eunuch performers 178n243, 190
during the cultural revolution 5
women 37
Zhang Sanfeng performance types 72
Mud-walking 139
envoys 141
solo dance rituals 151-154
armed escorts 173
Bruce Lee 203
ritual-theater 10-11
as a source of prowess 13-29
militia creation 23-29

pirates 46-59

possession 66, 102, 113, 122, 142-146, 150-153, 167-176, 183-186, 196, 233, 261

Princes
    Su, 34, 186-187, 191, 195-196,
    205, 208
    Duan, 34n42, 103, 186-187, 196
    Zhuang 34n42, 186-187, 196,
    207
    Rui 205

processions 14-15, 24, 109, 160, 168,
    173-174

prompt books *(jiaoben)* 89

Qi Jiguang 42, 46-73, 114
    Poem 53
    Tang Hao 103
    Appendix 117

Qigong Fever 105, 107, 107n159,
    213n314

Red Spears 17, 184, 200

redemptive societies 33n39, 203-204,
    203n300, 206n306
    mutual-aid 33, 176, 183-184, 166

Sanyijiao (Three-in-one Religion) 53-
    58, 93, 114 also see Lin Zhao'en

Schipper, Kristofer 127

Seidel, Anna 67

Shaolin 62n97, 63, 73, 76, 94, 110,
    124, 214, 236,
    reversing 228-231, 240

shenda (spirit-hitting) 26-27, 150

snakes (also *see nagas* and *dragons*)
    possessed 20, 142, 176
    snake body 129, 142-144
    snake spear 136n177 146-
    killing-subduing 138, 142
    with horns 153-154
    mime 155
    xingyi stamping 162-164

snakes (continued)
    as a symbol of Xuanwu 234

spirit mediums 21, 28-29, 71-72, 122,
    168-173
    fighting 18-19
    Lin Zhao'en fighting 55
    xian'er 69
    spinning 145, 261
    with pacifiers 146-148
    self-cutting 150-153
    Boxers 182-183

spirit writing 11, 57-58, 66, 69, 71-72,
    97-99, 203

stage combat 53, 63, 94, 235-236

starvation 153-155

Strickmann, Michel 127

Sun Lutang 204-205

Sun Wukong 25-26, 88, 132, 175,
    183, 212-213, 231, 233,

synesthesia 219-220

Tai Chi (Taijiquan, T'ai Chi Ch'uan)
    form names and meanings 78-89
    Tai Chi Classics 90-99

Taiyi
    Nezha's Secret Father 134
    principle of supreme unity (in
    ritual) 165
    sexual anxiety theory 133n174,
    210
    nixing (reverse path) 165, 232

Taiping (Great Peace) Rebellion
    10-11, 25, 182, 117

Tang Hao (historian) 46-47, 96n142,
    103
    and Xu Zhen 67n102
    and Gu Liuxin 46-47

Taoism *see Daoism*

theater/opera *(see performers, canonization, processions, Chinese Literature)*
as a source of prowess 13-31
use of Elixir Pill in 90-91

Thunder Gods (Lei Gong)
Ritual 23-29, 113, 132, 138, 142, 146, 234
Thunder Palm 156, 163
Garuda 97
on wind-fire wheels 159-162
Dragon Court 178

Traditional Chinese Medicine (TCM) 106, 220

Visualization
in Golden Elixir practice 66, 70, 212-238
fire 136n178
Chöd 156
guiging (ghost soldiers) 171
Zhenwu (Perfected Warrior) 216
cun 存 222

Wang Xiangzai 205

Weapons 146-158
Deer horns 150-155
wind-fire wheels 133-134, 136-137, 156-163, 142, 156, 177-180, 186, 230
Doulble-ended spear (Two headed Snake) 146-150
Chakram 156-157
Vajramushti 157
Giant Swords 146-168
Nezha's Ring (thunder hoops) 134, 154-158, 163

Wells, Marnix 45-46, 96, 115-119
Wile, Douglas 45n53, 52 ,67-68, 76-77, 93-97 118

Wokou (Water Lords) 51-52

Wong Shiu-hon 67

Wang Zongyue *see Yue Fei*

Wudang (mountain)
current issues109-111, 206n306
Zhang Sanfeng and 70, 76-77
passthrough gate 94, 109-111

Xiang Kairan 202-206

Xiao Haibo *(also see bapanzhang)* 207

Xingyiquan 59-63, 187n240, 204 *(also see Yue Fei)*
Xinyi (Liuhe) 59-63

Xuanwu *(See Zhenwu)*

Yan Zhiyuan 159

Yellow Crown (name for a Daoist) 192, 206 (also see *Daoism*)

Yin Fu 189, 191-192, 194, 196

Yiquan 205

YMCA Consensus (Young Men's Christian Association)
conquers China 30-38
muscular Christianity 102
missionaries 9, 30-33, 183-186
footbinding 104
resisting 100-111
divergent voices 198-208, 239

Yue Fei (Garuda) (Wang Zongyue) 97-99, 102, 159-193, 183, 239,

Yongle (Emperor of the Ming Dynasty) 49-50
sponsor of Wudang 110
in *Xiyangji* 43-45

Zhang Daoling 65, 69-70

Zhang Sanfeng 67-73
        in *Xiyangji* 41-48
        origin story *67-69, 76-77*
        as sexual trickster
        in redemptive societies 203-204
        Sanyijiao 56-63
        as a real person 205
        inventing neigong 228-230
        invulnerability 234
        persistance 239-240
        in the Tai Chi Classics 90-99
        Appendix 116-120

Zheng He (Admiral San Bao) 42,
        48-51, 58-61, 61n96, 114

Zhenwu (Xuanwu) 43, 76, 81-83, 88,
        95, 113-114, 234
        Black Flag 26-28,
        temple gates 186n263
        visualization 216

Zuowang (sitting and forgetting) 70,
        217-218

Lightning Source UK Ltd.
Milton Keynes UK
UKHW050629170322
400107UK00015B/1834